Emmanuel Chinedu Anagwo

The Nexus Between ICT and Liturgy

Africa in Theology – Theology in Africa
Afrika in der Theologie – Theologie in Afrika
L'Afrique en théologie – Théologie en Afrique

Edited by / Herausgegeben von / Edité par

Prof. Dr. Chibueze C. Udeani
(Würzburg / Nigeria)

Prof. Dr. Claudia von Collani
(Würzburg)

Prof. Dr. Andreas Heuser
(Basel)

Volume 5

LIT

Emmanuel Chinedu Anagwo

The Nexus Between ICT and Liturgy

Towards Consolidating Digital Worship in the African Context

LIT

This book is printed on acid-free paper.

Bibliographic information published by the Deutsche Nationalbibliothek
The Deutsche Nationalbibliothek lists this publication in the Deutsche Nationalbibliografie; detailed bibliographic data are available on the Internet at http://dnb.dnb.de.

ISBN 978-3-643-91622-8 (pb)
ISBN 978-3-643-96622-3 (PDF)

A catalogue record for this book is available from the British Library.

Contact:
Fresnostr. 2 D-48159 Münster
Tel. +49 (0) 2 51-62 03 20 Fax +49 (0) 2 51-23 19 72
e-Mail: lit@lit-verlag.de https://www.lit-verlag.de
Distribution:
In the UK: Global Book Marketing, e-mail: mo@centralbooks.com

DEDICATION

* This book is dedicated to my elder sister, Ezinne Theresa Nwamaka Ogige (Nee Anagwo);
* Also, to all clergy, consecrated men and women and the lay faithful who are authentic promoters of ICT for eworship.

ACKNOWLEDGEMENTS

In the words of Alfred North Whitehead, "No one who achieves success does so without the help of others. The wise and confident acknowledge this help with gratitude." Accordingly, my heart is filled with thanksgiving to all who helped, both directly and indirectly, towards the successful completion of this study. I must first and foremost thank God, the author of all, the source of all, and primordial communicator. I am eternally grateful for all the favours received in the course of researching on theme of the prospect of the digital worship that is dear to my heart ever since my official tertiary teaching profession in 2012. To my Local Ordinary, the Catholic Bishop of Nnewi, Most Rev. Dr. Jonas Benson Okoye and to the Emeritus Catholic Bishop of Nnewi, Most Rev. Dr. Hilary Paul Odili Okeke, I remain ever grateful for their fatherly care and support, especially in the school apostolate assigned to me. A million thanks to Rev. Fr. Prof. Ferdinand Nwaigbo for his scholarly direction and insightful comments, before writing the foreword. May the Good Lord bless you immensely for this invaluable help. Equally, my appreciation goes to my former Professors in Sacred Liturgy, Most Rev. Prof. Augustine N. Echema and Rev. Fr. Prof. Patrick C. Chibuko. Their guidance, inspiration and mentorship inculcated in me to always know the dynamism associated with the modern liturgy, even as one observes the liturgical norms and principles.

Special thanks to the Rector of the Catholic Institute of West Africa (CIWA), Port Harcourt, Nigeria, Very Rev. Fr. Prof. Jude Abidemi Asanbe and the Dean of Theology Faculty, Rev. Fr. Prof. Luke Emehiele Ijezie for their cordiality and words of encouragement. Rev. Fr. Dr. Peter D. Uchu and Rev. Fr. Dr. Victor U. Jamahh are my colleagues in the Sacred Liturgy Department, for their collaboration, companionship, and camaraderie, as we mentor the future liturgy experts and CIWA students in general. To my elder brothers and friends who have been a great source of pillar and support, Rev. Fr. Prof. Ignatius MC Obinwa and Rev. Fr. Dr. Peter Onwuka, I salute their fraternal care, solidarity, and sense of brotherhood. I am also grateful to my senior and contemporary colleagues. I must single out the following: Rev. Fr. Prof. Onyema Anozie and Rev. Fr. Asso. Prof. Inaku K. Egere. It has been a wonderful collaboration in the spirit of the Synod on Synodality, advocated by Pope Francis. Your encouragement and friendliness spurred me through the thick and thin of our teaching apostolate in CIWA. My unalloyed appreciation also goes to Rev. Fr. Paul Anyansi and Rev. Fr. Anthony Ifeanyichukwu Okeke who allowed me to spend part of 2022 summer vacation in their respective parishes, Our Lady, Queen of Apostles Catholic Church, Ilupeju, and Holy Spirit Catholic Church, Onireke (both parishes in Lagos Archdiocese), Lagos State, Nigeria. They provided an enabling environment to fine tune my materials for the subject matter. I owe a lot to them.

I cannot forget my classmates who watched my back and encouraged me in various ways, namely, Rev. Fr. Juventus E. Amadike, Rev. Fr. Victor A. Ezeanya, Rev. Fr. Dr. Peter Muojekwu, Rev. Fr. Prof. Ikenga K. Oraegbunam and Rev. Fr. Kenneth Okechukwu Ekekwe. For my siblings and their families: Ezinne Theresa Nwamaka Ogige (Nee Anagwo), Mr. Augustine U. Anagwo, Mrs. Monica N. Adumekwe, Mrs. Nkem Rita Ezenwa (Nee Anagwo), Mr. Joseph Chidiebele Anagwo, Mrs. Chika Orji (Nee Anagwo), Mr. Mike Ezenwa (Maco) and Chief Emeka Orji (Kotoka), may the blessings of God never depart from you. Eternal rest to my late parents, Mazi Gilbert and Madam Felicia Anagwo (Nee Egboluche) and my late sister and brother, Lady Kate Ohaekwe (Nee Anagwo) and Mr. Cyriacus Chukwuemeka Anagwo (Escort). To all my students and acquaintances who, while engaged in this research, helped with their books, encouragement, and good counsel, I say thank you. May God continue to keep you all in His love. Amen.

Emmanuel Chinedu Anagwo, PhD (Sacred Liturgy), PhD (Philosophy of Education), STL, MTh, MED, BTh, BPhil, BA, DIP. Edu, DIP. Lat.
Catholic Institute of West Africa (CIWA),
Port Harcourt, Nigeria,
17th October 2022,
Memorial of St. Ignatius of Antioch.

TABLE OF CONTENTS

ABBREVIATIONS

Acts	Acts of the Apostles
Can	Canon
CESACC	Centre for the Study of African Culture and Communication
Cf	Confer
CIWA	Catholic Institute of West Africa
Co	Company
Col	Colossians
Cor	Corinthians
Dan	Daniel
Deut	Deuteronomy
Dr	Doctor
DV	*Dei Verbum*
DVD	Digital Video Disc
Eccl	Ecclesiastes
Ed	Editor
EIA	*Ecclesia in Africa*
Eph	Ephesians
Etc	*Et cetera*
Exod	Exodus
Ezk	Ezekiel
Gal	Galatians
Gen	Genesis
GIRM	General Instruction of the Roman Missal
GSM	Global System for Mobile
Heb	Hebrews
HOD	Head of Department
Hos	Hosea
ICT	Information and Communication Technology (or Technologies)
Inc	Incorporation
Isa	Isaiah

Jam	James
Jer	Jeremiah
Josh	Joshua
Kgs	Kings
LG	*Lumen Gentium*
Macc	Maccabees
Mal	Malachi
Matt	Matthew
Mr	Mister
Mrs	Missis
Msgr	Monsignor
Neh	Nehemiah
No	Number
Nos	Numbers
NT	New Testament
OT	Old Testament
Pet	Peter
Prof	Professor
Ps	Psalm
Rev	Revelation
Rev	Reverend
Rom	Romans
Sam	Samuel
SC	*Sacrosanctum Concilium*
St	Saint
Kgs	Kings
TV	Television
Tim	Timothy
Tit	Titus
Vol	Volume
Wis	Wisdom

FOREWORD

This book, titled: *The Nexus Between ICT and Liturgy: Towards Consolidating Digital Worship in the African Context*, by Rev. Fr. Dr. Dr. Emmanuel Chinedu Anagwo, a trained liturgist and the current Dean of Students' Affairs at the Catholic Institute of West Africa (CIWA), Port Harcourt, Rivers State, Nigeria is both timely for our present age of digital generation, and relevant for the Church in Africa. A penetrating reading of the content will surely enable the reader to understand the deep and liturgical utility on the use of Information and Communication Technology (ICT) in Christian Worship in our daily life and across the whole world.

The reformed liturgy of the Second Vatican Council (*Sacrosanctum Concilium*) maintains that at the centre of Christian worship, the liturgy has a particular purpose and significance. The liturgy is the summit towards which all the activities of the Church and mutually all the activities of her members rotate. Fundamentally, the liturgy is the font and fountain from which all her powers and forces as well as that of all her members flow (*Constitution on the Sacred Liturgy*, no. 10). The primary aim of the liturgy is to put people with each other and in union with God. By her nature, the liturgy is communicative.

The word *source* shows how the liturgy is a wonderful source and fountain of our communication with God and communication of the young and old, rich and poor, sick and healthy, weak and strong as well as people of every nation, race, language and ethnic group. This is the primary aim of the author, namely, to put people in communication with one another and to open a communication channel through human beings with God: the Father who created us, the Son who redeemed us and the Holy Spirit who sanctifies us.

The element of the spoken Word of God in time, in the economy of salvation and spoken word of human beings in a place of worship form the nexus between the Liturgy and ICT. In time, the Word was made flesh (John 1:14). The taking flesh of the Word of God is what we re-enact in the liturgy with our communicative instruments. In the liturgy is the source of word. People re-enact the taking flesh of the Word with human words, as the beauty of language and with what is in the storehouse of ICT, spiritually, religiously, psychologically, and physically. During the celebration of the liturgy, ICT affects worshippers as persons in our entire beings, spiritually and religiously, as well as psychologically and physically.

This book is an invitation to pause and listen to what God is speaking to us in the liturgy through the language of digital communication. I am glad over Dr. Anagwo's effort at bringing out this digital oriented book. He has undoubtedly done a commendable work in developing the theology of the Word of God since his earliest days as a doctorant till the present day with academic rigour, scholarly creativity, liturgical muscles, and keen theological fervour. Dr. Anagwo deserves all appreciation! I recommend this book to all clergy, religious and the lay faithful in the Church. May this book inspire all readers with Christ-centred, spirit-filled, and people-oriented life in the active participation in the liturgy.

Rev. Fr. Dr. Ferdinand Nwaigbo,
Professor of Systematic Theology,
Emeritus Head, Systematic Theology Department &
Formerly, Dean of Theology Faculty,
Catholic Institute of West Africa,
Port Harcourt, Rivers State,
Nigeria,
28th October 2022,
Feast of Simon and Jude, Apostles.

PREFACE

Catholic Christianity is constantly growing in all ramifications. The recent advancement in computer and internet technologies is a case study for updating and liturgical renewal. From Johannesburg to Lagos, Cairo to Dakar, Kinshasa to Kigali, Nairobi to Accra, etc., the debate on how Africa worship should respond to the digital revolution is raging and imminent. As in every human endeavour today, ICT and Liturgy can have mutually beneficial relationships. The media environment may not change the heart of belief but does affect and effect the way the faithful think and act. The Church should explore the opportunities of the environment and not fear it. She has lived through the media changes before and guided by God's spirit, will continually find ways of fostering belief and life in Christ. *Ipso facto*, the Church should entrench the new media in more of its activities, pastoral strategies, and liturgical events. By seeking the face of God in cyberspace, the faithful afford God another opportunity to disclose Himself to them. Encouraging her members to seek God in bytes and bits, the Church needs to study how ICT functions and see how each of these forms of social media operates and find ways to utilize them in evangelisation, celebration, and worship.

Apparently, the faithful, especially the present youth, are growing in a world that has greatly and negatively changed. Many lack the positive quality of the holistic formation in morals, social, ethical, academic, and even liturgical. The writer observes the difficulties, the deficiencies, and the neglect they suffer, and the consequent characteristic tendencies associated with such downturn. This is evidenced in the high rate of passive participation in the Church's affairs. Lawrence Okwuosa rightly observes that: "Today, so many young men and women are leaving the Church in droves, with the accusation that the Church is dead, a reference to Nietzsche's uncomplimentary description of the Church. They complain that the Mass does not satisfy their spiritual needs and expectations. They are bored with the rudimental structure of the Holy Eucharist, which leaves little or no space for novelties and active participation of the lay people."[1]

---

1 Lawrence Okwuosa, "The Eucharist and Christian Formation" in Agatha Osarenkhoe (ed.), *The Voyage: A Publication of the Conference of Major Superiors of Nigeria*, Vol. 3, Jan. 2006, 40.

Drawing from this scenario, the Church in Africa remains at a precarious position. The need for guiding light, thinking aloud and prophetic import, is widely required today more than it was required a century ago.

Accordingly, Pope Benedict XVI rightly observes that: "The new technologies are not only changing the way we communicate, but communication itself…giving birth to a new way of learning and thinking, with unprecedented opportunities for establishing relationships and building fellowship."[2] Research suggests that interactivity in ICT also tends to increase the credibility of the message.[3] This is because the consumers are able to express their opinions of the facts and may get feedback. Hence, Bickart and Schindler suggest that business information presented in social media has a higher credibility than marketer-generated information. Gruen *et al.* identify a significant relationship between the knowledge exchange among consumers and the intentions to engage in word-of-mouth.[4] Similarly, electronic word-of-mouth is more credible if found on an interactive website, where consumers exchange information and opinions. These views can help the Church of today to identify and select the appropriate information to be presented online. As purveyors of ICT, the Church in Africa can borrow a leaf from them apply the principle in the gospel-related content posted online especially at it affects worship.

In its efforts, the study adopted descriptive and analytical stand, taking cognizance the overall development of ICT and Catholic liturgy. Uniquely, the book is an effort to note the possible errors on the use of ICT, indeed snares, in which participants are apt to get themselves tangled even when they are made in good faith. A critical look at the historical development of liturgical practices, for instance, from the Jewish worship through the Franco-Germanic and Roman liturgies and into the present era could help us to establish more firmly the rationale for historical formulation of rites and rituals. Despite faithfulness to tradition, liturgical practices have

---

2 Pope Benedict XVI, "Truth, Proclamation and Authenticity of Life in the Digital Age," on 45th World Communications Day, ((Vatican City: Libreria Editrice Vaticana, 2011).

3 See J. Beninger, "Personalization of Mass Media and the Growth of Pseudo-Community," in *Communication Research*, Vol. 14, Issue 3, 1987, 352-371.

4 See T. Gruen, T. Osmonbekov, A. Czaplewski, "eWOM: The Impact of Customer-to-Customer Online Know-how Exchange on Customer Value and Loyalty," in Journal of Business Research, Vol. 59, 2006, 449-456.

developed in the course of time and history. In the words of Pope St. John Paul II, "not all changes have always and everywhere been accompanied by the necessary explanation and catechesis; as a result, in some cases there has been a misunderstanding of the very nature of the liturgy, leading to abuses, polarization, and sometimes even grave scandal."[5]

It, therefore, makes a clarion call to prepare worshippers on the future use of ICT to plunge the Church to explore its richness and possibilities towards the evangelization and liturgical formation of the faithful. The increasing dependency of educational value in general on digital technology is inevitable as it is a powerful tool for enhancing quality in liturgical formation. Pastors or pastoral agents that fail to embrace this wind of change sooner or later will be living in the past and would be irrelevant to the system. Hence, those who engage in the pastoral ministry in urban parishes must meet them where they are; but those who equally engage with the rural parishes who are visual learners should also teach them accordingly.

Consolidating on the gains so far, every effort should be made by the parish administrators and pastoral agents to embrace ICT. The universal Church sees the social media as "Gift of God"[6] which is in accordance with the divine plan which one must cooperate to attain salvation. It is therefore tragic, in some quarters, that African Catholic worship in our time and within the sub-Saharan Africa is being reduced to analogue Church instead of a digitalized worship. Some worship centres in South Africa, Cameroun, Kenya, Ghana, Nigeria, to mention but a few, minimally harness the vast opportunities for evangelization with ICT in Africa. Some Catholic pastors and worshippers are at their lowest ebb in terms of using only bulletin, announcement boards, archaic and outmoded means of communication with less concern to promote digital worship that are in line with an integral spirituality, correct liturgical and doctrinal principles. What beholds us today is estrangement from the wave of globalization that recognizes the cyberspace, as another Christian community, even as they minister to the physical congregation.

---

5 Pope John Paul II. *Ad Limina Address* (Vatican City: Libreria Editrice Vaticana, 11th July 1998).

6 Second Vatican Council, *Communio et Progressio* (Pastoral Instruction on the Means of Social Communication), in Austin Flannery, (ed.), *Vatican Council II*, (Dublin: Dominican Publications, 1987) 2.

A lot of misconceptions and misinterpretations by some scholars, theologians, scientists, liturgists, religious leaders, and others, either due to ignorance or selfishness (to remain relevant) have most unfortunately resulted in untold abuses, aberrations, falsifications, stagnation, and persecution. Those who have dared to challenge the *status quo*, by answering the divine call of increase, multiply and subdue the earth for humanity's benefit (Gen 1:28), are tagged as leftists, modernists, atheists, etc. Nonetheless, the Church should rise to the challenge of the modern means of communication to utilize the benefits in the proclamation and the celebration of the Word of God for liturgical formation of the worshippers for the 21st century Catholic Christianity. In this regard, Pope St. John Paul II exhorts the bishops to listen to the younger Catholics who were expressing desire for more reverent and dynamic liturgy of our time: "the young are summoning the whole Church to take the next step in implementing the vision of worship which the Council has bequeathed to us. Unburdened by the ideological agenda of an earlier time, they are able to speak simply and directly of their desire to experience God, especially in prayer both public and private. In listening to them, dear Brothers, we may well hear "what the Spirit is saying to the Churches" (Rev 2:11).[7]

ICT remains one of the inventions and innovations of humanity in the world of communication. It may be used to instruct the faithful on their faith, to enhance evangelization strategies; above all, as a source for liturgical formation. These advantages of the new media offering new platforms for formation notwithstanding, ICT has, however, posed some challenges to liturgical norms and ethos. For authentic active participation to evolve, celebrants and participants should be concerned about what tomorrow would be. Preparing the worshippers on the responsible use of ICT for liturgical formation will give them access to a sensory-rich world of information made more attractive with full-colour, graphics, video, and stereo sound, will ensure that their positive prospects are well harnessed and maximised; at the same time, narrowing the liturgical challenges they present against liturgical principles, especially against distractions and exclusivity of liturgical objects for worship alone. Even as we thank God

---

[7] Pope St. John Paul II, "Pope Tells WYD Youth that Salvation is an 'Invitation to be Part of a Love Story" from https://twitter.com/hashtag/Panama2019 accessed on 28th September 2022.

for the gift of mass and social media, parents, teachers, pastors and pastoral agents must teach people especially the young people in the more mature way with the use of ICT.

Random sampling from the faithful who are digital natives in our liturgical celebrations shows that they expect us to teach, using the tools they understand and are familiar with and prefer to communicate with. If the Church in Africa refuses to form and inform worshippers especially the young ones, on the last day, she will be charged as guilty. Surely, the Church would feel guilty before the Lord Jesus Christ if she did not utilize this powerful means human skill is daily rendering more perfect in our world today. It presupposes more training in the use of ICT by pastors and pastoral agents and urges them to be in tune with the latest digital technology around the world in order to engage them in the onerous task of their liturgical, doctrinal and faith formation. The book is a welcome addition and another clear indication of the continuing interest of scholarship in issues that enhance the worship-life of the Church. It ably focuses attention on a fundamental and very significant aspect of the nexus between ICT and liturgy which many contributors since the Second Vatican Council have often presumed. Although ICT has been able to transform and the turn the world into a global community, the book maintains that such breakthroughs must be matched by liturgical principles, otherwise it will be tantamount to cataclysmic destruction of liturgical heritage and patrimony.

The title of this book elucidates the essence of what the book seeks to trumpet: addressing the dearth of the ICT usage in some liturgical celebrations in African context. The seven (7) chapters of the book invite the reader to a fresh appreciation of an enquiry into the digital revolution in liturgical celebration, x-raying the mutual relationship between the ICT and the Catholic liturgy. The Church in Africa must harness the airwaves which have led to the proliferation of both public and private audio-visual means of mass communication for deeper evangelization. They can serve as a rich and trustworthy reference point and a spiritual "Global Positioning System" (GPS) for Christian life and spirituality. The book has a well-structured introduction, offering the reader a gist of each chapter and an evaluation of each chapter.

In the first four (4) chapters, the book discusses the use and abuse of ICT for Catholic worship. The book argues that modern liturgical celebrations are not possible without the help of information technology, which is having a significant impact on the *modus operandi* (mode of operation) of worship today for the evolution of active, full, and conscious participation of the worshippers, advocated by the reformed liturgy of the Second Vatican Council. Nonetheless, the freedom of ICT in the liturgy must be used with great circumspect, adhering to the basic liturgical principles and norms. This is to forestall applications that may likely prove harmful, a source of distraction and passive participation in the liturgical worship.

The fifth chapter explores a great treasure-trove of theologico-liturgical insights from the exegesis of ICT on the Second Vatican Council's interdisciplinary document titled: *Inter Mirifica* 13. It is also supported by the lessons emerging from its analysis with biblical foundations, patristic and magisterial teachings as well as some contemporary views that explored the *status* on the use of ICT in the Catholic liturgy. The author, in the exegesis, expounds attractively and lucidly four themes such as the means of social communication to be at the service of the Church, the Church to ensure that the integrity of moral and religious progress is not compromised, pastors of souls to be zealous in using these media for preaching the Gospel, and the laity to use the media to bear witness to Christ. Chapter six (6) is titled, "The Future of the Digital Worship for the Church in Africa Today" and the author advocates that the African continent, rather than crying wolf, should chart a new course for the future, that is ICT savvy complaint, do her research and findings and come up with ICT complementary procedures that take into consideration the African concerns. This is not in any way a push for an independent Church but downloading the universal principles for the Church in Africa. According to Patrick C. Chibuko, "The Church requires a functional liturgy that is not restricted to the cathedrals and adorned with elegant ceremonies. She needs a liturgy that extends to wherever the people are in their contexts."[8] It presupposes that the Church's contents online should be relevant to the local community and related to their growth in faith. They should be effectively used; yet, maintaining the spirit of the mission of the Church.

---

[8] Patrick C. Chibuko, "Foreword" in Emmanuel C. Anagwo & Kelechi Anyanwu (eds.), *Theory and Praxis of Sacred Liturgy in Nigeria: A Festschrift in Honour of Most Rev. Prof. Augustine Ndubueze Echema*, (Umuahia: Sons Digital Press, 2021) xvi.

Since "only the best is good enough for God," they must ensure the growth of the faith and its practice among the people.

Chapter seven (7) is the appraisal of the entire book, pointing out the possible nexus between ICT and liturgy as quite revealing and rewarding. While using the mass and social media, the Church in Africa must rise to the challenge of evolving a perfect, smooth, and effective transmission of liturgical celebration and formation by connecting, collaborating, and creating the new social media with worshippers. She needs to enter the modern media marketplace where she must aggressively compete with other groups for minds, hearts, and values. Some of the recommendations to salvage the crisis and chart roadmaps of prognosis for the future of the digital worship in the African context include proper training of the ministers to be ICT complaints savvy, need for substantial fund for the procurement and maintenance of ICT, parish pastoral plan to adequately integrate ICT, need to develop a model youth Mass, setting up the media office in the parish and diocesan levels. Others include establishment of diocesan and parish ministers of ICT, annual Week of ICT at the parish and diocesan levels respectively, increased ICT-thematic homilies and need for a periodic ICT-penitential service. When the appropriate spirituality of the ICT is faithfully adhered to, it will enable the faithful to appreciate the digitalized worship, live it authentically and thereby making it an effective, joyful, meaningful, relevant, and worthwhile path to God.

Consequently, one can surmise that as a well-researched and a practical manual, anchored from lenses of the Second Vatican Council's interdisciplinary document titled: *Inter Mirifica* 13, with special predilection on the liturgy, this book is the fruit of scholarship and pastoral interest of the author. It pays attention to detail which is so important in preparing liturgical celebrations and is balanced with sensitivity to liturgical and contextual needs. Both the Catholic traditions and the renewal of the liturgy are respected. Thus, being available to the ecclesiastical authorities and official sources, the book offers ready access to information not easily gained on digital worship to evolve 21st century African Catholicism. This book will make a vital contribution not only to scholarship in liturgical studies in Africa but also as a catalyst towards a simplified consolidation, to the practice of Christian worship in the world today.

CHAPTER ONE

GENERAL INTRODUCTION

Background to the Study

The globalization of the 21st century has brought about digital influence in almost every facet of human existence including Catholic worship. The world, as it is today, is very advanced in technology and in order not to be left behind nor become irrelevant in this era, one has to be up to date with regard to new methods of operations especially with technological gadgets. The liturgy, an ancient phenomenon, still exists in this "computer age" because it keeps readjusting herself and adapting to the contexts in which she finds herself. Indeed, the Catholic Church has always held firm ideology that she must rise and explore the possibilities of the modern means of communication to e-worship if she wants to be relevant today. Emmanuel Olusola avers that, "...to be relevant to the people of this age, while not losing her credibility, liturgical celebration of the Church must speak the language of the modern person. When an analogue Church communicates with a digital congregation, the result can only be imagined."[1] As one of the voices of the Church in Africa, some years ago, the communiqué of the Catholic Bishops' Conference of Nigeria (CBCN) on "The Word of God and the Building of the Nigerian Nation" recognized the need for the Church to be alive with the people she has come to evangelize. The Nigerian hierarchy acknowledges God's word in worship to be a living and growing thing.[2]

Over the centuries, Christian liturgy has undergone a great deal of change and development. If the liturgy is to remain alive and in touch with people,

---

1 Emmanuel B. Olusola, "The Christian Liturgy in the Age of Info-Technology: Prospects and Challenges" in Luke Ijezie *et al.* (eds.) *Theology and Liturgy in the Life of the Church Proceedings of the 26th Annual Conference of the Catholic Theological Association of Nigeria* (CATHAN) 2012, 270.

2 Catholic Bishops' Conference of Nigeria (CBCN) "The Word of God and the Building of the Nigerian Nation" Communiqué at the end of the First Plenary Meeting, Abuja March 2009.

it must also express itself anew in the age of info-technology. The liturgical celebration for the Church must begin to speak the language of the digital world if she wants to be relevant to the people of this digital age. In 2010 World Day of Communications Message, Pope Benedict XVI affirms that:

> The increased availability of the new technological demand greater responsibilities on the part of those called to proclaim the word, but it also requires them to become more focused, efficient and compelling in their efforts. Priests stand at the threshold of a new era: as new technologies create deeper forms of relationship across greater distances, they are called to respond pastorally by putting the media ever more effectively at the service of the Word.[3]

As purveyors of ICT, the Pontiff's clarion call is for the Church to employ and significantly use the new media at the service of the liturgical worship. The Church and her mode of worship should not allow the present info-technological innovations to pass by without tapping these resources in a meaningful way that her members will find resonance with the eucharistic liturgy. Accordingly, it cannot be gainsaid that ICT is one of the inventions and innovations of humanity in the world of info-technology. It may be used to instruct worshippers on their faith, to enhance evangelization strategies; above all, as a source for liturgical formation. These advantages of the new media offering new platforms for formation notwithstanding, ICT has, however, posed great challenges to liturgical norms and ethos. For active participation to evolve, celebrant and participant should be concerned about what tomorrow would be. Preparing worshippers on the responsible use of ICT for liturgical formation will give them access to a sensory-rich world of information made more attractive with full-colour, graphics, video and stereo sound. It will ensure that their positive prospects are well harnessed and maximised; and at the same time, narrowing the liturgical challenges they present against liturgical principles, especially against distractions and exclusivity of liturgical objects for worship alone. Even as we thank God for the gift of mass and social media, parents, teachers, pastors, and pastoral

---

3 Pope Benedict XVI, *Priests and Pastoral Ministry in a Digital World: New Media at the Service of the Word* (44th World Communication Day, 2010) in http://w2.vatican.va>documents>hf-b, accessed on 8th August 2022.

agents must teach people in the more mature way with the use of ICT. Worshippers, especially the youths who are "digital natives" in our liturgical celebrations, expect them to teach using the tools they understand and are familiar with and prefer to communicate with. If the Church refuses to form and inform them, on the last day, she will be charged as guilty. As Pope St. Paul VI postulates that the "Church would feel guilty before the Lord if she did not utilize these powerful means, human skill is daily rendering more perfect."[4] Admittedly, it calls for more training in the use of ICT by pastors and pastoral agents and urges them to be in tune with the latest digital technology around the world in order to engage worshippers in the onerous task of their liturgical, doctrinal and faith formation.

Consequently, the Church has for centuries consistently and jealously invested a lot of energy in preserving the deposit of faith in every matter that touches the liturgical worship. Ultimately, they are oriented towards the eternal worship and celebration of the Lamb. Almost sixty years after the promulgation of *Inter Mirifica* on 4th December 1963, by the Second Vatican Council, in the light of the present-day development in communication technology,[5] what is the future of African Catholicism. In the words of John Lukwata:

> Africa has witnessed a liberalization of airwaves which has led to the proliferation of both public and private audio-visual means of mass communication. Moreover, the existing constitutions of many African states also guarantee and respect the freedom of speech. Hence, the Church can harness these means for deeper evangelization.[6]

---

4 Pope Paul VI, Apostolic Exhortation on *Evangelii Nuntiandi* (Evangelization in the Modern World) in http://w2.vatican.va/content/paul-vi/en/apost_exhortations/documents/hf_p-vi_exh_19751208_evangelii-nuntiandi.html accessed on 17th April 2022.

5 Second Vatican Council, *Inter Mirifica (Decree on the Means of Social Communication)*, in Austin Flannery (ed.), *Vatican Council II* (Dublin: Dominican Publications, 1987) 1.

6 John Lukwata, "Church and Mass Media: Harnessing Opportunities for Evangelization in Eastern Africa" in in *African Ecclesial Review* (AFER) Vol. 57, Nos. 3 & 4 Sept/Dec. 2015, 152.

Indeed, the debate on how African worship should respond to the digital revolution is a recurring decimal. Since it is clear now that ICT and Liturgy can have mutually beneficial relationships, the Church in Africa should entrench the new media in more of its activities, pastoral strategies, and liturgical events. After all, we live in times of great change in society and in the Church. Some questions are begging for answers: “What kind of liturgies are we proposing for the future?”, “What is the compatibility ratio between ICT and Liturgy today?”, "Do we have liturgical guidelines on the use of ICT in the liturgical celebrations of the Catholic worship?"; "To what extent do we employ ICT in Catholic worship?"; "Do we use the ICT as a faith practice or a mere familiar practice to worship God?"; ""Do we approach the gadgets of ICT as a faith practice or a conventionally familiar practice?"; "Do we connect the Word of God in faith projected with ICT, ipad, screen or as a familiar routine?"; "Do we have a designated place for the agents of the ICT to stay and cover the liturgical ceremony in our parish Church?"; "Is the Catholic Church really doing enough to address the challenges in order to explore the merits of ICT in the Eucharistic liturgy?" These and more are some of the questions to be addressed by this book.

Statement of the Problem

The dearth of information resources for the Church had been the bane of the 21st century Christianity. The era is characterised by an array of social media innovations being shaped into powerful internet communications platforms. While using the mass and social media, the Church must rise to the challenge of evolving a perfect, smooth, and effective transmission of liturgical formation to worshippers by connecting, collaborating and creating the new social media with them. It is therefore tragic, in some quarters, that African Catholic worship in our time and within the sub-Saharan Africa is being reduced to analogue Church instead of a digitalized worship. Some worship centres in South Africa, Cameroun, Kenya, Ghana, Nigeria, to mention but a few, minimally harness the vast opportunities for evangelization with ICT in Africa. Some Catholic pastors and worshippers are at their lowest ebb in terms of using only bulletin, announcement boards, archaic and outmoded means of communication with less concern to promote digital revolution that are in line with an integral spirituality, correct liturgical and doctrinal principles. What beholds us today is estrangement from the wave of globalization that recognizes the cyberspace, as another Christian community, even as they minister to the physical congregation.

Liturgical principles that guide the use of social means of communication abound to bear fruits of active participation. Liturgical norms and prescriptions acknowledge modern communication gadgets but emphasize that whatever must be used on the altar be strictly and exclusively blessed and dedicated for the service. Thus, the use of ipad, iPhone, galaxy, etc cannot replace Lectionary, Book of Responsorial Psalms/Songs, Book of the Gospel, etc. So liturgical ministers, both major and minor, must always use proper book designated for their functions to proclaim the word, although modern technology can be used to magnify their voice and visibility. The world today is geared towards social media. We live in an environment of e-world. Everything goes internet today. However, ICT must not be followed sheepishly. The key to this study is *anamnesis* (remembrance). It studies an *anamnesis* of a person which means a recall, a re-enactment. Not by ways of repetition but recalling or remembering what happened in the past. Liturgical celebration does not celebrate an ideology. It celebrates someone in His Paschal Mystery. And the Paschal Mystery is re-enacted in the liturgy. And doing what Christ did in the past, it has the same efficacy now. And the liturgy does that in a vicarious capacity.

Unfortunately, modern liturgical celebrations are not possible without the help of information technology, which is having a significant impact on the *modus operandi* (mode of operation) of worship today for the evolution of active, full and conscious participation of the worshippers advocated by the reformed liturgy of the Second Vatican Council.[7] However, the freedom of ICT in the liturgy must be used with great circumspect. This is because the usage of these technologies is revolutionizing the liturgical norms and rules, raising some issues and challenges for the glorification of God and the sanctification of the people (*glorificationem Dei et sanctificationem populi*). But it has much good as well. Experience has taught that the baby must not be thrown away with the bathing water. Nonetheless, as laudable, and good ICT, in recent times, worshippers have observed with dismay

[7] Second Vatican Council, *Sacrosanctum Concilium*, (The Constitution on the Sacred Liturgy) in Austin Flannery (ed.), *Vatican Council II*, (Dublin: Dominican Publications, 1987) 14.

some problems, aberrations, dangers and challenges pulp up by its usage. Hence, there are some challenges, amplified by disillusionment caused by the brazen abuse by both the clergy and impostors who have deployed the privacy of the platforms for commercialization of religious worship, that the Church is been confronted, calling for effective use of ICT. So, Christians in Africa yearn for a Church that understands the dialects of the time. They yearn for a Church that is revolutionary, dynamic, and pastoral.

Aim and Objectives of the Book

In recent years there has been a groundswell of interest on how ICT can best be harnessed to improve the efficiency and effectiveness of the Catholic liturgy. The past three decades have seen the rapid development of ICT. We may have become overwhelmed with digital revolution; hence, media literacy and impact are only emerging. While the nexus of ICT may seem obvious, the deep connections, the nature of these connections and the many possibilities for the 21st century e-worship are yet to be significantly explored. The book examines the possible nexus and complementarity between the use of ICT and Catholic liturgy. While exploring ICT for e-worship, the book intends to advocate on adherence to guidelines on their use in liturgical celebrations. Accordingly, the book attempts to expose the meaning, theology, forms, methods, and abuses in ICT. At the end, it is hoped that this book would re-direct everyone to the right track on the simplified consolidation of the principles guiding the use of ICT for the Church in Africa and for the universal Church. The study sought to achieve the following specific objectives:

- Discuss the nature of ICT.
- Examine the different types and forms of ICT.
- Discuss the nexus between ICT and Catholic worship.
- Highlight the abuses associated with the use of ICT in the Catholic liturgy.
- Discuss the liturgical principles that can influence the application of ICT at Christian worship.
- Demonstrate the different ways the future of the digital worship affects the Church in Africa.

Research Questions

The entire work is going to be guided by research questions with a view of setting a template for liturgical catechesis that would enable the faithful better appreciate the Catholic liturgy. As such, some questions are generated because of the problems to address the subject matter:

- What is the nature of ICT?
- What are the different types and forms of ICT?
- What are the possible connections between ICT and Catholic worship?
- What are the abuses associated with ICT in the Catholic liturgy?
- How would the liturgical principles influence the application of ICT at Christian worship?
- How would the future of the digital worship affect the Church in Africa in different ways?

Scope and Limitations

The area of study is searching for the nexus between ICT and Christian worship, under the banner of the Second Vatican Council's document titled: *Inter Mirifica* 13, with specific reference to the Church in Africa. This means where the people are; after all, context is sacrosanct and cannot be negotiated. Anything coming for the context is original. When research lacks context, then whosoever exercises becomes cerebral, that is, just intellectual and only materials for shelve and findings become esoteric. It is also within the context that mutual enrichment/commitment of African theology is accomplished.

However, the concept of ICT and Liturgy in general was also studied. In the search for the nexus, the writer anchored his study from sound liturgical principles for a balanced understanding. The book examines the unapparent relationship of ICT and liturgy in the light of evangelization in the digital age. It argues that ICT is a human activity and that human beings create culture to which, interestingly, they are subject. The Christian worship is propagated through evangelization, which is an activity of communicating the Gospel of Christ, using inherent symbols or media.

Besides the scarcity of books and articles on mutual relationship between ICT and Liturgy, there was also difficulty of finding books treating ICT in the Catholic liturgy in particular unlike ICT in the Christian worship, which are usually private and unpublished. Faced with such limitations, this work lays no claim to exhaustiveness, nor does it pretend to be a final word on the issue at stake. It sets out to deconstruct and construct a protype to exist between ICT and Catholic liturgy.

Significance of the Book

The significance of any study lies in its usefulness, particularly in its subject matter. This study restricts itself to the principles guiding the application of ICT to liturgical celebrations as clearly stated in the Second Vatican Council's document titled: *Inter Mirifica* 13. Admittedly, it leads the reader to discover that we have entered a period in history not unlike that at the close of the twentieth century – an era in which an array of social media innovations is being shaped into powerful internet communications. The global village continues to plunge deep and deeper into wide-reaching social and religious media literacy movement. These phenomena have clearly affected how most of us live our lives and relate to others and ultimately to God. In this way, the study is informative not only in a general way, but it also interests the pastor of souls; highlighting, as it does, the need to engage the faithful more seriously at worship. It is also an eye opener to liturgical ministers to the extent these gadgets of ICT can be used in the Catholic liturgy.

Accordingly, the book shows the Catholic liturgy has not only been on the negative and very destructive effects of ICT in our relationship with one another and God. The Church has also given specific instructions which, if followed, would minimise considerably, if not eliminate, the dangers of passive participation in liturgical celebrations. It offers the opportunity of freeing worshippers held in bondage of the slavery of ICT by ignorance to what extent the teachings of the Church permit their application in Christian worship. Hence, if ICT is properly used, it will facilitate active participation, as demanded by the reformed liturgy of the Second Vatican Council and remains a plausible method to harvest converts and talents for Jesus Christ outside worship (*extra missa*) and during worship (*intra missa*). This study therefore is a veritable resource material to all, especially the clergy, religious men and women, the lay faithful, all genuine worshippers, and indeed, to anyone who wants to be informed and formed on the proper application of ICT at the Catholic worship. Although the study focuses on the Church in Africa, it would obviously be beneficial even beyond the continent of study.

The study is envisaged to be an ingenious contribution and masterpiece to the emerging digital twist and to liturgical scholarship. Since nobody has written a book of this magnitude for the Church in Africa and beyond, it is a ground-breaking record to broaden liturgical lines of inquiry in this new vista of study. This book is set to make a vital contribution not only to scholarship in liturgical studies in Africa but also to the practice of Christian worship in the world today.

Method of the Book

The scientific methodology of descriptive analysis, utilizing ICT in teaching and learning has been articulated and pivoted in the Socio-Cultural Theory which was propounded by Lev S. Vygotksy, a psychologist in Russia in 1934, who began his work following the Russian Revolution of 1917. This is in a bid to arrive at a plausible solution to the problems raised. Reviewing of the works of scholars who previously dealt on the subject matter, collection, and consultation of materials from other sources were included, but not limited to journals but also to the internet sources. The Theory of Vygotksy emphasizes how an individual's social and cultural worlds impact development. In other words, a child's social world is guided by language, and children use language to understand and experience their world. Eventually, language they hear (and other cultural tools, symbols, systems, and practices) becomes internalized and helps them to control their behaviour. Expository-analytical method was also used in chapter two to four in order to streamline and harvest a good knowledge of the theological and liturgical discourse with a view to dissect the nexus between ICT and Catholic liturgy. Moreover, the study also employs the liturgical exegetical and analytical methods to address the subject matter in chapter five. Chapter six is on the blueprint for the future of the digital worship for the Church in Africa whereas chapter seven offers practical recommendations and conclusion.

Definition of Terms

The title of this book has some key words that should be delineated for clarity's sake. To facilitate a deeper understanding of the study, the following terms are defined: ICT, Liturgy and African Context.

ICT

ICT has been variously described and defined; yet each definition falls short of sufficiently capturing the profundity and depth of what it entails within a few lines of a definition. Suffice it here to present the most outstanding ways of understanding ICT. ICT is an acronym that stands for 'Information and Communication Technology (or Technologies).' It applies to online resources, digital resources, network resources or computer resources. Generally, the term ICT designates systems or vehicles or channels for the transmission of information or entertainment-"the means of social communication" in the Second Vatican Council's definition.[8] It consists of radios, televisions, newspapers and magazines (or the press in common parlance), books, motion pictures-films and hoardings, records and tapes, cell phones, the use of SMS, internet e-mail, parish/diocesan/congregation websites, VCD, to mention but a few.

As instruments of social communication, they have as their aim "unity and advancement of men living in society...."[9] Therefore, they perform four primary functions, namely, informing, educating, entertaining, and serving the economic system by delivering an audience to the advertisers. Osita Agu further notes that ICT deals "with the use of electronic, computers and computer software to convert, store, protect, process, transmit, retrieve and to distribute information."[10] The impact of the media on the society cannot remain unnoticed as it serves to inform, educate, and entertain people. Hence, utmost function of the media in a society is to provide news and

---

8 *Inter Mirifica* 1.

9 Second Vatican Council, *Communio et Progressio* (Pastoral Instruction on the Means of Social Communication) in Austin Flannery (ed.), *Vatican Council II*, (Dublin: Dominican Publications, 1987) 1.

10 Osita Agu, "Uses and Applications of Information and Communication Technologies in Broadcasting", in Ike S. Ndolo (ed.), *Contemporary Issues in Communication and Society*, (Enugu: Rhyce Kerex Publishers, 2011) 122.

information to the masses. This accounts why this present era is also called information age.

The digital media, most times, influence people's opinions; shape their choice making, actions, etc. The effects pervade the society like a mist; not only in matters concerning public opinion or political issues but in matters of the development of personal lifestyles and tastes; possible inducements to violence, and influences upon consumer behaviour and the sensibilities and dispositions of the people. In short, they have become an indispensable part of the society and religious activities. In the context of this study, ICT in Christian worship/theology is interchangeably used to refer to cyberspace,[11] cybermedia, cyberworld, cybertheology, e-worship, electronic church, online evangelization, virtual space, virtual worship or online worship, as any form of liturgical worship uploaded and made available in the web (internet), in order to reach a greater number of people other than those physically present.[12] But for these e-channels and Apps to function, they still need electronic devices such as telephones and digital cameras, android/Apple phones and live-streaming gadgets, tablets and iPads, computers, smart radio and Television sets..

---

[11] The prefix, "cyber" is derived from cybernetics (coined by Norbert Wiener from Greek cybernetics in 1948) which means the science of communications and automatic control systems. It presently denotes how a new world is built with the help of digital technology. Common usages include cyber culture, cyberpunk (a society largely controlled by computers), and cyberspace. The term "cyberspace" represents the new ideas and phenomena which emerged with the phenomenal growth of internet and digital communication. Cyberspace exists entirely within a computer space, distributed across networks. Cyberspace is a name of a real, but non-spatial world. Cyberspace is a catchall term for the many ways people communicate with their computers. It is a "space" in the sense that for many people the internet is an imaginary world that they enter through their computer.

[12] Examples include Live-streamed/Television Masses, Pre-recorded and Televised Masses, Online Audio and Visual Devotions, Online Catecheses, Online Faith programmes and concerts, Online Prayer Meetings/Groups, Online Adoration of the Most Blessed Sacrament, Online Homilies and Reflections, Holy pictures/posters and Online Seminars and workshops. To propagate these online faith-based programmes, online channels and handles are needed. These include Faith-based Phone Apps, Websites and blogs, YouTube Channels, Facebook pages, Instagram handles, Twitter handles, and Electronic Applications that permit texts/audio-visual communication.

Liturgy

Since the Second Vatican Council, the word "liturgy" has become a common term in the Catholic Church as well as the Lutheran and Episcopal Communions, for the public prayer of the Church which is not a private devotion. As such, no one is permitted to add, subtract, or modify the liturgy because of personal whims or taste.[13] The discipline of the liturgy assures its conformity with the teaching of Christ and His Church. While other forms of prayer are available, praiseworthy, and a part of Christian life; none of them is like the prayer of the Church. Liturgy, which is also understood and interchangeably used as divine liturgy, divine worship, sacred liturgy, Catholic worship, solemn liturgy, and liturgical worship, is the customary public worship done by the Catholic religious group. Liturgy is thus considered as the gathering of people from different age groups, place, and cultural backgrounds, as the Church prays in the Eucharistic Prayer III: "and you never cease to gather a people to yourself, so that from the rising of the sun to its setting a pure sacrifice may be offered to your name."[14]

The importance of the liturgy to the life of the Church is delineated in the reformed liturgy of the Second Vatican Council. In the earthly liturgy, worshippers have a foretaste of that heavenly liturgy. All who profess the faith are nourished with the Word of God and Eucharist. In them, the faithful learn their duties as Christians, in their witness to works of charity. They reiterate the message that sacred liturgy is the summit towards which the entire apostolic activity of the Church is directed and the font from which all her power flows.[15] Sacred liturgy is therefore the official prayer of the Church rendered to God with prescribed formulary or ritual. It is the symbolic action intended to mediate the lives of worshippers, lives of remembrance and hope, or praise and thanksgiving, lives of repentance and forgiveness and lives of service grounded in the shared life-experience of those who have communion in God's Spirit through Jesus Christ. The

---

13 SC 22.

14 *The Roman Missal Renewed by Decree of the Most Holy Second Ecumenical Council of the Vatican, Promulgated by Authority of Pope Paul VI and Revised at the Direction of Pope John Paul II, English Translation According to the Third Typical Edition* (henceforth The Roman Missal) (Nairobi: Paulines Publications Africa, 2011) 577.

15 *Sacrosanctum Concilium* 10.

Catholic faithful must be prepared for the celebration of the sacred liturgy by a deep faith and true repentance. The dismissal mandate commissions them to live out the fruits of the celebration by engaging in works of charity, piety, and justice to renew the face of the earth.

Thus, it means the celebration of the liturgy of the Mass, the Divine Office and administration of the Sacraments. Later the “para-liturgical” was developed, which means forms of worship and practices that are outside the liturgy but related. They are otherwise known as devotions or devotional practices which arose out of volition and personal piety. The insight by the reformed liturgy of the Second Vatican Council is quite concise. That liturgy is the summit and source (*culmen et fons*) of Christian life and spirituality.[16] It teaches that with Christian faith, the divine worship we offer, and the work of our redemption are all condensed in the liturgy. The faithful use the liturgy to express the mystery of Christ in their lives and to manifest the true nature of the Church to the world.

In this regard, evangelization is the proclamation of the Good News of Jesus Christ (his birth, person, life, death, burial, and resurrection) and the kingdom of God (God's rule or reign in the world and over his people), by the Church and individuals. There is no doubt that print, radio, and television, indeed, all forms of mass media, have allowed this Good News of Jesus Christ to be proclaimed and celebrated all over the continents for centuries. Francis Cardinal Arinze further remarks that: “Proclamation is thus carried out in various ways such as homily, catechesis, radio and television, talks, books and other writings, religious plays telling our colleagues about the Catholic faith and in general, the use of the modern media to spread the Good News of salvation in Jesus Christ for all humanity.”[17] The advancement of ICT has brought about social media, derived from the social software movement, a collection of internet websites, services, and practices that provide a method of communication that is fast, powerful and interactive with the potential to reach millions of people at a low-cost enabling Christians to easily engage in dialogue and relationship building with people next door or around the world. Since the ICT's inception, its potential for magnifying various outreach efforts has been limitless, tantalizing and encompassing.

---

16 *Lumen Gentium* 11, *Sacrosanctum Concilium* 10, *Catechism of the Catholic Church* 1324.

17 Francis Arinze, *The Eucharist and Mission* (Onitsha: Invoice Master, 2005) 12.

Unfortunately, this potential has remained largely untapped in the Catholic worship, with the celebration of most churches in Africa still at the analogue; if at all they have, using their parish websites much less than the more accessible church brochures and programmes. They are not updated when they exist at all. So, if ICT is abundantly used, as digital media, it will facilitate active participation for Jesus Christ both outside and during worship. This book discusses how ICT, in the use of media as power point displays, slide shows, video cameras, ipads, overhead projectors, etc can positively or negatively contribute to mar communication and celebration of the word of God and the sacraments of the Church. Their influences are enormous since they create a lot of possibilities and innovations.

African Context

African context embraces two words: African and Context. Africans are mainly inhabitants of the African continent, the second largest continent in the world. It is made up of about fifty-three (53) countries, excluding the West Sahara, which consists of five geographical sub-regions, namely, the Central Africa, East Africa, North Africa, South Africa, and West Africa with an estimated population of about 1.34 billion inhabitants as of 2020.[18] In 1900, an estimated 2 million Catholic faithful lived on the African continent. Today, that number stands at about 236 million.

Whereas the word "Context" is not easily defined since it seems simple but very important. Often, experts take for granted the context and do their reflection as they deemed fit and as such, they become esoteric to the people. Context has to do with the people, where they live or work. It is in their local environment. It is all about the people, their cultural, socio-economic and political situations. These greatly influence worldview and determine their value for them. Accordingly, the theologian must take cognisance of the reality of the context as he/she goes about his/her reflection. In the words of Patrick C. Chibuko, "Theological research without context remains celebral and sterile."[19] Undoubtedly, cognisance of the context is imperative because no two contexts are completely the same;

---

18 Source: 2022 United Nation World Population Prospects.

19 Patrick C. Chibuko, *Dynamics of the Liturgy in the COVID-19 and Post-COVID-19 Pandemic Era: Implications for the Church in Nigeria (1st Inaugural Lecture)* [Port Harcourt: CIWA Publications, 2021] 3.

though, they may show some similarities. The worldview of a people who are largely farmers will surely be different from the perspective of a community that is largely dominated by herdsmen. In both contexts, we can be sure that their value of things would be different, though some semblances may be noticed.

It becomes an intellectual error to use a context or to judge one context to be better than the others. Each context is peculiar. This is what some of the early missionaries missed when they arrived Africa. They misjudged the African context, giving the impression that God was absent in their context and so they have come to insert, or "incarnate", as it were, God into the African culture. Admittedly, context is not entirely a human creation. Although, human factors would have necessitated the situation of a given context, every context is first and foremost a creation of God. God reveals Himself to His people in their own context. He speaks to them in a language that they understand and through the means available to them. To this end, a scholar should find meaning in the context of the people rather than give or impose meaning into a context. The Second Vatican Ecumenical Council discusses more in this idea of context in her Pastoral Constitution of the Church in the Modern World titled: *Gaudium et Spes*. In this document, the Council Fathers made it abundantly clear that the Church even though is not of this world, should by no means be isolated from the world. Her teachings and preaching of the Gospel should be made readily comprehensible to the different contexts of the human society.[20]

Often, this admonition is not taken seriously. We still find scholars, theologians and liturgists wanting to impose the Western context into the African context. They want the people to worship God exactly the way the Europeans worship God. Many at times, not to worship in the European fashion is seen as idolatry. This is a wrong judgement. A look at context, each context would reveal that no one context is bereft. Each context has its own rich peculiarities, and the experts need to acknowledge that, appreciate it and harness it for a richer reflection. In the study, context refers to the circumstances that formed the setting for an event, statement or idea or terms in which it can be fully understood. From the perspective of Christian worship, our study here needs to be largely located and understood from the African setting especially from the suburbs in South Africa's townships to the crowded Ajengule or Mararaba in

---

[20] *Sacrosanctum Concilium* 4.

Abuja/Nasarawa, or Cairo or Kinshasa to the villages and poor neighbourhoods in much Africa. In recent times, there have calls for scholars to increase the African contributions in different areas of life.

Accordingly, African worship is a gathering of the Church, an assembly duly convoked for the purpose of praying to God in the African context. Africa ranks high among the religious countries in the world. Worship was the centre and life-wire of their existence.[21] Their culture was inspired and directed by their religious beliefs and Africans are traditionally, notoriously and profoundly religious people as John Mbiti would surmise.[22] Churches, mosques and *juju* (traditional) temples dotted the streets of the continent with mammoth crowd as congregation and adherents. On weekly, monthly, and yearly bases, they troop *en masse* to worship God. Most of them are prepared to spend interminable hours there and even for all sorts of "prayer meetings and sacrifices."

Thus, African worship seeks to celebrate with the people so as to make them at home with it. In a digital age, this is realizable due to the use of the various signs and symbols of ICT that are common to the people's cultures in both teaching and celebrating with them.[23] The Fathers of the Second Vatican Council also recognized the role that culture has played in assisting the Church in her work of evangelization whey they remarked that "the Church has…utilized the resources of different cultures in its preaching to spread and explain the message of Christ…in the liturgy and in various aspects of the life of the faithful."[24] This initiates a process of interaction and integration between Christian Gospel and a particular culture. In order to achieve this objective, there is need to safeguard the integrity of the Gospel value and to encourage sensitivity to various cultural heritage.

Nonetheless, the religious life of every group of people is embedded in their culture. Each person is borne into a particular culture like Christ who was borne into Jewish culture. What this means is that one is first and

---

21 See Hilary Paul O. Okeke, *Living Our Culture in the Light of Faith Pastoral Letter* (Nnewi: CathCom Publishers, 2015) 16.

22 John Mbiti, *African Religions and Philosophy* (London: Heinemann Education Books, 1969) 1.

23 Patrick C. Chibuko, *Paschal Mystery of Christ: Foundations for Liturgical Inculturation in Africa* (Frankfurt: Peter Lang, 1995) 5.

24 Second Vatican Council, *Gaudium et Spes* (Pastoral Constitution on the Church in the Modern World) in Austin Flannery (ed.), *Vatican Council II* (Dublin: Dominican Publications, 1987) 5.

foremost a cultural person before he/she becomes a religious. Christianity, therefore, becomes meaningful and relevant when expressed in the culture of the people since culture has something positive to offer to Christianity. The element to consider relevant and positive to every culture must be exploited, assimilated, and integrated by the Church. Generally, not being unaffected from the global village, characterized by internet explosion, African liturgy is a lively worship facilitated also by the good use of ICT. It stands to evoke greater commitment among the faithful to permeate their life. Their celebration is rooted on the dynamics of the people who are vibrant. In worship, the use of music, hymns, songs, band, sprinkling of holy water, application of modern social media, etc portends the tendency to encourage active participation in the liturgical and para-liturgical celebrations. Invariably, the use of Holy Bible, hymnals, involvement of everybody and ICT will also advance the spirit of an integral participation.[25]

Division and Content

Given the above multifaceted configuration, the entire book is developed into seven chapters with an introduction and conclusion. Chapter One is the foundation chapter, introducing the rest of the book, amplified with the product of the background to the study. It traces, right from the Great Commission of Jesus Christ, that we should take the Gospel to the ends of the earth through various evangelization strategies and activities. ICT has proved to be one of the most efficient and reliable means of communication. The aim and objectives, research questions as well as the methodology, scope and significance were highlighted. Furthermore, the terms used in the topic of the book are defined to give a proper understanding and meaning to it.

Chapter Two made a general excursus on the themes of ICT and Catholic Liturgy. It makes an interesting study especially on the evolution of the concepts and affirms the need for the contemporary Church to continue the vast occasion of opportunities in these lenses. The opinions and authorities, historical development in the digital revolution were reviewed. The chapter

---

[25] Emmanuel C. Anagwo, *Active Participation in the Eucharistic Celebration* (Port Harcourt: University of Port Harcourt, 2013) 109-110.

examines the existing literature, within the reach of the writer, on the general perspectives between ICT and Liturgy

Against the backdrop of the above background, Chapter Three discusses the search for the nexus between ICT and Catholic worship. The mutual relationship is expended under *anamnesis*, person, and event-based lenses. Lessons from COVID-19 pandemic Era with the thrust of ICT were expounded. Chapter Four is on the use and abuse of ICT in liturgical celebration today. The chapter is an effort to note the possible uses and abuses or errors on the use of ICT, indeed snares, in which participants are apt to get themselves tangled even when they are in good faith.

Chapter Five is the liturgical exegesis on the use of ICT with the *magna charta* (great chart/blueprint), cited in the Second Vatican Council's interdisciplinary document titled: *Inter Mirifica* 13. Chapter Six casts a message of hope for the future of e-worship in the 21st century African Christianity. The chapter offers a demonstrative model of how the Church in Africa can be salt and light in bringing about pastoral and liturgical transformation in Africa through digitalized worship and a critical and constructive engagement with machinery of ICT. Chapter Seven, the last chapter, espouses practical recommendations and the conclusion of the study.

The central point of this book is that there is a mutual relationship between ICT and Liturgy, which in partnership, mutual support and collaboration would certainly benefit the worshippers. None should downplay the other. Admittedly, liturgy primarily is for worship; secondarily, teaching takes place there too. Ordinarily, liturgy is not only an ambient of worship but also one of enlightenment, education, instruction, and formation in social, moral, and religious values. The Fathers of the Second Vatican Council rightly posited:

> Although the sacred liturgy is above all things the worship of the divine Majesty, it likewise contains much instruction for the faithful. For in the liturgy God speaks to His people and Christ is still proclaiming His gospel. And the people reply to God both by song and prayer. … Thus, not only when things are read "which were written for our instruction" (Rom. 15:4), but also when the Church prays or sings or acts, the faith of those taking part is

> nourished and their minds are raised to God, so that they may offer Him their rational service and more abundantly receive His grace.[26]

Let us now see the general understanding of ICT and Liturgy in their evolutional study to the Church and the Society.

[26] *Sacrosanctum Concilium* 33.

CHAPTER TWO

DIALECTICS OF ICT IN THE CATHOLIC LITURGY

The importance of ICT and Catholic liturgy has never been undermined in the Church. The Church cherished and still cherishes her liturgical life since it is her very soul and life-wire. The liturgy celebrates the Paschal Mystery which is the foundation for the Church. The Church exists as a continuous proclamation of the fact that Christ has died, Christ is risen, and Christ will come again. Liturgy is but a living celebration of this fact, a proclamation in time of a timeless reality. Liturgy is the indescribable encounter of the corporeal and the incorporeal in real time – a meeting point of the divine and humanity. The totality of this encounter is unique. ICT uniquely embraces the processes for utilizing Information and Communication Technology (ICT) in the Catholic liturgy by the Church who lives amidst a 'mediated' generation that is amply exposed to the audio-visual media and its sensorial language. This chapter reviews the flurry of literature that abound on the dialects of ICT in the Catholic liturgy. The methodology employed here is that of reviewing the literature by theme, in a bid to articulate the thoughts of scholars on the matter at hand.

Theoretical and Liturgical Construct of Using ICT

Communication is an essential component of everyday life among human beings. It does not only express the way of life of people but also their worldviews, perspectives and interpretations. Information and Communication Technology (ICT) is a means of global communication that has attracted usage from multitudes of people, groups, organizations, parastatals, and associations. As the name suggests, it embraces electronic devices that enable an individual to have access to information, store information and retrieve information after a while. Since communication is the ability to express and convey our ideas from one person to the other for the purpose of enlightenment, self-fulfilment and empowerment, it is an umbrella term that includes all communication and information devices or applications such as computers, internet, radio, television, cellular phones, iPhones, network hardware and software, satellite systems and the various services and applications associated with them, tablets, ipads, smart phones, DVD/VCD players, video games, interactive smart boards, audio, microphones, speakers, computer-aided instructions and projectors, among others. Increasingly, ICT is being applied successfully in instruction, learning, assessment, and formation. The use of ICT can provide a context for collaboration, co-operation, and positive learning experience among young adults. ICT provides unique opportunities for scaffolding and supporting learning/worshipping for people with special learning needs and from culturally or linguistically diverse backgrounds. ICT provides a variety of ways for people to weave together words, pictures, and sounds, thereby providing a range of ways for them to communicate their ideas, thoughts and feelings.[1]

The theoretical and liturgical framework of utilizing ICT in teaching and learning has been articulated and pivoted in the Socio-Cultural Theory which was propounded by Lev S. Vygotksy, a psychologist in Russia in 1934, who formulation his thesis, following the Russian Revolution of 1917. Vygotksy's works became popularly known in 1961. It became the foundation of much research and theory in cognitive development over the past several decades, particularly of what has become known as Social Development Theory. The Theory emphasizes how an individual's social and cultural worlds impact development. In other words, a child's social world is guided by language, and children use language to understand and experience their world. Eventually, language they hear (and other cultural tools, symbols, systems, and practices) becomes internalized and helps them to control their behaviour.[2]

Essentially, the theoretical and liturgical framework of developing worshippers' socio-communitarian participation can highly be encouraged by putting it into practice through the use of ICT equipment tools in forming and informing liturgical experiences. It is a truism that media technologies

---

1 See M. P. Kaaindio, & M. N. Wagithunu, "Integrating Information Communication Technology Skills in Preschool Education in Kenya" in *Mediterranean Journal of Social Sciences*, 5 (5) 89-102.

2 See Emmanuel C. Anagwo, "The Value of Liturgical Catechesis for Formation and Renewal of Young Adults: Challenges for Utilizing ICT in Nigeria" in *Discovery and Empowering African Youth* (*Jos Studies*), Vol. 26, May 2018, 44.

have accounted for substantial time spent by some people. The degree of interest and attachments some people placed on the media, if not properly checked and manipulated, adverse consequences are bound to arise. Be that as it may, ICT is also a potentially powerful enabling tool for liturgical worship. They have impacted positively in every aspect of human existence thereby creating a powerful tool for change in how human beings pass on information, process information, and carry out their daily transactions. Richard Leonard opines: "No one who takes postmodernity seriously underestimates how important the media are in relation to every part of people's lives."[3]

To understand ICT as a social network, it calls for a re-examination of the nature and definition of community. Community has been approached as a spatial, social, and value-laden construct. The understanding that communities have moved from a geographical focus to become dispersed networks of support and sociability has urged researchers to study computer networks as social networks and a new form of community. ICT networks have become an increasingly relevant way for people to maintain social order. Being a social network, they have a communal orientation. To maintain an efficient, effective, and proficient liturgical relevance in this digital age, the Church's liturgical catechesis must be conscious of the signs of the time and speak the language of the digital age.

However, worshippers have never fully learnt the workings of liturgical catechesis and consequently, have not learned to participate fully and actively and consciously. To forestall these defects, this book advocates for the theoretical and liturgical construct of using of ICT for formation and renewal of worshippers. After all, if Jesus Christ had lived in this modern age, He could have probably told a parable like: "The kingdom of God can be compared like a smartphone or an ipad which a wise businessman/woman found, covered it, goes off and sells everything to acquire it." Or better, it can read: "The kingdom of God can be compared like a wireless network which draws all kinds of people globally to connect with each other."

---

3 Leonard, Richard, "'Light! Camera! Worship! The Cinema and its Challenges to Roman Catholic Worship in Postmodernity" in Keith Pecklers (ed.), *Liturgy in a Postmodern World*. New York: Continuum (2003) 27.

Development of Means of Social Communication in General

The Fathers of the Second Vatican Council underlined the Church's stand on the effective use of the media in our modern world, when they said: "All the children of the Church should join, without delay and with the greatest effort in a common work to make effective use of the media of social communication in various apostolic endeavours, as circumstances and conditions demand."[4] Earlier the Church understands it that the history of human communication is something like a long journey, bringing humanity "from the pride-driven project of Babel and the collapse into confusion and mutual incomprehension to which it gave rise (see Gen 11:1-9), to Pentecost and the gift of tongues: a restoration of communication, centred on Jesus Christ, through the action of the Holy Spirit. It was Pope Celestine VI who said that: "Every history is sacred history…Every history is a Gospel…Eliminate God from history and you will not be able to understand even the history of man which is just an episode, a chapter, a reflexion of the history of God."[5] The concern here is to see how history, when properly applied in this context, leads to a better understanding of the development or evolution of the means of social communication.

The first period of means of communication could be traced to orature (oral tradition). From time immemorial, it was the primary means of communication, transmitted across generations by spoken means, as opposed to the written, word. Essentially, orature encompasses diverse genres. This includes myths (stories to explain mysteries in human experience), legends (story with historical core surrounded by fantasy), fables (moral tales), and folktales (stories to entertain riddles, proverbs, and praise poetry) whether spoken, recited or sung. Across the world, and the African ethnic groups share a tradition of heroic tales told with the means of epic poems, including songs, salutations, blessings, narratives, oracles and oaths, incarnations (and even rumours in a negative sense). Some of these epics recount tales of real-life stories of heroes and heroines. In his article titled: ""Church and Mass Media: Harnessing Opportunities for Evangelization in Eastern Africa," John Lukwata declares that: "The oral culture is still alive in Africa today. It has survived the pressure of

4 *Inter Mirifica* 13.

5 Pope Celestine VI, *The Letters of Pope Celestine VI to all Mankind*, English Edition (Vatican City: Libreria Editrice Vatican, 1948) 128.

globalization. It also plays a role in the way people use the new communication technology."[6]

Actually, oral tradition was also the normal mode of communicating the teaching of a master in the ancient world. The use of papyrus was widespread writing but was clumsy and expensive. Using a stylus to a clay tablet worked, but once the day dried, no "corrections" or "edits" could be made. Writing on a scroll made of an animal skin was certainly an improvement but was limited. The widespread use of papyrus for the ancient world was like the coming of the internet in the modern world – a virtual explosion of written communication evolved.

With the emergence of great teachings captured in written form, ancient writers continued to be sceptical of using the written word. This is because it fell far short for the communication of treasured knowledge. Church historian, Eusebius, relates this thinking from the fragments of *papias*. According to him, "I will not hesitate also to set down for the benefit, along with the interpretations, all that ever I carefully learnt and carefully recalled from elders, guaranteeing its truth.... For I supposed that things out of books did not profit me as much as the utterances of a voice which liveth and abideth."[7]

A celebrated Latin adage holds that: *Quod scripsi, scripsi* (what I have written, I have written). Admittedly, it was a maxim credited to Pontus Pilate in the Bible in response to the Jewish priests who objected to his writing on the sign (*titulus*) that was hung above Jesus Christ at his Crucifixion. Conversely, when experiences and ideas are not written down, they cannot be preserved and passed on to later generations. Over centuries, this style of writing and copying of texts hardly changed. When Christianity was state religion and became public under Emperor Constantine, copying of texts was done in monasteries and kept in libraries.

The second and most important period in the development of the means of communication, as the medieval period, came with the invention of moveable letter for printing by Johannes Gutenbergy in the year 1455. The printing press that uses the letters are made of iron plate that can be changed in a frame made of wood was developed for the first time. Indeed, it was a

---

6 Lukwata 150.

7 Commentary on Eusebius' Ecclesiastical History 3.39 from https://biblicalscholarship.wordpress.com/2020/01/03/commentary-on-eusebius-ecclesiastical-history-3-39/ accessed on 15th September 2022.

breakthrough, not only in communication technology, but also in the further development of human thinking such as in philosophy and theology. This is anchored on the fact that for the first time, the same texts became easily available to everyone. The same form (and text) could be multiplied as many times as they are demanded by people. The advancement is that instead of having only one single copied text, plenty were made available.

Again, these texts were identical with the original and not altered or changed by any copying mistake by hand. Thus, for the first time in the history of the Church, unified texts for liturgy became available. This led to the unified Missal of Pope Pius V. Before then, there were many local liturgies which could be unified with this printing method, promoting the liturgy of the city of Rome for the universal Church.

The new printing method also facilitated the process of sharing new ideas in Christian worship. It was this method which helped Martin Luther (1483 to 1546) and his companions in a special way to spread the Reformation without the Catholic Church realizing at that time the "Copernican Revolution" in communication technology. In the sixteenth century, Martin Luther and other reformers called the Church to a recovery of liturgy's rightful place within the community's life with intelligible vernacular worship, active participation and 'worldly preaching' as the twentieth-century Lutheran pastor, Dietrich Bonhoeffer would assert.[8] Although the Council of Trent refuted the reformers, centralized Catholic worship with a new emphasis on rubrics and the liturgy remained the property of the clergy, until the advent of the Second the Second Vatican Council (1962-1965).

Back to our subject matter, let us illustrate with statistical data. From an average of some 40 new book titles a year in 1500 (before the Reformation), this changed to 111 titles in 1519 (two years after the Reformation) and 498 in 1523, 418 of them from Protestant origin. Revelatory, Luther's "Sermon on Indulgence and Grace" was reprinted 12 times in 10 months from March 1518 onwards. The text had 25 editions within the first two years. Luther's discussions with Eck in 1518 sold 1,400 copies within a few days at the Frankfurt Trade Fair the same year.

Accordingly, with the invention a completely new profession was born, the printer. Printing and publishing became a booming business. It was not any more in the hands of the monasteries and monks but run by

---

[8] Quoted by Keith F. Peckler (ed.), in "Introduction" to *Liturgy in a Postmodern World* (London: Continuum, 2003) 1.

professionals to make money and to develop their business. Indicatively, the first printer in England, William Caxton, started his press by 1476 in London at Fleet Street. The quarter of the clergy were the only ones who could read and write those days.

Obviously, the new method of printing that new developments in thinking in philosophy, theology, and worship. With the greater availability of books and printed material and a lower price through more developed techniques slowly also other groups of people had access to printed materials. This was further promoted after the obligation for schooling to learn to read and write was introduced by different countries after the French Revolution (1789). Newspaper and periodicals became available to ordinary people beyond the "upper class." Thus, the "market" grew bigger and bigger far beyond books.

By modern age, another development of communication technologies means was added with Film (1895), Radio (1906) and Television (1940s). These developments of social media blitz added with video and sound to the communication possibilities. An important moment in the development of these possibilities is the invention of the transistor by Bell Laboratories (1947) which made Radio and even Television more easily available on very small devices and without the need for complicated technology. Computers[9] and Internet added to a further development towards Cyberspace and Virtual Reality which bring us, in the words of Pope St. John Paul II, into a "New Culture." The first commercial computer, though debatable, was the UNIVAC I. It was developed by John Eckert and John W. Mauchly in 1951. It was designed by the Census Bureau to predict the outcome of the 1952 presidential election. Subsequently, the next twenty-five years, mainframe computers were used in large corporations to do calculations and manipulate large amounts of information stored in the databases. Supercomputers were used in science and engineering, for designing aircraft and nuclear reactors, and for predicting worldwide

[9] A computer is a programmable electronic device that performs mathematical calculations and logical operations, especially one that can process, store and retrieve large amounts of information very quickly. Personal computers are also employed for manipulating text or graphics, accessing the Internet, or playing games or media. The main components of a computer are: i) a central processing unit (CPU); ii) a monitor; iii) a keyboard; iv) a mouse. Originally, the first computers were the size of a large room, consuming as much power as several hundred modern personal computers. Later, computers have become smaller and much more powerful that it was before.

weather patterns. Later, minicomputers were introduced in the early 1980s in small businesses, manufacturing plants and factories, private and public companies.[10]

Since the 1950s, four generations of computers have been developed. Each generation reflected a change to hardware of decreased size but increased capabilities to control computer operations. The first generation used vacuum tubes, the second used transistors, the third used integrated circuits, and the fourth used integrated circuits on a single computer chip. Today, still in the experimental stage, there are advances in artificial intelligence that will minimize the need for complex programming to characterize the fifth generation of computers.[11] Ever since the dawn of the 21st century, ICT has continued to engender rapid transformation in the world including in worship.[12] ICT does not refer to the computer alone as is erroneously believed by some educationists, theologians and scholars; but refers to those channels through which communication is made and information circulated. These include computer ROMS, television, telephones, GSM phones, projectors, audio-visual, video tapes, video machines, recorder (tape & video), filmstrip, cameras, etc.[13] ICT affects Gospel communication as well. Without going into the nitty-gritty of the computer advancement, let us see how this ICT can be viewed as a special gift of God.

ICT as a Gift of God

Like other academic and disciplines of life, there is also a growing interest in the use of ICT in the liturgical worship today. This is true especially among young people, but also among the older generations of Catholic

---

10 In 1973, Martin Cooper was the first man to demonstrate a hand-held cellular phone. It had a battery, a radio and a microprocessor (mini-computer). New Yorkers were shocked and gaped in amazement when they saw Cooper making a phone call on the street.

11 History of ICT (Information and communications technology) from https://www.sutori.com /en/story/history-of-ict-information-and-communications-technology--N7J51bQqSU7vLWc Vfdn5M9qa accessed on 15th August, 2022.

12 Loenard Ilechukwu & Rose Uchem, "Application and Role of ICT in Religious Education" in *Research on Humanities and Social Sciences,* 4 (4) (2014).

13 Ilechukwu & Uchem, Application and Role of ICT in Religious Education (2014).

worshippers. This development is preponderantly on account of the fact that info-technology related issues have become a much-talked topic as they occupy space in almost all facets of life. Today, the world is carried about almost in every pocket, hand-bag, home, Church, office and cars as mobile phones, television cable networks, CD's, DVD's MP3's and MP4 players, computer and its internet social network service programmes such as E-mail Wizard, Facebook, 2-Go, GIGO, WhatsApp, Twitter, SnapChat, BlackBerry Messenger, WIFI, Google-Chrome, Imo, Instagram, Yahoo messengers, to mention but a few. Different cultures and economic systems around the world are becoming connected to each other because of the influence of large multi-national companies and improved communication systems. In fact, every domestic trend is becoming globalized. We now have such acronyms as global crisis or problem, global recession, global sickness, global crime and very soon we are going to have new global inventions introduced among others such as global cough, cry or even laughter.

Prior to the revolution in ICT, liturgical assembly especially the pastor and parents could monitor the media so that the young ones heard, watched and read only what was deemed appropriate for them. The lament is that today, none of that is the case anymore; largely because of the role that technology has come to play in our lives. Opinions on this internet usage ranges from utter condemnation to glorious celebration. Evidently, the ICT has come to stay for good with its numerous benefits, for instance, as means of new evangelization in the digital age[14] and liturgical formation, by simply pressing and manipulating the right buttons. ICT, as a Gift of God, underscores the essentials on the new media as a gratuitous gift of God. It is anchored on the understanding that no one has right to this gift of God. It is only by judiciously using it that one can merit it.

As with other social media, even when condemning dangerous abuses, the Church has taken a fundamentally positive approach to the internet and ICT. In this way, quoting Pope Pius XII's 1957 Encyclical Letter, *Miranda Prorsus*, the Pastoral Instruction on the Means of Social Communication, *Communio et Progressio*, published in 1971, underlined that point: "The Church sees these media as 'gifts of God' which, in accordance with His

---

[14] See Inaku K. Egere, "Social Media and Mission-Based Marketing Approach for New Evangelization in the Digital Age" in *African Ecclesial Review* (AFER), Vol. 57, Nos. 3 & 4, Sept./Dec. 2015, 186-205.

providential design, unite men in brotherhood and so help them to cooperate with his plan for their salvation."[15] Indeed, ICT is a gift of God to the whole world, the world to which He has created and gave humanity dominion. For instance, we have the divine mandate to increase, multiply and subdue the earth for human beings' benefit (Gen 1:28). ICT is the symbol of God who communicates, and He is the communication per excellence. It can be used to communicate the message of God and Christ to the world. The Church sees the web as a missionary territory with people in need of salvation. She uses the ICT as a modern pulpit to reach out the people in the cyberspace. Ronald J. Allen, in his essay titled: "Preaching on Social Issues" prophetically and prudently notes that: "God seeks a social world in which all relationships are loving and just. The pulpit that is silent on social issues frustrates the purposes of God."[16] That is a stark reality before every worshipping community today. Indeed, ICT has become the fastest means of communication that could be employed to reach millions of people in the shortest possible time.

ICT is a gift to the world because it can be used to make people to be mindful of being good, as demanded by God. It is meant for the good use of everyone irrespective of his/her race, tribe or status. ICT is solicitous for the wellbeing of all God's people and so it is helpful too for those who are weak in faith, distressed and troubled as well as those who are strong and cannot be shaken. As custodians of faith and morals, the Church has always shown special interest in the use of modern gadgets of communication at the service of the Gospel. Pope St. Paul VI, in his Encyclical Letter titled: *Evangelii Nuntiandi*, further stresses that:

> In our age which is characterized by the mass media, we must not fail to avail ourselves of the media…The Church would feel guilty before God if she did not avail herself of these powerful instruments which human skill is constantly developing and perfecting…In them she finds a new and more effective form, a platform or pulpit from which she may address the multitude.[17]

---

15 Joseph Migga Kizza, *Ethical and Social Issues in the Information Age* (New York: Springer Media, 2003) 13.

16 Ronald J. Allen, "Preaching on Social Issues" in *Encounter* 59.1-2 (1998) 61.

17 Pope Paul VI, Encyclical Letter, *Evangelii Nuntiandi* 45.

Accordingly, if the recent trend in the media blitz and information technology is anything to go by, then the Church cannot continue to remain oblivious of the landmark this gift of God which continues to be used among the people of this age for evangelization and allied purposes. Digital media, as a divine art, can be used to extend the glory of God, edify, and sanctify the faithful through live streaming of ritual actions and religious materials such as homilies, doctrinal and liturgical catechesis. In his 2009 Message for the World Communications Day, Pope Benedict XVI avers that, "These technologies are truly a gift to humanity, and we must endeavour to ensure that the benefits they offer are put at the service of all human individuals and communities, especially those who are most disadvantaged and vulnerable."[18]

ICT is a gift of God to the whole world, because it is a symbol of unity as well as an instrument for forging the chain of unity, which binds all His people together as one. In a world that is bitterly divided, in a continent that is groaning under the yoke of racial, ethnic and religious conflicts, in a community that is suffering as a result of useless bickering that widens even further the divisions of ethnicity, ICT can be used as a symbol of unity as well as the instrument by which the world is brought to unity. After all, if Jesus Christ had lived in this digital age, He could have probably told his disciples a parable that would sound like: "The kingdom of God can be compared like a wireless network which draws all kinds of people globally to connect with each other."

Jesus makes it clear that the devil, as cunning as he is, cannot succeed if it is divided against itself. How much more necessary is it the case that those who work for the enthronement of all that is good and right must be united if they are to succeed. The priest is to be the arrowhead in securing unity in the world. The universal Church sees the social media as "Gift of God" which is in accordance with the divine plan which one must cooperate to attain salvation. The Church should rise to the challenge of the modern means of communication to utilize the benefits in the proclamation and the celebration of the Word of God for liturgical formation of the worshippers as we move forward towards the 21st century Christianity.

---

18 Pope Benedict XVI, *New Technologies, New Relationships: Promoting a Culture of Respect, Dialogue and Friendship* (43rd World Communication Day, 2019) in http://w2.vatican.va>documents>hf-b accessed on 8th September 2022.

Cyberspace vis-à-vis New Evangelization

In recent times, discussions on evangelization *in lieu* of cyberspace must take note of Emmanuel A. Badejo's paper titled: "The Role of the Media in Evangelization: Opportunities and Challenges." As communication is one of the most critical dimensions to the process of evangelization, he notes that: "Evangelization, in simple terms is the dissemination of the Gospel to the ends of the earth for the purpose of drawing humanity closer to God, to live a life of holiness, 'so that all might be saved" (John 3:16).[19] Pope St. Paul VI further describes it thus:

> Evangelization means bringing the Good News of Jesus into every human situation and seeking to convert individuals and society by the divine power of the Gospel itself. At its essence are the proclamation of salvation in Jesus Christ and the response of a person in faith, which are both works of the Spirit of God. It must always be directly connected to the Lord Jesus Christ. 'There is no true evangelization if the name, the teaching, the life, the promises, the Kingdom and the mystery of Jesus of Nazareth, the Son of God are not proclaimed.[20]

After two thousand years of Christianity, there are still many people that have not heard about the Good News of Jesus Christ. St. Pope John Paul II puts it very well in his Encyclical Letter titled: *Redemptoris Missio*, when he said, "The mission of the Redeemer is far from completion…"[21] Christians are therefore called to be witnesses of Christ to the ends of the world. Pope Francis, in his brilliant Apostolic Exhortation titled: *Evangelii Gaudium* (The Joy of the Gospel), corroborates that the Church must rediscover the richness and beauty of Christ and His Gospel which is beautiful in the liturgy. He remarks: "Evangelization with joy becomes beauty in the liturgy, as part of our daily concern to spread goodness. The Church evangelizes and is herself evangelized through the beauty of liturgy,

---

19 Emmanuel A. Badejo, *The Role of the Media in Evangelisation: Opportunities and Challenges* in *www.recowacerao.org* accessed on 18th October 2021.

20 *Evangelii Nuntiandi* 22.

21 Pope John Paul II, *Redemptoris Missio, Encyclical Letter on the Permanent Validity of the Church's Missionary Mandate* (Vaticana: Libreria Editrice, 1990) 1.

which is both a celebration of the task of evangelization and the source of her renewed self-giving."[22] We can rightly sum up the three objectives of mission thus: 1. To proclaim the Gospel to all people; 2. To help bring about the reconversion of those who have received the Gospel but live it only nominally; 3. To deepen the Gospel in the lives of believers. Evangelization is therefore rooted in the 'Gospel' (Good News) and because it calls the believers, even if they are uncomfortable, to live the faith of their baptism more openly and to share it more freely.[23] The New Evangelization "Calls each of us to deepen our faith, believe in the Gospel message and go forth to proclaim the Gospel. The focus of the New Evangelization calls all Catholics to be evangelized and then go forth to evangelize. In a special way, the New Evangelization is focused on re-proposing the Gospel to those who have experienced a crisis of faith. Pope Benedict XVI calls for the re-proposing of the Gospel 'to those regions awaiting the first evangelization and to those regions where the roots of Christianity are deep but who have experienced a serious crisis of faith due to secularization'. The message of Jesus Christ needs to be re-sown and watered for those who have already heard Christ's call, but who have not been fully evangelized or catechized.[24]

Accordingly, Teresa Okure points out that the New Era of Evangelization was the theme of a National Catholic Seminar held at the Pastoral Institute, Ibadan in 1984. During the seminar, evangelization was described thus: "The term "evangelization", generally connotes the work of preaching the Gospel and spreading the faith in order either to win converts to Church or to consolidate the faith of those already converted. In Nigeria the former is said to belong to the old era of evangelization, the latter to the new era."[25] Pope St. Paul VI further describes evangelization in these words: "The Church, the family of God on earth is on mission-evangelization.

---

22 Pope Francis. (2013). *Evangelii Gaudium, Apostolic Exhortation on the Proclamation of the Gospel in Today's World* (Vaticana: Libreria Editrice, 2013) 24.

23 For a detailed study, Emmanuel C. Anagwo & Peter O. Umekwe, "Enhancing Evangelization and Inculturation through the Print Media in Nigeria" in Emmanuel C. Anagwo (ed.), *Journal of Inculturation Theology*, Vol. 18, No.2, 2021, 257-273

24 Pope Benedict XVI, Reflection at the Synod of Bishops on New Evangelization, (Vatican City: Libreria Editrice Vatican, 2012).

25 Teresa Okure, "A New Testament Perspective on Evangelization and Human Promotion" *in Journal of Inculturation Theology,* Vol. 1, No. 2, 1994, 126.

Catechesis is certainly an integral part of the mission since catechetical instruction is "a means of the evangelization that must not be neglected."[13]

It is a serious endeavour which demands that those engaged in it are people (men and women) radically committed to Christ. The agents of catechesis are catechists. *Lumen Gentium* asserts that, "The apostles were the first catechists; they proclaimed the mystery of Christ so that those to whom it was proclaimed would experience the joy and peace that comes only from Christ. The apostles' activities as catechists were a response to the charge of Christ: 'Go therefore, make disciples of all nations' (Matt 28:19). All catechetical principles flow from this missionary charge addressed to all members of the Church.[26] As early as middle 19th century, there were some Africans who responded to the same divine charge as catechists, freely making themselves instruments of Christ. To this day, the response has not ceased. *Ad Gentes* is the Second Vatican Council's decree on missionary activity. It establishes, "Evangelization as one of the fundamental missions of the Catholic Church and reaffirms the tie between evangelization and charity to the poor. *Ad Gentes* also calls for the formation of strong Christian communities as well as strong relations with other Christians. Finally, it lays out guidelines for the training and actions of the missionaries.[27]

Today, with evangelization in cyberspace, missionary work has taken a new dimension. Before now, some older worshippers who did not believe in modernism, (such as with the use of television and the internet), as they viewed them as channels to pollute or corrupt the human soul. However, they have now embraced it wholeheartedly and use it to spread the Gospel to the whole world. This is in *tandem* with the doctoral thesis of Charles Boampong Sarfo titled: "Eucharistic Celebration and Cyberspace in the Light of *Sacramentum Caritatis* 57: A Study in Kumasi Ecclesiastical Province, Ghana." He asserts that the study was to critically assess the values in the digital media for a fruitful participation in the Eucharistic celebration with an increased liturgical spirituality in the Kumasi Province, Ghana. It also assessed whether the Church sees the web as a missionary territory with people in need of salvation and how she is using the various

---

26 *Lumen Gentium* 17.

27 *Ad Gentes* from https://dbpedia.org/page/Ad_gentes accessed on 18th October 2021.

opportunities of the internet as modern pulpits to reach the millions of the faithful.[28]

Granted that online evangelization is becoming the order of event; they are still people who are very slow in their openness and willingness to engage in dialogue and adapt the *modus operandi* to better speak to the faithful in a language they can identify and engage with. Though some Church documents recognize the cyberspace as having serious implications for evangelization, little or no effort has been expended to explore the rich reservoir of this technology. Little or no effort is done to prepare the Church's personnel for media work ahead, etc. For the Church to be excluded from the social media as all dimensions of Church life are influenced by technology could lead to marginalization and irrelevance especially for those territories without borders. Accordingly, the words of Manuel Castells, in his celebrated book titled: *The Internet Galaxy: Reflections on the Internet, Business and Society,* are relevant to them:

> In a global economy, and in a network society where most things that matter are dependent on these internet-based networks, to be switched off is to be sentenced to marginality…the cumulative effects of these mechanisms of exclusion divide people around the planet…between those connected in the global networks of value-making…and those switched off from these networks.[29]

Essentially, the Church should reflect seriously and critically on how best she can employ the technology at her disposal. Though she is not to follow every fad and fashion, she has to be discerning and open to the possibilities that there is still much to be learnt and used in the liturgical celebration and the proclamation of the Gospel. The Church, of course has been a great herald of the necessity of her mission to the world through the media; but with this move, she became flesh in the Twitter world. The BBC's David Willey, in Rome, says that the Vatican has long shown interest in using the latest communication technologies to spread the faith with the inventor of

---

28 Charles Boampong Sarfo, JNR, "Eucharistic Celebration and Cyberspace in the Light of *Sacramentum Caritatis* 57: A Study in Kumasi Ecclesiastical Province, Ghana," Unpublished PhD Dissertation (Port Harcourt: CIWA, June 2019) vi.

29 Manuel Castells, *The Internet Galaxy: Reflections on the Internet, Business and Society* (Oxford: Oxford University Press, 2001) 277.

radio, Guglielmo Marconi, setting up Vatican Radio in 1931.[30] Indeed, God is present wherever His people are, and if we agree that those who use the media are also children of God, then God can also incarnate in the media.

Now, how can the Church evangelize her members present in the many media platforms today if not by making her presence to be felt therein? The world of mass media also has need of Christ's redemption.[31] This is Digital Incarnation whereby Christ's redemptive presence is deeply advanced in the media space. In the Second Vatican Council Document on "the Means of Social Communications," the Church recognizes the importance of the various media platforms present in that time. She also noted how they can be used to reach and influence human society. The document further states:

> Among the wonderful technological discoveries which men of talent, especially in the present era, have made with God's help, the Church welcomes and promotes with special interest those which have a most direct relation to men's minds, and which have uncovered new avenues of communicating most readily news, views, and teachings of every sort. The most important of these inventions are those media which, such as the press, movies, radio, television and the like, can, of their very nature, reach and influence, not only individuals, but the very masses and the whole of human society, and thus can rightly be called the media of social communication.[32]

Following from this, the Church outlines the media platforms available in those times. Now, the list seems to have widened to include both Mass Media and Social Media platforms. Today, examples include the popular ones such as Twitter, Facebook, Instagram, and YouTube. Admittedly, the task of evangelization is the primary Mission of the Church. In his paper titled: "Community and Social Interaction in Digital Religious Discourse in Nigeria, Ghana and Cameroon," I. Chiluwa observes that for digital

---

30 https://www.bbc.co.uk/news/world-europe - 20581755 accessed on 12th December 2021.

31 Pope John Paul II, Apostolic Letter, *Rapid Development, To those Responsible for Communications* (Vatican City: Libreria Editrice Vaticana, January 24, 2002) no. 4.

32 *Inter Mirifica* 1.

worship, the real goal here is to connect with people that are not seen in person to build a relationship that could potentially result in the regular face-to-face encounter. Historically, Online awareness among Nigerians began in 1991 with the activities of Nigerians in diaspora, particularly the USA with the creation of the first online community known as "Naijanet." This online practice continued to grow. What facilitated it majorly were the various online activities by Diaspora Nigerians through communication by emails which led to a "Virtual Nigeria." As greater interest in the social media increased, especially with divergent views and interests on social matters, new virtual communities were formed. This would lead religious institutions and Pentecostal churches who believed that the Internet was a fulfilment of prophecy as an instrument for the dissemination of the Gospel in the last days to begin to take the advantage of the new media to propagate their activities. The Redeemed Christian Church of God hosted its first website in 1997, Christ Embassy in 2000 and Deeper Life Bible Church in 2001.[33]

According to Peter Onyekachi Ezekoka, in his article titled: "ICT as an Agent for E-Worship in Nigeria," the Catholic Church under the umbrella of the Catholic Bishops' Conference of Nigeria (CBCN), and many dioceses would follow some years to launch their own websites. For those Catholic dioceses, parishes, and private/public associations of the faithful in Nigeria who are yet to take the bold step and join the moving train in launching their websites, he strongly argued that they do so. As a possible means of evangelization, they should also constantly update them since those websites might represent the first impression people would have about their dioceses and parishes. Assuredly, church programmes, events and informing contents should serve to help online visitors to participate and benefit from them.[34]

---

[33] I. Chiluwa, "Community and Social Interaction in Digital Religious Discourse in Nigeria, Ghana and Cameroon," in *Journal of Religion, Media & Digital Culture*, Vol. 2, Issue 1, 2013, 11-13.

[34] Peter Onyekachi Ezekoka, "ICT as an Agent for E-Worship in Nigeria" in Emmanuel C. Anagwo & Kelechi Anyanwu (eds.), *Theory and Praxis of Sacred Liturgy in Nigeria: A Festschrift in Honour of Most Rev. Prof. Augustine Ndubueze Echema* (Umuahia: Sons Digital Press, 2021) 432-433.

ICT and Liturgical Formation

Relatedly, the use of ICT offers almost limitless capacity for information gathering, entertainment, social interaction and above all, liturgical formation. The goal of liturgical formation is to lead the people to maturity in faith and effective participation which when translated into active life means a living faith and better human person and ultimately would lead to salvation. This is the mission of the Church on earth, a mission to *salum animarum* (save souls). Admittedly, the liturgy provides avenues for worthwhile transmission of knowledge, values, and skills to take place. We have chosen to regard the formation that takes place within it as 'liturgical formation.' It embraces not only the religious, didactic, and evangelizing instructions during liturgical worship, but also the general educational effort of liturgical educators and scholars. Christopher Woods rightly notes that the concept of liturgical formation is multi-faceted, with many schools of thought, and preferences of individual liturgists; as such, various understandings abound, which demand further explanation and expansion.[35] Suffice it here to present three of the most outstanding ways of understanding liturgical formation.

First, liturgical formation, according to Mark Earey in his celebrated chapter in the edited book *Liturgical Formation and Education of the People of God in Worship-shaped Life,* refers to the preparation of those who come to worship God, in the sense of deepening people's understanding.[36] Here liturgical formation is an essential part of liturgical catechesis. Consequently, some key principles might be: educating people to recognize the signs, symbols, and depth of the mystery and history of the liturgy, which have become hidden in recent years; sharing and exploring liturgical 'grammar' at whatever point in their lives people become Christians, and continuing this as their Christian faith progresses and unfolds; considering new ways of ensuring that the riches and beauty of the Christian liturgies do not become fossilized or, at worst, extinct. This is in *tandem* with the words of Pope Francis in his recent Apostolic Letter,

---

[35] Christopher Woods, "Liturgical Formation: What is it and why is it important?" in http://www.westcott.cam.ac.uk/liturgical-formation accessed on 30th August 2022.

[36] M. Earey, *Liturgical Formation and Education of the People of God in Worship-shaped Life.* Ruth Meyers and Paul Gibson (eds). (London: Canterbury Press, 2010) 43.

Desiderio Desideravi (On the Liturgical Formation of the People of God) that: "I simply desire to offer some prompts or cues for reflections that can aid in the contemplation of the beauty and truth of Christian celebration."[37]

Second, liturgical formation refers to those who 'preside' at the liturgy or lead God's people in worship. This includes: the planning and performance of liturgical worship; an exploration of the history and development of Christian worship from the very roots of the early Church; a thorough and dynamic understanding of and confidence in using the variety of the *Common Worship* library. Liturgical formation is not only a requirement for ordained ministers. It is also urgently needed for those training to be readers, non-ordained worship leaders, as well as current clergy.[38] Third and finally, liturgical formation is part of the life-long pilgrimage of faith. The recurring question here is: What does this worship *do* to me or to us? The key to answering this question will include an understanding of the pattern of a liturgical day, a liturgical week, and a liturgical year. Also in scope: the ways in which a liturgical cycle resonates with one's personal life, and with the physical seasons of the year; the relationship between pastoral care and sensitively planned and performed pastoral liturgies (especially baptisms, marriages, and funerals), as these are frequently occasions in which a larger part of the community become worshippers; and the missionary importance of a warm, welcoming liturgy which touches the mystery of God; yet, brings Christ close to each one of us personally.[39]

Therefore, liturgical formation ensures the mastery of the genius of liturgical worship, rites, gestures, postures, symbolisms, and liturgical texts. One of its rich values is that the faithful are provided with the information and understanding of what happens in the liturgy, to be able to translate it into their daily lives. The reformed liturgy of the Second Vatican Council makes clear the awareness that goes with what we celebrate: "that the liturgy may be able to produce its full effect, it is necessary that the faithful come to it with proper dispositions, that their minds should be attuned to their voices, and that they should cooperate with divine grace lest they receive it in vain."[40] This means that liturgical orientation should transcend

---

[37] Pope Francis, Apostolic Letter, *Desiderio Desideravi* (On the Liturgical Formation of the People of God), (Vatican City: Libreria Editrice Vaticana, 29th June 2022) 1.

[38] Woods, "Liturgical Formation."

[39] Woods, "Liturgical Formation."

[40] *Sacrosanctum Concilium* 11.

sentimental religiosity, and embrace a religiousness that is solidly anchored in the reality of life and the world. Accordingly, Romano Guardini (1885–1968) corroborates the understanding as an education to unite our heart and voices to the *Ecclesia orans* (praying Church).[41]

Generally, liturgical formation flourishes in theological courses, and at colleges, seminaries, religious houses, regional training partnerships, and dioceses. This area of study specifically reflects on the education, training and enriching of those who lead God's people in worship, of all the baptized people of God, and of others who participate in worship. This education and training can bring about a participative and collegial community organization. All genuine liturgical formation involves not only doctrine, but also practice. In liturgical worship, there is a web of unity between principle (theory) and practice. The Church tries to accommodate the two, joining the theoretical aspect with the practical realm—theories must be matched with praxis.

Liturgical formation is a way of learning about faith, of knowing who God is, and how we relate and respond to the One who gave us life and who sustains our lives. During his general audience in St. Peter's Square at the Vatican City, Pope Francis pinpointedly notes that a major theme highlighted by the reformed liturgy of the Second Vatican Ecumenical Council was that the liturgical formation of the lay faithful is "indispensable for a true renewal."[42] The Pontiff further states the necessity that the Council Fathers were "strongly driven by the desire to lead Christians to an understanding of the grandeur of the faith and the beauty of the encounter with Christ, with the guidance of the Holy Spirit, an appropriate renewal of the liturgy."[43] People worship to stand in relationship with God, and so participation is important. Active participation is not something added to the Eucharistic liturgy simply to enliven the liturgy; it is fundamental to how people express themselves as members of the Body of Christ.

---

41 Quotation from Sartore, "Pastoral Liturgy," in Chupungco, *Handbook for Liturgical Studies*, 74.

42 Pope Francis, "Stop Taking Smartphone Snapshots During Mass, Pope Says" in National Catholic Reporter, https://www.ncronline.org/news/vatican/francis-chronicles/stop-taking-smartphone-snapshots-during-mass-pope-says accessed on 25th September 2022.

43 Pope Francis, "Stop Taking Smartphone Snapshots During Mass, Pope Says".

Liturgical formation is certainly an integral part of this mission since liturgical instruction is a means of evangelization. This radical commitment is lacking among some worshippers because of the means to elicit this formation. ICT application can be designed as a very nice avenue of disseminating the liturgical formation of the faithful. This will go a long way to counter anomalies of "violence and pornography applications" that are scattered in the society today. As a panacea to the trend, good instructional talks and audio-visual applications can be forwarded online. After all, one outstanding characteristic of mind is the photographic capacity. The sense of sight is a powerful one and this strength has been highlighted by those who wish to underscore the fact that the touch screen of ipad, android and smartphones rely on the sense of sight to communicate. Visual information creates awareness when ICT shapes ideas through imagination and intellect. It articulates experiences, struggles and aspirations. Beyond language, the most common way of identifying people, organizations, institutions, and societies is through signs and symbols. These can be illustrated with different liturgical colours and symbols.[44]

Ordinarily, ICT is designed as a touch device with the interface for finger integration. The composition of ICT is such that it is easier to share information therein with others. One outstanding usage, one may argue, is that the liturgical books, like any other books, are essentially used to conserve and transmit information. In the same way, the electronic tablets like ipads do the same function even with some added advantages. For instance, a tablet can contain all the ritual books in one place and allows the celebrant to switch the text from one language to another whenever there is need to do so as well as enlarge it to the size or change to font of their comfort level. It can also help in the singing of unfamiliar hymns as the congregation reads from them.

Although, ICT and its related gadgets are very expensive to buy and maintain, coupled with the shortage of power supply in Africa, the Church must rise up to the challenge of our time. This is because the dignified and fitting use of it for liturgical formation is a task that must be addressed with greater urgency if the Church is to remain relevant to the digital era. Pope

---

[44] Bridget O.N. Nwanze, "Art, Media and Literature as Catalysts of Socio-Political Change: The Nigerian Experience and the Role of the Church" in Bona Ikenna Ugwu, *Politics, Social Change and the Church in Nigeria Acts of the 12th SIST International Missiological Symposium, 2007* (Enugu: Kingsley's, 2011) 122.

St. John Paul II, in his *Ad Limina Address,* exhorts the bishops to listen to the younger Catholics who were expressing desire for more reverent and dynamic liturgy of our time: "the young are summoning the whole Church to take the next step in implementing the vision of worship which the Council has bequeathed to us. Unburdened by the ideological agenda of an earlier time, they are able to speak simply and directly of their desire to experience God, especially in prayer both public and private. In listening to them, dear Brothers, we may well hear "what the Spirit is saying to the Churches" (Rev 2:11).[45]

It is, therefore, on the need for the ICT to be at the service of liturgical formation of the people that challenges the Church to urgently consolidate its usage as one of the inventions and innovations of humanity in the world of communication to instruct the worshippers on their faith, speedy evangelization and liturgical resources for breviary, homilies, reflections, missal, lectionary, etc. With regard to the liturgical books (like Lectionary, Roman Missal, Prayer of the Faithful), the *General Instruction of the Roman Missal* (GIRM) states that these books, used to proclaim the Word of God, should be "truly worthy, dignified and beautiful."[46] This insight, from the GIRM, means that the liturgical books are thus expected to be handsomely and attractively bound being destined to be used at the worship of God who desires simply the best from us. As they would be carried in procession, they should be ornamentally presentable as befitting the worship of the Most High, maintaining, of course, the characteristic features of the Roman Liturgy, namely, noble simplicity, brevity, sobriety and practicality. When ICT is to be used, it must not detract from liturgical decorum. The *corpus* of decorum comes to the faithful through tradition and in many cases made binding by the disciplinary instruction of the *Magisterium*, for instance, as highlighted by the canonical and liturgical

---

45 Pope John Paul II. *Ad Limina Address* (Vatican City: Libreria Editrice Vaticana, 11th July 1998).

46 *General Instruction of the Roman Missal* (GIRM) (Nairobi: Paulines Publications Africa, 2003) no. 349.

legislations in *Redemptionis Sacramentum*[47] and *The General Instruction of the Roman Missal.*[48]

Undoubtedly, since liturgical formation is the key to the formation of the whole human person, geared towards his/her eternal destiny, which is eternal happiness in God, with the aid of ICT for liturgical formation, the worshippers would be able to develop the sense of liturgical responsibility, right use of freedom and active participation in the religious life of the Christian assembly. A responsible use of ICT will ensure that their positive elements are well harnessed; and maximised and at the same time, narrowing the liturgical challenges they present against liturgical principles, especially against distractions and exclusivity of liturgical objects for worship alone. The watchword is that the use of ICT must be threaded with caution to achieve great success in her evangelizing mission through the use of means of social communication, "by which they will not suffer danger as they use the media, like salt and light, add savour to the earth and light to the world"![49] The clarion call, if understood, would contribute to rescue worshippers towards proper goals for worship in the liturgy. For instance, one outstanding practical use is that priests and other pastoral agents can use ICT to send emails and texts, audio or video messages for liturgical formation. These engagements with both the traditional and new media will go a long way in enhancing the ministry of liturgical formation. Worshippers need to be properly taught through liturgical formation. Such catechesis and formation can be given and facilitated with the aid of ICT.

Active Participation in the Light of ICT

It is certainly correct to agree with Anscar J. Chupungco that the ultimate aim of the liturgy is to create the worship that the faithful are able to identify with and claim as their own; a liturgy in which the texts, gestures and feasts "evoke something from the people's history, traditions, cultural patterns

---

47 Congregation for Divine Worship and the Discipline of the Sacraments, *Redemptionis Sacramentum* (*On Certain Matters to be Observed or to be Avoided Regarding the Most Holy Eucharist*), (Okpuno: Fides Communications, 2004).

48 *The General Instruction of the Roman Missal* (GIRM) (Nairobi: Paulines Publications Africa, 2003).

49 *Inter Mirifica* 24.

and artistic genius."[50] Authentic suited ICT complaint liturgy fosters active and fruitful participation and geared toward the building up of the assembly. Active participation is one of the basic themes in the reformed liturgy of the Second Vatican Council. It is a means toward the achievement of the transformation and development of a true Christian spirit. It demands the worshippers' entrance into the very mystery of God with the totality of their being to become part of the event being celebrated. The participation should be full, conscious and active.[51] To participate fully means that the assembly is to come to the liturgy as human beings with all the faculties that make them human- body, soul and spirit. It implies using all the human senses and dimensions that are available to the faithful to take part in the liturgy.

To participate consciously means the assembly has to be aware of what it has been convoked to do. This demands attentiveness and a genuine understanding of the meaning of texts, rites, words, actions, gestures, etc., used in the liturgy. Active participation means that the assembly to take part in the liturgy actively through external expression such as acclamations, responses, hymns, gestures and bodily movements.[52] These are to spring from their interior dimension of their being. In the bid to achieve this noble objective, the Conciliar Fathers urged the observance of a reverential silence which aids the participant's interiorisation of the worship experience. This implies that the assembly come, not to have fun in the name of active participation, but to have a right internal disposition, with their minds attuned to their voices as they cooperate with the grace of God through Christ in the Holy Spirit. Here, ICT contributes a lot to boost the system through the good use of the modern gadgets such as power point and projector, screen and television. Worshippers can come to be lively and active in the Church during liturgical celebration.[53]

---

50 Anscar J. Chupungco, *Handbook for Liturgical Studies; Fundamental Liturgy*, Vol. II (Collegeville, Minnesota: Liturgical Press, 1998) 339-340.

51 *Sacrosanctum Concilium* 14.

52 Emmanuel C. Anagwo, *Active Participation in the Eucharistic Celebration* (Port Harcourt: University of Port Harcourt, 2013)12.

53 Emmanuel C. Anagwo, "Active Liturgical Participation and Collaborative Ministry in Nigeria" in Benedict E. Ukutegbe, Emmanuel C. Anagwo & Victor U. Jamahh (eds.), *Active Participation and the Church in Nigeria, Proceedings of the Annual Conference of the Catholic Liturgists' Association of Nigeria (CALAN)*, (Warri: Vinnyl Communications, 2017) 49.

The Conciliar Fathers maintained that the right and duty of the people to participate actively in the liturgy stem from their baptism and the fact that the Church is a priestly and a kingly people.[54] Participating in the liturgical act cannot be optional since it is through such participation that the human person is transformed in Christ's likeness. It is the baptismal character that makes any action truly participatory. By its very nature, spectatorship is not acceptable. In his celebrated book titled: *The Mass*, Guy Oury avows that by virtue of active participation "no member of the church can be content to stand aloof, observing the sacred action coldly as though he or she was a total stranger to it. The mystery of the Mass should permeate the being of every member of the Church who is present."[55]

The above notwithstanding, participation in the liturgy should not only be active or external but interior or intelligent as well. This demands that participants should not only have knowledge of their role at Mass by heart but must be intrinsically connected to every word they utter, and every posture, gesture or movement perform. To ensure a fruitful and true participation, "the words of the mouth must come from the depths of the heart, must be an inner prayer, otherwise the most 'liturgical' Mass is nothing but sounding brass or a twinkling cymbal and an abandonment before the face of the Lord."[56] According to the book titled: *Liturgical Participation: An Ongoing Assessment*, Frederick McManus maintains that Christ's faithful are not to be spectators at the liturgical function but to be fully involved not only by external expression but also by interior participation in the paschal mystery of Christ.[57] Balthasar Fischer, in his article, "Active Participation in the Mass," avers baptism as the means that enables the faithful to acquire the right to full and active participation. They are encouraged to "play their parts once again, should think, act, pray, sing, offer, and most important of all, eat jointly with the priest at the holy table."[58]

---

[54] *Sacrosanctum Concilium* 14.

[55] Guy Oury, *The Mass* (New Jersey: Catholic Book Publishing Corp, 1988) 34.

[56] Balthasar Fischer, "Active Participation in the Mass," in Alfons Kirchgaessner (ed.), *Unto the Altar: The Practice of Catholic Worship* (New York: Herder and Herder, 1963) 172-173.

[57] Frederick McManus, *Liturgical Participation: An Ongoing Assessment* (Washington DC: The Pastoral Press, 1988) 10.

[58] Fischer, "Active Participation in the Mass" 172.

In spite of the good use of ICT, an intelligent participation calls for a disposition where the heart and mind are so awake, alert and engaged in the rite. It demands a certain transparency in the rites for the worshippers to be actively involved. Intelligibility ought not remove the sense of the mystery from worship. So, liturgical participation, as public worship, needs ICT to boost the activity through their service and good application. In this highly recommendable, engaging and thoroughly liturgical participation, it brings to the fore the urgent need to change the perception of the lay faithful as a "spectator or silent observer" at Mass to that of an active, full and conscious participator by introducing some ICT gadgets into the liturgy without necessarily altering its basic framework. ICT helps to promote active participation in the liturgy when properly utilized. For instance, modern means of communication like sound system can help to reach out vast majority of people with ease. Undoubtedly, ICT has helped to bring the world together like a global village. It is the key because it disseminates information to millions of persons with just a click of the mouse and is a wonder to behold. This has enlarged the number of participants tremendously.

Through multi-media means like audio-visual aid, ICT has made learning very easy and the Catholic faith more interesting especially among children and the youth who are the digital natives. When the evangelizer speaks the language they understand, it gives them a sense of belonging and arouse their interest and curiosity about the things of God. Despite the relationship formed between liturgy and ICT, it must be categorically stated that the liturgy must not be a slave to ICT. Rather ICT must be at the service of liturgy. The major goal of ICT is to make the people participate fruitfully in the liturgy. Anything beyond this philosophy of life should not be accepted. Every liturgical celebration must be geared towards interior transformation (*metanoia*). And this must be to the glorification of God, the edification and sanctification of the people of God (*glorificationem Dei et sanctificationem populi*).

Active participation within the horizon of ICT is best captured in the multi-sensate. As a model of participation, it presupposes the fact that human imagination may be excited by a variety of stimuli. The point of stress includes both non-verbal dimensions of participation observed in liturgy like the postures and gestures, signs and symbols, etc; and verbal dimensions like all communication and information devices or applications such as computers, internet, radio, television, cellular phones, iPhones, network hardware and software, satellite systems and the various services and applications associated with them, tablets, ipads, smart phones, DVD/VCD players, video games, interactive smart boards, audio, microphones, speakers, computer-aided instructions and projectors, among others. Accordingly, US Bishops' Document on Church Art and Architecture titled: "Built of Living Stones" rightly states that,

> ...artworks consisting of technological and interactive media, such as video and other electronically fabricated images, may also be appropriate for sacred purposes. Subject to the same criteria of suitability as other sacred art, technologically produced works of art can point toward sacred realities even though they do not possess the more enduring form, colour, texture, weight, and density found in more traditionally sacred art.[59]

When audio-visual aid technology contents are presented to the congregation, they help to facilitate their understanding of the Mass better. In this way, it facilitates the active, conscious and full participation of the liturgical assembly. According to Edward McNamara, in his article titled: "Follow-up: On Banners, Overhead Projectors and PowerPoint Displays," it has also made it cheaper as the parish does not have to invest in hundreds of weekly bulletins or expensive missal.[60] Through the use of the sensate (taste, sight, touch, smell); kinetic (body movement) and emotion, liturgical participation is enhanced. Examples of multi-sensate include kneeling, standing, signing of the cross, imposition of hands, genuflection, to mention but a few. Multi-sensate, however, can degenerate into ritualism since the assembly may be engaged in a practice without knowing its signification. Ongoing catechesis can help to stem the tide of extremism in this regard, as the experience of COVID-19 pandemic shows.

---

[59] US Bishops' Document on Church Art and Architecture, "Built of Living Stones" nr. 163 in http://www.usccb.org/liturgy/livingstonesind.shtml, accessed on 23rd August 2022.

[60] Edward McNamara, "Follow-up: On Banners, Overhead Projectors and PowerPoint Displays" 8th June 2010 in http://www.zenit.org/article-29678?l=english accessed on 20th August 2022.

Lessons from COVID-19 Pandemic Era with the Thrust of ICT

The world has greatly learnt of the importance of digital worship from the experience of lockdown and restrictions imposed by the COVID-19 (Corona Virus) pandemic. During his Inaugural lecture titled: *Dynamics of the Liturgy in the COVID-19 and Post-COVID-19 Pandemic Era: Implications for the Church in Nigeria,* Chibuko avers that, "In seeking for a practical liturgy that suits the troubled era of COVID-19 is far from twisting the arm of the classical liturgy of the Church. Instead, it is to challenge theologians and liturgists to rediscover the hidden potency, capabilities in the existing liturgy and aptly apply them."[61] It is an opportunity to explore the latent potencies yet to be fully explored in the context of the digital revolution. In his article titled: "Sacred Liturgy and COVID-19 Pandemic Era Guidelines and Lessons by the Church in Africa", the writer rightly notes that the emergence of COVID-19 pandemic has now formed part of the challenges of ICT to religious worship.[62] It has reshaped, moderated and left an indelible mark on humanity. It is a global pandemic that has occurred over the width and breath of the world affecting exceptionally high proportion of the world's population. It has brought about new ways of doing things which, notably among them, included wearing of facemasks, keeping social distance, frequently washing of hands with running water and sanitizing them and other surfaces, increased usage of social media network platforms, spending of less time at public gatherings and with a regulated number of people in attendance, etc. In another context, in his article titled: "Adopting New Ways of Celebrating the Word of God in a Pandemic Era," the writer notes that:

> In the contemporary society, one of the significant modern means to communicate the Word of God is the social media: newspapers, magazines, radios, televisions, tapes and internet facilities. Social media platforms have become the wonder of development today and have pervasive influence on our world. Prior to the pandemic era and even more because of social distancing, they are becoming

---

[61] Chibuko, *Dynamics of the Liturgy in the COVID-19 and Post-COVID-19*... 92.

[62] For a detailed study, see Emmanuel C. Anagwo, "Sacred Liturgy and COVID-19 Pandemic Era Guidelines and Lessons by the Church in Africa" in *Vidyajyoti Journal of Theological Reflection*, Vol. 86, August 2022, 605-618.

> the fastest means of communication that could easily reach millions of people in the shortest time. It should be used to disseminate mystagogical catechesis.[63]

Nonetheless, due to the dynamism and complex nature of the sacred liturgy, numerous adaptations and provisions were made by the Church to respond to the challenge of the COVID-19 pandemic. In the words of Ferdinand Nwaigbo, in his celebrated book titled: *The Holy Spirit and the Youth in Africa in the Era of COVID-19*:

> Theologically speaking, the presence of sickness in the contemporary world is evidence to God's requirement from us of faith and obedience and testimony to human solidarity in sin and susceptibility to infection and disease, and to the parasitism, corruption and decay which at present are visible in our fallen world (Romans 8:18-25).[64]

The Church as a caring mother does not keep mute in the face of all these or any suffering person in the world. *Gaudium et Spes* makes it crystal clear that: "…the joy and the hopes, the grieves and the anxieties of the men of this age, especially those who are poor or in any way afflicted, these are the joys and hopes, the grieves and anxieties of the followers of Christ."[65] Beyond the scientific efforts at medications to remedy the Corona Virus pandemic, the Church keeps cooperating with science and intensifies her prayers for the healing of her people and the land through the sacred liturgy. It is common knowledge that every opportunity should be maximised by Christians to a life of witness. Be it moments of joys or sorrows, glorious times or trying times, the demand is the same. The pandemic era offers an avalanche of opportunities of witnessing Christ through her sacred liturgy. It is certainly correct to agree with the conclusions of ChukwuEmekalum Nwosuh that:

---

63 Emmanuel C. Anagwo, "Adopting New Ways of Celebrating the Word of God in a Pandemic Era" in Clement Obasi (ed.), *Bigard Theological Studies (BTS)*, January-June 2022, Vol. 42, No.1, 20-35.

64 Ferdinand Nwaigbo, *The Holy Spirit and the Youth in Africa in the Era of COVID-19* (Mauritius: Blessed Hope Publishing, 2020) 205.

65 *Gaudium et Spes* 1.

> The coronavirus may certainly not be a form of divine visitation, but like every crisis, it offers us an opportunity to reappraise and rediscover the value and importance of liturgical actions and in fact, the liturgy itself. If we succeed in doing this, we will benefit immensely as a Church from a scourge that holds nothing but death and doom.[66]

The measures adopted to mitigate against the scourge of COVID-19 throw up a number of challenges to the Church in Africa. We have no doubt that the faith of the Christian assembly is like "the proverbial egg that must be handled with care." The challenge remains that the celebration of the sacred liturgy in Africa frequently involves large gathering of people. It involves frequent body contact. This creates an avenue for the spread of the virus. Indeed, the challenges of the liturgical celebrations are both immediate and remote. Immediate challenge has to do with the observance of all those healthy measures at the Eucharistic sacrifice of the Mass while the remote hinges on the catechesis that must prelude protocol guidelines to be observed at the Eucharistic liturgy. Ministers of hospitality could also be trained to direct people properly. Such catechetical matters, for the Church in Africa, should be more proactive not reactive.

One of the outstanding lessons of COVID-19 pandemic and lockdown brought out more the relevance of e-worship and how the available social media platforms can be used in the propagation of the Gospel message and in staying close to one another in spirit. Admittedly, the present online of the Church in Africa offers some respite and peace to the nation's online space and provided the nexus that can unite people from different ethnic, social, economic and faith backgrounds. It is an opportunity worthy of exploration to sustain the celebration of the sacred liturgy in a post Corona Virus era. Pastors of souls and pastoral agents can create their own websites, pages or platforms, Facebook groups, chat groups, YouTube, Podcast, LinkedIn, Pinterest, Google, Skype, Blog cites, etc. and through these platforms share the Word of God, liturgical catechesis, inspiring stories, their homilies, talks, sermons and reflections with the faithful of the parish/station on account of social distancing or any part of the world they

---

[66] ChukwuEmekalum Nwosuh, "On Dispensing with the Kiss of Peace: Seeking Creative Liturgical Actions" Dominican Institute, Samonda, Ibadan, Nigeria, Unpublished Paper, 2nd May 2020.

may be at the material time in question. They can also send daily and Sunday reflections through emails, text messages and social media like Facebook, WhatsApp, Twitter, Imo, chatrooms, to nourish and sustain the means of disseminating and celebrating the sacred liturgy. Elsewhere in his article titled: "The Value of Liturgical Catechesis for Formation and Renewal of Young Adults: Challenges for Utilizing ICT in Nigeria," the writer argues that the Church can use screen projectors and power point displays to show hymns, readings, homily, announcements, etc., as liturgical aids to facilitate the understanding of Mass, liturgical catechesis and encourage integral and effective liturgical celebration.[67]

Live streaming is also another important aspect of using the social media platforms. As some worshippers are prevented because of ill health or the observance of social distancing, they are interested in watching video and clips. Parish/station events like Sunday homilies, Church programmes and exciting events can be covered in video and images and posted to them *via* social network sites. This is because videos and other forms of visual presentation could be effective pedagogical tools to celebrate sacred liturgy because of its capacity to surmount social distancing imposed on the people because of the demands of the pandemic period. However, we must caution that virtual worship cannot substitute for in-person celebration and participation in the sacraments and sacramentals.

However, of all the challenges against the validity of church online, one that cannot be left out is the challenge many participants bring upon themselves. This is the challenge of trying to replace physical worship with e-worship. Some use e-worship or 'church online' as simply a matter of convenience. Even when there might be no factor that militates against their physical presence in Churches around them, some e-worshippers prefer to remain in the convenience of their homes, and sometimes choose to worship in their pyjamas rather than get dressed and participate in the local church. Peter Onyekachi Ezekoka, in his paper titled: "ICT as an Agent for E-Worship in Nigeria" warns that

> …e-worship is not meant to replace, but only to complement physical worship. Surely, there are situations and challenges that can create more e-worshippers more than physical worshippers ...

---

67 Anagwo, "The Value of Liturgical Catechesis for Formation and Renewal of Young Adults…" 47-48.

> situation such as was imposed on the world recently by the COVID-19 pandemic, but it needs to be stressed that when people can worship physically, they should gladly do so.[68]

The danger that an extreme interest in e-worshippers can create is a disregard of physical worshippers, especially the physically challenged, sick and elderly people who, sometimes, have no access to the e-world or find it complicated to use. The difficulty might lie in them not being learned and lettered enough or not being proficient enough to understand how the internet world works. So, they feel anxious over it. They have a great number of people, almost at an equal plane with the young people who clamour for social media blitz. They remain the Church's treasure, and the Church does not neglect them, because their grief and concern is the grief and concern of the Church too; especially those who are poor or in any way afflicted (in this case, with lack of ICT proficiency). The joys and hope, grief and anxieties of these followers of Christ reflect the joys and hopes, the grief and anxieties of the Church.[69]

The Church should remain alive to all these challenges as she continues to minister to her children online. Being the moral conscience of the society, the Church has been equipped to call on all peoples to come together in order to fight these challenges. The principle moral responsibility for the proper use of the media of social communication falls on all the stakeholders, liturgists, liturgical team planners, newsmen, writers, actors, designers, producers, displayers, distributors, operators and sellers, as well as critic and all others who play any part in the production and transmission of the Eucharistic celebrations. The Public authority too is bound by special responsibilities in view of the common good, to which these media are ordered, to protect and safeguard true and just freedom of information, and to encourage spiritual values, culture and the fine arts and guarantee the rights of those who use these media.[70]

---

68 Ezekoka, "ICT as an Agent for E-Worship in Nigeria" 426-427.

69 *Gaudium et Spes* 1.

70 *Inter Mirifica* 11-12.

Evaluation

This chapter reviewed literature under the dialectics of ICT in the Catholic liturgy. There was a critical review of the fundamental pedagogies in the Theoretical and Liturgical Construct of Using ICT, Development of Means of Social Communication, ICT as the Gift of God, Cyberspace vis-à-vis New Evangelization, ICT and Liturgical Formation. Active Participation in the Light of ICT and Lessons from COVID-19 Pandemic Era with the Thrust of ICT. All affirmed that ICT is a veritable instrument towards effective formation and renewal in the Christian faith. This is anchored on the understanding that they must permeate and pervade the spiritual, pastoral, catechetical, social, moral, and religious aspects of their lifestyle. We are more convinced than before on the need to step up the grooming of the young adults who are digital natives and other worshippers to evolve their formation and renewal in the 21st century Christianity. Since the Church cannot and should not abandon them, it is important that their liturgical celebration and formation should be facilitated through the employment of the language, category, and framework of techno-science in conveying the truths of faith to the people of our time.

Accordingly, the pastoral agents must adapt to the new reality despite the challenges, huddles and difficulties of ICT. If they transmit their liturgical formation with an outdated cultural baggage and a vocabulary that is archaic and in a style that is grating, then only a few, if any, on the online participants will have the receiver tuned in to accept and appropriate the fruits of the formation and renewal. The chapter advocates that digital technology be effectively used to develop the faithful in such areas as their liturgical formation, rituals, gestures, postures, characters, attitudes, among others, which is also a way of promoting effective and integral liturgical participation. In this way, it will go a long way to rediscover and empower them to maximize their potentials and vocational discernment. However, pastors and pastoral agents, among others, should collaborate to invest time and money to adequately fund programmes towards liturgical catechesis which will aid the procurement of the essential ICT tools for the liturgical formation and renewal of the faithful. While the arguments of the book may not be exhaustive, they raise enough incisive questions and prodding for further discussion and for genuine formation and renewal for the faithful.

The above literature review examined the scholarly contributions of some authors, with the affirmation, that the Church should rise to the challenge of the modern means of communication to utilize the benefits in the proclamation and the celebration of the Word of God for liturgical formation of the worshippers. The authors above were chosen and reviewed on account of the limited scope of study. Besides the study has to justify its reliability on the study of the search for the nexus between ICT and Catholic liturgy. To the best of the materials available to the writer, none of the authors combined the study of both ICT and Catholic liturgy, from the singular scholarly viewpoint, as a researchable topic, for the Church in Africa. Only the the thesis of Charles Boampong Sarfo, JNR. Eucharistic Celebration and Cyberspace in the Light of *Sacramentum Caritatis* 57: A Study in Kumasi Ecclesiastical Province, Ghana. Unpublished PhD Dissertation, June 2019, who is the current Assistant Secretary General, Catholic Bishops' Conference of Ghana, comes here to consolidate this stance. Sarfo's thesis was originally written as his doctoral thesis and successfully defended in the Sacred Liturgy Department of the Catholic Institute of West Africa (CIWA), Port Harcourt, Nigeria (an affiliate of the University of Calabar (UNICAL), Nigeria), lasted for only three years (2016 to 2019). But this is one of the areas that the writer has decided to research on since 2012 when he took up his teaching appointment in CIWA. The writer has written more than four articles on the subject matter.[71] Over the years, he also has taught the course on "LIT 5271/6271: Liturgy and ICT" for masters and doctoral programmes respectively.

---

[71] For a detailed study, consult Emmanuel C. Anagwo, "ICT in the Catholic Worship: Some Pastoral Issues and Implications Today" in *Journal of Inculturation Theology*, Vol. 14, No.1, 2013, 50-71; Emmanuel C. Anagwo, "Preparing the Youth on the Use of ICT for Liturgical Formation: A Challenge for the Church in Nigeria" in *Koinonia*, Vol. 7, No.5, June 2017, 37-55; Emmanuel C. Anagwo "Ipad at the Service of Liturgical Formation of the Youth" in Luke Ijezie *et al.* (eds.) *Youth Formation & Globalisation in the Nigerian Context", Proceedings of the 32nd Annual Conference of the Catholic Theological Association of Nigeria* (CATHAN) 2017, 419-434; Emmanuel C. Anagwo, "The Value of Liturgical Catechesis for Formation and Renewal of Young Adults: Challenges for Utilizing ICT in Nigeria" in *Discovery and Empowering African Youth* (*Jos Studies*), Vol. 26, May 2018, 37-54; Emmanuel C. Anagwo & Peter O. Umekwe, "Enhancing Evangelization and Inculturation through the Print Media in Nigeria" in Emmanuel C. Anagwo (ed.), *Journal of Inculturation Theology*, Vol. 18, No. 2, 2021, 257-273.

Besides, some of the scholars, whose works have been reviewed focused exclusively on either ICT in education or allied disciplines. There is need for a study that is focused on the mutual relationship and similarities between the two dependable variables. Such a study will be more and far-enriching enterprise for theoretical and practical advancement of worship life of the Church. This current research hopes to fill in this gap that exists in the current scholarship in order to advance a future for the digital worship for the Church in Africa.

CHAPTER THREE

THE SEARCH FOR NEXUS BETWEEN ICT AND CATHOLIC LITURGY

This pivotal chapter searches for the possible nexus between ICT and Catholic liturgy. Probing into this goldmine, it underscores that like a great wave, modernization has swept many parts of the world through internet, television, and media blitz. Today, we do not talk about only e-banking, e-dividend, e-ticket, e-culture, e-parliament, e-farming, e-naira, e-book, e-tag, e-learning, e-library, e-priest, but also e-worship.[1] E-worship embraces the application and use of electronic devices such as overhead projector and screen, slide show, ipad, etc in the course of the liturgical celebration to facilitate liturgical prayers. The use of ICT in the liturgy has ritual configurations. Ultimately, care must be taken so that the principles of liturgy, laid down to govern worship are not compromised nor disregarded because ICT has to be employed.

Mutual Relationship Between ICT and Liturgy[2]

ICT and Liturgy can never be at loggerheads when the principles of science and worship are well spelt out, understood, and adhered to by both disciplines. These departments are complementary and are in search for truth in different realms of life, namely, natural and supernatural. For some school of thought, Liturgy seems to be at loggerheads with ICT; but in truth,

---

1 See Walter C. Ihejirika, *The e-priest: The Identity of the Catholic Priest in the Digital Age* (Owerri: Edu-Edy Publications, 2011). In this book, the concepts and instruments of the new ICT are used as symbols and metaphors to explain the life and ministry of priests.

2 Insights used to address some of the issues on the mutual relationship between ICT and Liturgy are influenced by the article of Patrick C. Chibuko, "Information and Communication Technology (ICT) in the Liturgical Life of the Christians Today: An Anglophone West African Response" in Emmanuel C. Anagwo (ed.), *Journal of Inculturation Theology*, Vol. 16, No. 2, 2019, 140-155.

the purpose is the same: to seek the ultimate truth, the meaning and reason of all we see or imagine. Both solicit exceptionally brilliant faculties such as intensified concentration and constant application. This illuminates why both the ICT users, and the worshippers experience the same type of fulfilment bliss when they perceive the truth. The difference lies in the paths they pursue; ICT submits the theory it postulates to experimental verification, whereas Liturgy rest on implicit faith.

Accordingly, ICT and Sacred Liturgy have common features which can be expanded and exploited towards understanding how the former can lead to the latter. Life provides stages as one moves from one step to another. The liturgy, which is the celebration of the Paschal Mystery of the passion, death, resurrection, and ascension of the Christ into glory, remains the inestimable treasure of the Church. The liturgy makes the Church, builds it up, constitutes it, nourishes it, assures its growth, and manifests its true nature. It is the source and summit of the Christian life. It is the summit towards which all the activities of the Church are directed; it is also the fount from which all her power flows. For the goal of apostolic endeavour is that all who are made sons and daughters of God by faith and baptism should come together to praise God during worship, to take part in the sacrifice and to eat at the Lord's Supper.[3]

While we may have become overwhelmed with digital revolution, media literacy and impact are only emerging. The liturgy opens a cyberspace for the intertwining of heavenly truths and earthly realities in such a way that the earthly is dynamically oriented to the heavenly realities. Whereas, for another school of thought, the nexus between ICT and Liturgy may seem obvious, the deep connections, the nature of these connections and the many possibilities for the 21st century e-worship are yet to be significantly explored. As we examine the possible nexus and complementarity between the use of ICT and Catholic liturgy, the ready question that comes to mind is: Is there really any relationship between liturgy and ICT? If yes, to what extent can ICT be used in the liturgy? From onset, we must assert that there is a relationship. ICT and Liturgy have common features which can be exploited in understanding how the former can enhance the latter. Let us briefly discuss them under *anamnesis*, person, and event-based categories.

---

3 *Sacrosanctum Concilium* 10.

Anamnesis

A key relationship between Liturgy and ICT is *anamnesis* (remembrance). Liturgy is celebrated in remembrance of a person (Jesus Christ) who is the founder of all the sacraments, celebrated in the liturgy. And He is present in full body, soul and divinity in the sacrament of the Holy Eucharist which is the source and summit of our Christian faith.[4] At every liturgical celebration, especially the sacrifice of the Holy Mass, the sacrifice of Christ is re-enacted in an unbloody manner. Christ, already at the Last Supper, asked his disciples, *Hoc facite in meam commemorationem* "to do this in memory of him" (Mark 14:22-24, Luke 22:19, and 1 Cor 11:23-25). In the words of Wendelin Köster, in his paper titled: "Recovery Collective Memory in the Context of Postmodernism,"[5]: "The demand of Jesus, 'Do this in memory of me!', was at once the igniting spark of the memory power of the Church, and its content." This facilitates the powers of concentration. In the physical aspects of concentration, the people react to an invitation and come together in person and in one place, forming an assembly. And whenever the sacrifice of the Holy Mass is celebrated as an assembly, Christ's mode is being carried out and the event of the Last Supper is brought back to life.

In the same way, ICT has capacity of storing information and bringing them to life later in life. It is true that man/woman is given to forgetfulness. Because of this, he/she needs something to store information, so that when it is needed later in life, it can be retrieved and the memory still fresh. A good example here is the video tapes of priestly ordination, religious profession, anniversaries, church dedication, Chrism Mass, pastoral visit of the bishop, and so on. These videos help to keep alive memories that would have been ordinarily erased within a twinkle of an eye. In his article titled: "Information and Communication Technology (ICT) in the Liturgical Life of the Christians Today: An Anglophone West African Response," Patrick C. Chibuko rightly observes that specific life experiences leave evergreen memories behind. These memories condition, determine and influence one's behaviour a great deal even in the present. He remembers:

---

4 *Sacrosanctum Concilium* 10.

5 Wendelin Köster, "Recovery Collective Memory in the Context of Postmodernism," in Keith Pecklers (ed.), *Liturgy in a Postmodern World* (New York: Continuum, 2003) 33.

> ...with joy, his priestly ordination in 1983 which was recorded with the then high-quality video camera into VHS cassette. Since then, he relays it at each anniversary and recalls with thanks and gratitude to God for the gift of priesthood, the sacrifices of his people, the bishop who came to his home town for the rite, the challenging homily that still spurs him on today, the welcome address with all the good wishes, admonitions of his people, the faces of his friends and benefactors who honoured him that day with their prayers, presence and presents. This same experience could very well apply to every Christian in the reception of any of the sacraments like Baptism, first Holy Communion, Confirmation, Holy Matrimony, anniversaries, and several other landmark celebrations worthy of remembrance.[6]

So, liturgy is essentially a religion of remembrance. It constantly reminds the believers of the wonderful works of God both in the Old and New Testaments and in their present situations within the narrative redemption of God's plan. The remembering characteristic feature of Christianity arises from the imperfect nature of humanity. One of such is the capacity to forget easily. Generally, humanity is easily given to forgetfulness. This is because the memory, as the seat of remembering, can disappoint. Accordingly, "it is an imperfection in practically every human being to forget, to be constant in inconstancy, to be consistent in inconsistency."[7] Down through the ages, various mechanisms have been devised to checkmate human forgetfulness through documentations and writings. One recalls the Shema Israel, as recorded in Deut 6:4, and the incident of the Last Supper with the injunction, "Do this in memory of me" Today, ICT has facilitated the mechanism of improving the human capacity to keep and preserve records for contemporaries and posterity. The memories of a well celebrated and participated worship will advance eloquent echoes in the quality and exemplary living standards of the people. Essentially, liturgical celebration is all about *anamnesis,* re-enactment. Due to the fact that human beings are often given to short memories as earlier hinted, ICT in all its ramified

---

6 Chibuko, "Information and Communication Technology (ICT) in the Liturgical Life..." 140.

7 Chibuko, "Information and Communication Technology (ICT) in the Liturgical Life..." 140-141.

gadgets could serve as suitable means for remembrance in worship.

Person Based

It is true that liturgy celebrates not a thing or an ideology; rather, it is a person-based religion and celebration. In liturgy the person of Jesus Christ is celebrated. His life, ministry, suffering, death and resurrection are all celebrated. Liturgy is generally understood as the official worship of the Church. In his Encyclical Letter, *Mediator Dei*, Pope Pius XII expresses the correct idea of the Church as the Mystical Body of Christ. According to him, "The Liturgy is nothing more nor less than the exercise of the priestly function of Christ."[8] It is the public worship of the people of God, prayer in action. It is the prayer of Christ and His members. In this regard, this classical definition by Pope Pius XII says: "Liturgy is the public worship which our Redeemer as the Head of the Church renders to the Father as well as the worship which the community of the faithful renders to its Founder, and through Him to the Heavenly Father. It is, in short, the worship rendered by the Mystical Body of Christ."[9] The richness of this understanding is expressed on the notion that it is Christ who is rendering this worship and we the members of His Mystical Body are participating in this worship of Christ to the Father. It, therefore, means that in liturgy the faithful (Body of Christ) continue to render that worship in memory (*anamnesis*) to God and implicitly through the power of the Holy Spirit who is always at work in the Church.

According to the reformed liturgy of the Second Vatican Council, we see the centrality of the Person and work of Christ to the liturgy.[10] The liturgy is all about Christ and the work of salvation He came to achieve on behalf of mankind. In this regard, following Patristic terminology, Christ is seen as the physician and medicine of both the corporeal (bodily) and non-corporeal (spiritual) aspects of humanity. Consequently, Christ operates in and heals both of these dimensions of our human existence. This has been made possible thanks to that perfect union that exists between Christ and His Father and which Christ communicates to us and effects in us. That

8 Pius XII, *Mediator Dei (The Sacred Liturgy),* (Boston: St. Paul Editions, 1947) no. 20.

9 Pius XII, *Mediator Dei* no. 20.

10 *Sacrosanctum Concilium* 10.

perfect union has also made it possible for Christ to achieve our perfect reconciliation with the Father and communicate to us the fullness of divine worship. This perfect reconciliation with the Father was achieved for us by Christ through the Paschal Mystery of His Passion, Death, Resurrection and Ascension into glory.[11] Consequently, the redemptive work of Christ is a fundamental and indispensable core of the plan and history of salvation. That redemptive act of Christ is what the liturgy commemorates and which the Church continues.[12] The Liturgy re-enacts that plan and continues it. What is commemorated and communicated in the liturgy is Christ, the fullness of God's revelation and the work of salvation He achieved on behalf of humanity.

Similarly, ICT is people oriented.[13] This is because it is geared towards making people understand what is happening around them very clearly. ICT focuses mainly on improving people at every age, to adapt to the reality of their age. We should make extensive use of new media in order to create, connect and collaborate with people and lead them up to the Paschal Mystery of Jesus Christ, for example, Broadcasting or sharing of homilies in worship on WhatsApp, Instagram, YouTube, Telegram, etc. But we need to be careful of uncritical, uncensored, verified messages being disseminated. That liturgy is very cautious about the use of privacy. ICT invades privacy especially the sacrament of reconciliation. Christian worship offers a kind of liturgy does not compete with events like Facebook, etc. That liturgy offers a kind of prayer of who we are in our deepest identity, the beloved of God. This does not mean dispensing of the

---

11 This meaning of the sacrament of reconciliation, and indeed all the seven sacraments, can be illustrated with the analogy of the proverbial story of an elephant and an ant. The ant wanted to cross a shaky bridge but could not do it. Since an elephant wanted to cross the same bridge, she perched on the ears of the elephant. After crossing the shaky bridge, the ant exclaimed: "We have done it." In other words, when we perch on Christ, we can access the merits of the sacraments.

12 *Sacrosanctum Concilium* 6.

13 Etymologically, the word liturgy is derived from two Greek words *laos* - people; and *ergon* - work. It meant the public function performed for the public welfare until it assumed a sacred dimension later in its historical development. An outstanding notion of liturgy flows from the letter to the Hebrews where Christ's sacrificial or priestly offering became the *leitourgos* of the Sanctuary (8:2). Christ is the liturgy the people celebrate, he is the melody of people's hymn, and he is the centre of the people's celebration.

avenues which the new media offers. But that those avenues are subordinated to the Gospel. Here, liturgy and ICT find a relationship to communicate the message of God effectively to people of every age; hence, ICT should be encouraged to the extent that it does not constitute distraction or promote passive participation.

Event Based

Liturgical celebration, especially the sacrifice of the Holy Mass, re-enacts the events of the Paschal Mystery of Jesus Christ. This event which took place over two thousand years, still comes afresh in our minds when celebrated. Accordingly, Patrick C. Chibuko observes that the Paschal Mystery forms the central point of the Christian mystery and faith. Every Christian theology or praxis has its foundation in the Paschal Mystery of Christ which embraces His passion, death and resurrection.[14] Evidently, it not only forms the foundation of the faith of the Church, but also remains the source from which the Church draws its vitality. The Church is built, sustained, nourished, and survived on this unique mystery of Christ. Essentially, Paschal Mystery is the whole experience of Jesus Christ in the flesh. This is the mystery of the incarnation and redemption. It refers to the whole drama of humanity's salvation which embraces the history of the suffering, death, resurrection, and ascension of Christ into glory. It is the continuation in time of the mystery of salvation brought about by God throughout His encounter with humanity. The theology of Easter *Triduum* can only be located with the Paschal Mystery for as Paul said, if Christ died and did not rise, our faith would have been futile, and our situation hopeless (1 Cor 15:14-15).

Through the liturgical celebrations, the Church constantly relives this event of the mystery. Down the ages, she makes a memorial, a commemoration, a re-enactment, an '*anamnesis*' of this mystery particularly in the sacraments, and her other liturgical celebrations. In the words of Dom Odo Casel the "Paschal Mystery is experienced through the liturgy in which Christ Himself is present and active through the Church

---

[14] Patrick C. Chibuko, *Paschal Mystery of Christ Foundation for Liturgical Inculturation in Africa* (Frankfurt: Peter Lang, 2001) 7.

and the Church acts with Him."[15] Christian worship has its full goal attained in the Eucharist because the "fullness of Glory" is found in Christ's self-sacrifice. Everything stems from it. *The Catechism of the Catholic Church* in quoting *Sacrosanctum Concilium* says that the Eucharist is the source and summit of all Christian life.[16] Every other sacrament, sacramentals and ministry in the Church is geared towards it. In fact, the Holy Mass is that unbloody re-enactment of the paschal event.

Granted that there were no cameras to record them, the events were documented as veritable information for the Church of today. This kind of documentation is a type of ICT. It helps to keep memory alive. If these events were not transmitted from oral source later to documentation era, no one would have known about it. But ICT helps the events of the liturgy to be stored and whenever needed, retrieved for consumption. By so doing, the nature of man/woman who is ordinarily given to forgetfulness can be salvaged.

From the foregoing, we can adduce that ICT has remained a great asset to Catholic worship in recent years, and the mutual benefits that can accrue to both means through more formidable partnership in the future look promising. Both are not inimical with each other; rather, are intertwined. Both are essential for the humanity's welfare and ascent to God. There is a long path ahead, both in fields of ICT and Liturgy. There are worlds beyond worlds to be unveiled, tapped and maximized. If life on our planet is accident or created by God, it is possible by the same postulate that it can also exist elsewhere. Sooner or later, we will resolve the mystery. Then, at some point ICT and Liturgy will perhaps meet. Until then, the search must go on, as one enriches the other; as well as respecting the other in areas of no compromise. A healthy collaboration and connection between the two would facilitate an integral and effective liturgical participation and advancement of humanity.

---

15 Quoted by Ignatius Puthiadem, *Christian Liturgy: The Representation of the Greatest God – Human Story* (Mumbai: St. Pauls Publications, 2002) 21.

16 *Sacrosanctum Concilium* 10.

Dynamics of E-Era with Reference to the Liturgy

The intermingling of ICT and Liturgy has become an affirmation of the immanent and the transcendent God who is constantly at work. Words are inadequate to qualify the range of ICT strides of modern society. The world of digital worship has impacted significantly on the lives of modern society especially the young through various strands of gadgets, soft wares and applications. Unthinkable feats sixty years ago are now possible through the media. There is no gainsaying that the media has simplified life, improved human, interpersonal and communal relations. According to Pope St. John Paul II:

> The world of communications is the first Areopagus of the modern age, unifying humanity and turning it into what is known as a 'global village'. The communications media have acquired such importance as to be for many the chief means of information and education, of guidance and inspiration for many people in their personal, family and social behaviour. In particular, the younger generation is growing up in a world conditioned by the mass media.[17]

There is hardly any part of human endeavour that has not been impacted by media technology and digital constructs. With electronic communication *via* internet, there is a gradual shift from the world of physical materials and books to digitalized versions. In this digital age, a lot of electronic devices abound in everyday life-giving rise to some being used in Christian worship and prayer. We shall briefly explain those electronic devices as they affect and effect liturgical worship.

E-Liturgical Books

These are situations when liturgical books of hard covers are not used in the liturgy. Instead, the use of soft copy through the internet facility/electronic device of a particular gadget of ICT is used. In his article

---

[17] Pope John Paul II, *Redemptoris Missio* Encyclical Letter (1990) 37 in http://w2.vatican.va/content/john-paul-ii/en/encyclicals/documents/hf_jp-ii_enc_07121990_redemptoris-missio.html. accessed on 15th April 2022.

titled: "The Dignity and Place of Liturgical Books in Sacred Liturgy: An Evaluation in the Light of Digital Revolution" Benedict E. Ukutegbe observes that famous books in various disciplines are now being converted to digital formats as e-books and e-libraries with the internet serving as a catalyst. It is little wonder then that even religious and theological materials have caught the bug. The area of liturgical books has not been insulated as there is now an array of applications (apps) and other digital format products of Liturgy of the hours, the Roman Missal, Roman Ritual, Lectionary on ipad, e-readers like Kindle, tablets, and even mobile phones. Environmental impact concerns, portability and convenience tip the balance in favour of these electronic media products.[18] He further states that:

> Churches especially in urban parishes float projection screens as liturgical aids to facilitate participation of the faithful. The faithful who are media savvy also resort to their phones preloaded with apps containing liturgical texts, lectionary, hymns, etc and cling to them with some sentimental attachment of a tech trendy world. In many urban parishes, priests, religious men and women and the laity are now seen openly using these media appliances and applications in the celebration of the liturgy. A priest in transit for example finds it more convenient to pray the liturgy of the hours with an ipad or mobile phone than carrying the printed Breviary. While private usages for the purpose of study and private prayers may seem convenient and escape scrutiny, their usages in the liturgy have generated debates as to their suitability for the liturgy.[19]

In the strict sense, liturgical books are books specially designated to be used at worship. By their nature, they are made and bound solely for use in the liturgy. These books are specially blessed. By blessing, they are set apart

---

[18] Benedict E. Ukutegbe, "The Dignity and Place of Liturgical Books in Sacred Liturgy: An Evaluation in the Light of Digital Revolution" in in Benedict E. Ukutegbe, Emmanuel C. Anagwo & Victor U. Jamahh (eds.), *Abuse in the Liturgy and the Nigerian Context Today, Proceedings of the Annual Conference of the Catholic Liturgists' Association of Nigeria* [*CALAN) 2018*], (Benin City: Floreat Systems Printing Press, 2018) 106.

[19] Ukutegbe, "The Dignity and Place of Liturgical Books in Sacred Liturgy" 106-107.

solely for use at the liturgy. Each is distinct and meant for a specific purpose and for the ritual within the liturgy. Unlike liturgical books, e-liturgical books are ambivalent because they do not exist in hard form (copy) but are contained in an electronic device. Since such devices are not blessed, the reverence due to such books are lost. *The General Instruction of the Roman Missal* states that since liturgical books especially the Roman Missal (the Sacramentary) and Lectionary are used to celebrate the Eucharist and proclaim the Gospel, they have a revered status. Accordingly, they should be made beautiful and elegant, so that they can sometimes be carried in procession too.[20] The implication of using e-liturgical books means flaunting this principle. An ipad or smartphone cannot be carried in procession because they have multiple uses that make them unsuitable for such sacred function.

E-liturgical books cannot also stand the test of time like hard copies of the Book of Gospel, Lectionary or Roman Missal. This is because as compatible devices, they are susceptible to virus attack and power failure. At the time of use, one may unfortunately observe that the particular document is corrupt. E-liturgical books can also easily be deleted and discarded which is not the case with hard copy of liturgical books. Again, the same ipad/phones used to read the Gospel or preside at Mass can be used to do social networking, downloading videos, watching good and bad movies, making useful and 'useless (mundane/profane) calls,' etc. This calls for reflection by technology experts to see if they can manufacture ICT products that can easily be exclusively used for liturgical purposes and so set apart for a sacred status. Meanwhile, although, e-liturgical books are not encouraged, they can be made available for the lay faithful's participation and especially for liturgical studies. Again, for serious reasons/circumstances such as distant travel, eye challenge, pandemic and other emergency situations, certain e-liturgical books like the Missals and the Divine Office could be used for liturgical celebrations.

E-Confessions

This is the situation when an individual wants or requests to have his or her sacramental confessions heard over the phone call. The sacrament of

---

20 GIRM no. 349.

reconciliation is one of the seven sacraments of the Church. It has been known by various names: Conversion, Penance, Confession or Forgiveness. Although, the preferred term nowadays, as Austin Echema would say, is "Reconciliation" because the conversion of a sinner, the penance or satisfaction that the person makes, the confession of the sins so committed and even the forgiveness received by the penitent, are all always related to reconciliation with God, with the Church, in the home, the neighbourhood, the school, the workplace, indeed the world at large.[21] Since it is one of the Sacraments of Healing in the life and ministry of the Church, it refers to that sacrament by which sins committed after Baptism are remitted if and when the sinner performs certain acts and receives absolution from a qualified priest. The ultimate purpose is for the reconciliation of the faithful to God and the Church. Indeed, reconciliation gives priority to God's gracious love which, in Christ, draws Christians who have fallen to sin into a life-giving communion. This communion transforms them into the likeness of Christ, frees them from sin and leads them into a life of love and communal charity.

The Catechism of the Catholic Church corroborates the fact that this sacrament is called reconciliation because it imparts to the sinner the love of God who reconciles (see 2 Cor 5:20).[22] Furthermore, whoever lives by God's merciful love is ready to respond to the Lord's call to be reconciled to his or her brothers and sisters (see Matt 5:24). Thus, if Christians love their neighbour, they will not feel comfortable until such neighbours are treated in a just and fair manner. That is what the sacrament of reconciliation celebrates since liturgy essentially celebrates what the Church believes, hence, the wise dictum "*lex credendi, lex celebrandi, lex vivendi*" (what the Church believes, she celebrates, and she lives out). Christians who are united and reconciled will obviously support one another and together act for change in the society. The bond of Christian charity demands that one should share with others. It sets an obligation before the Church, both local and universal for peaceful co-existence.

By its nature, it requires person to person contact. Indeed, the sacrament of reconciliation is a very delicate one that needs to be handled with great

---

21 Austin Echema, "The Sacrament of Reconciliation: Implications of the New Term" in *Journal of Inculturation Theology*, Vol. 4, April 1997, 42.

22 *The Catechism of the Catholic Church* [CCC] (Nairobi: Paulines Publications, 2001) 1443.

care. Here, the penitent pours out his/her entire self to God without any reservations and the priest listens empathically and reprimands as well as encourages the penitent to persevere. This priest does that with a smile of the loving father and warm touch during absolution. Nothing is too sinful nor secretive to mention in the course of confession and the priest is bound by the seal of confession to ensure everything that happens at the confessional remains there. This is not possible with e-confession. Admittedly, every phone call has a third party and could be recorded and saved. Between the caller (sender) and the receiver (recipient), there is what is called a "Gate Keeper". The gatekeeper is responsible for editing and filtering of the call or message before passing it to the receiver.

Accordingly, ICT gadgets have main servers from where any information that has passed through them can be retrieved. The machine is not bound by any oath or seal to choose whom to access it or not. Once anyone has access to know what to do or better still, the right button to press, then very sensitive information can be hacked, and the seal of confession breached. When such situation occurs, the electronic device is not blamed because it is not bound by any seal of secrecy. E-confessions do not warrant proper disposition of the confessor and the liturgical decorum necessary for the celebration of the sacrament. The priest may be driving, taking his bath, eating or playing games. In fact, while it is possible to pray for and with a person in a situation of sin or worry or anxiety, it is completely not permissible to listen to one's confession through any means of modern communication. Hence, e-confession should be totally discouraged.

E-Congregation

E-congregation (E-worship, Online Worship or online Church) refers to the situation where the faithful worship with the aid of electronic device instead of being physically presence in the Church. The device could be used at home, office, school, market, etc. However, the reformed liturgy of the Second Vatican Council, in its document *Sacrosanctum Concilium,* calls for active, conscious, full and socio-communitarian participation in the liturgy which requires physical presence.[23] The public nature of the liturgy requires the physical presence of its participants. In unison, they lift

---

[23] *Sacrosanctum Concilium* 14.

their eyes, hearts and minds to God in faith and charity. The physical presence of worshippers at liturgical worship sessions also helps to build a Christian community that do things in common. It cements the union of Christ's faithful as brothers and sisters. For instance, the community dancing and singing with one voice is joined in one faith, one Baptism and one God in happy expression of this togetherness where everybody is equal in the sight of God (see Acts 2:46-47).

An e-congregation prevents this public nature of liturgy that requires physical presence from happening. It allows participants the opportunity of worshipping from their comfort zones. When we leave our home and proceed to the Church, it is a symbol of making a journey of faith to seek out Christ. The redemptive presence of God is re-enacted through presence in the Church. The incarnation took place through the movement of the Son of God taking flesh in history and dwelling among us. Through bodily movement and procession, one joins in this redemptive work. Gerard van der Leeuw aptly says that:

> ...in the Bible, movement is everything. God is movement. His spirit broods over the waters of chaos, his pillar of fire leads through the desert, his prophets bring disquiet to a people that loves quiet, his Son comes down to earth, his spirit drives. His creation is no clumsy piece of work, but a progression into the world.[24]

But it is not possible when participation in the liturgy is e-congregation. When one is physically present at the liturgy, it is expected that one responds to the parts of the Mass as designated, but in the case of an e-congregation that sense of obligation might not be there and one's participation might end up being more of watching instead of worshipping.

E-Choir

E-choir (E-music) is the situation when a choir records songs to be used in different occasions during the liturgical worship and stored and retrieved for such occasion. Recognising the importance of singing in the liturgy, the

---

[24] Gerard van der Leeuw, *Sacred and Profane Beauty: The Holy in Art*, trans. David E. Green (New York: Holt, Rinehart and Winston, 1963) 20.

instruction on Music in Liturgy (*Musicam Sacram*) observes that liturgical worship is given a more noble form when it is celebrated in song, with the ministers of each degree fulfilling their ministry.[25] This is completely absent in e-choir. In e-choir, the songs used at liturgical celebrations are recorded songs played with aid of musical machines such as VCD, DVD, etc. Although the songs may be relevant to the celebration, the context, situation, season and even purpose for the song may defeat its being used for another celebration. E-choir does not envisage the active participation of the congregation. Accordingly, the song recorded in the evening may be conveniently used in the following morning. The worshippers become more of listeners instead of encouraging active participation in the songs.

Musicam Sacram encourages that at least one or two properly trained singers should be available.[26] The e-choir does not involve physical person leading in singing instead, an electronic device is used. Besides, e-choir requires the use of electricity to reproduce songs. In the event of power outage or failure, the prepared/recorded songs could be disorganised. This can cause distraction and confusion in the liturgy. Relatedly, owing to the complexities of ICT equipment, it can develop system/mechanical fault; thus, it leaves everyone in the dark.

Again, with e-choir, it is possible that a particular song recorded for a funeral liturgy may inadvertently be played during the reception of the Holy Communion. Accordingly, with e-choir, a wrong song may be played/intoned against the one planned because of the absence of the person who should operate the system. This dampens the spirit of the liturgy at each celebration. Songs that belong to a particular season may be played in the Church in a different season. Hence, it is strongly recommended that where possible, the physical presence of the choir for a liturgical celebration, even if they are few, should be encouraged.

E-Fundraising

E-fundraising (Electronic Fundraising, E-donations, or E-Tithing) in the Church is new way of elevating debts from the Church where money is transferred into the account of Church through electronic device. This is

---

25 Music in Liturgy (*Musicam Sacram*) 21.
26 Music in Liturgy (*Musicam Sacram*) 21.

very necessary with the introduction of e-naira by the Federal Government of Nigeria from 1st October 2021. However, it should not be done during the homily nor before the liturgy of the Eucharist. This can be in during announcement or after post communion prayer. When parishioners did not come with offering but have decided to monetize it, they can do or make a transfer of the money into the Church account and send their electronic receipt to the priest WhatsApp number/text messages or finance officer of the parish/station/diocese. But this should not, in any, distract the flow of the Eucharistic liturgy if trained personnel are used. Preferably, the transfer should be made into the Church account before someone joins at the Eucharistic liturgy at the beginning and not during the Mass. This is to forestall distraction. Again, it is not advisable after Mass because it will no longer be part of the sacrifice at Mass. Admittedly, what is offered through e-fundraising should be part of the sacrifice of the Mass and what was not offered cannot be categorized as such.[27]

It has become necessary to develop and create a finance department in every parish Church where none is existent. The nomenclature does not really matter as far as it engages in meeting the practical needs of the poor, the marginalised like the children of the imprisoned who belonged also to the most vulnerable folks of the parish and society at large. In some parishes it is entrusted to a few members of the parish council. This arrangement can well be improved upon and given a priority in the parish because of its practical and evangelization values. The sources of income to this department could be very much widened through well organised and co-ordinated ICT facilities where donations to this purse are not only in kind but above all in cash through online donation. It will go a long way in the generation and sustainability of parish/diocesan funds.

Types of ICT for Catholic Liturgy

There are several ways ICT can be used for liturgical formation of the worshippers especially the youth who are 'digital natives' or 'digital generation'. ICT during worship takes various types and appears under

27 For a detailed study, see Emmanuel C. Anagwo, *New Trends of Fundraising in Christian Worship: The Nigerian Pastoral Experience* (Berlin: Peter Lang International Publisher, 2022) 100-101.

various names: power point, video and sound clips, animation, e-learning, Facebook, and teleconferencing. From onset, we must underscore that the list is not exhaustive but stems from the pastoral, academic and life-experience of the writer. Let us now briefly discuss the constituent parts of the types of ICT for Catholic liturgy, one after the other.

i) Power Point (Banners, Overhead/Screen Projectors and PowerPoint Displays): ICT can be used to support homilies, talks, sermons, etc which presents the results of thematic work, group or individual work. Power Point presentation and presentations made on smart board in archives which were available through website and/or platforms.

ii) Video and Sound Clips: Computer equipment for video and sound editing makes it possible for learners to produce audio-visual materials and audio recording. Video footages and audio recording clips may be used by pastors or pastoral agents to provide feedback. Some of the catechetical and liturgical instructions can be put in video and audio clips. For instance, a video clip of the liturgical symbols, seasons or ritual colours, postures, gestures, and liturgical movement can go viral among the youth.

iii) Animation: Parishes can use different computer programmes and web pages to animate issues which they want to show and explain to the worshippers especially the youth. The idea behind this is to make the liturgical formation more concrete. This way of working could be found in many different themes of the Church's teaching such as: life, ministry, passion, death, resurrection and ascension of Jesus Christ.

iv) E-Learning: This is another way of using ICT for liturgical formation especially using Ipad and android phones. Parishes can link up to a particular website and individual youth also book on to different stations to receive liturgical formation and catechesis. A good example is the website called "youngandcatholic.net" designed to disseminate Catholic faith and doctrines. At the universal level, we have Catholic Resources on the net. This contains wide variety of texts such as Latin liturgical texts, patristic documents, Council of Trent, Vatican II, and other papal documents. It includes links to homepages of dioceses, online bibles and so on. Vatican Home Page uses www.vatican.va/, the homepage for the See of Rome with links to various Roman dicasteries and current papal documents available in many languages. Other parishes, cooperate bodies and spirited individuals can emulate such and establish their own websites accordingly.

v) Facebook: Facebook dominates the social media advertising business, reportedly collecting more than $1.5 billion in 2010, mostly for display advertising on its pages. The mission of the Church can also extend in this area, as an indispensable milestone for evangelization. Admittedly, Walter Ihejirika explains Facebook as: "a digital photo album like traditional photo album which we normally show to friends when they visit us. Now my friends and relations do not need to physically visit me before they can view my latest pictures - they can do so by registering on Facebook."[28] We can have a Facebook account of the parish/diocese, and some can be dedicated specially for the youth. Every diocese and parish can also have a page and monitor the content, in this age that one cannot easily stop hacking but can counteract them. Like the writer who weekly posts Sunday reflections on his Facebook page,[29] daily homilies may also graphically be posted with pictures to disseminate Christian message.[30]

vi) Teleconferencing: This has played an indispensable role in liturgical formation. Though mostly used in the secular society, it is a method of using technology to bring people's ideas together despite geographical barrier. There are several varieties of teleconferencing which usually include a large screen and video cameras that can send live pictures and online system to record communication among participants.

Forms of ICT for Catholic Worship

Today, the Church has at her disposal a variety of means of ICT for social communication. As highlighted by Antony Mayfield, in his work titled:

---

[28] Ihejirika 84.

[29] Over six years now, the writer has successful used his Facebook page to post his homilies on Sundays. On two occasions, when my laptop had technical faults, I was inundated with calls and messages by both priests, consecrated men and women as well as the lay faithful. This confirms that people really read and hope on those homilies even when they do not comment or react on them. Today also, some priests and even religious men and women post their reflections daily on both Facebook, WhatsApp, and YouTube. This is a welcome development! It is, indeed, a virtual pulpit as against the physical pulpit to preach the Gospel to those on the territory without borders.

[30] Emmanuel C. Anagwo, "Preparing the Youth on the Use of ICT for Liturgical Formation: A Challenge for the Church in Nigeria" in *Koinonia*, Vol. 7, No.5, June 2017, 48.

What is Social Media? there are six forms of social media: social networks, blogs, wikis, podcasts, forums, and microblogging.[31] Let us briefly discuss each of them.

i) Social Networks: A social network is a website that allows people with similar interest to come together and share information, photos, and videos. Those who engage in social networking may be doing so as a personal, business, or religious enterprise. These sites allow users to build personal web pages and then connect with friends to share content and communication. The biggest social networks are *MySpace, Facebook* and *Bebo*. These are useful in mobilizing social actions such as prayers, short scripture passages and instilling a sense of fellowship.

ii) Blogs: The word 'blog' refers to a shortened form of its original name, "weblog." These weblogs allowed early internet uses to "log" the details of their day in diary-style entries. Often, blogs allow readers to comment, to be familiar whereby they form communities around popular blogs. Perhaps the best-known forms of social media, *blogs* are online journals, with entries appearing, beginning with the most recent. These provide avenues through which thought-provoking homilies and inspirational stories and testimonies can be shared among believers.

iii) Wikis: A wiki is website or online resource that can be edited, updated, and deleted by its relevant users unlike a blog that is a personal website usually created by an individual or multiple users. Such websites allow people to add content to or edit the information on them, acting as a communal document or database. The best-known *wiki* is Wikipedia, the online encyclopaedia which has over 2 million English language articles. The Church can use wikis to document official accounts of its historical events and to elucidate on its documents, decrees, and other messages from the Church's leaders.

iv) Podcasts: A podcast is a programme made available in digital format for download over the internet. Examples include an episodic series of digital audio or video files that a personal user can download to their personal device and listen when they choose. As audio and video files, they are available by subscription through services like *Apple iTunes*. *Podcasts*

---

[31] Antony Mayfield, *What is Social Media? iCrossing ebook* from https://www.coursehero.com/file/6882077/What-is-Social-Media-iCrossing-ebook/ accessed on 25th August 2022.

are useful in sharing pre-recorded homilies and Mass proceedings, among other Church events.

v) Forums: These came about before the term "social media" and are a powerful and popular element of online communities. These are the communities that organize and share particular kinds of content. The most popular content communities tend to form around photos (Flickr), bookmarked links (delicious) and videos (YouTube). The Church can use forums to elucidate on issues that may need deeper theological explanations over time. These include those issues that call for the Church to publicly declare its position, among others.

vi) Microblogging: As an online broadcast medium, it exists as a specific form of blogging. A micro-blog differs from a traditional blog because its content is typically smaller in both actual and aggregated file size. So, this is a social networking combined with bite-sized blogging, where small amounts of content ('updates') are distributed online and through the mobile phone network. Microblogs "allow users to exchange small elements of content such as short sentences, individual images, or video links,"[32] which may be the major reason for their popularity among the people. These small messages are sometimes referred as micro posts. Twitter is the clear leader in this field.[33]

Evaluation

This chapter affirmed the need for a continual search for the mutual relationship between ICT and Catholic Liturgy. After all, liturgical celebration means re-enactments of the person of Christ in his salvific acts. ICT records, stores, protects, processes, transmits, retrieves, and distributes information and memories of the celebration of the Paschal Mystery of Christ. It cannot claim to be of object of celebration but simply a modern means to facilitate the celebration and re-enactment of attentive celebration. ICT qualifies only as means to an end and not the end itself. Nonetheless, the liturgy of today must catch up with the new trends. To do the contrary would mean singing outside the choir. The liturgy would simply make

---

32 J. Aichner & F. Jacob, "Measuring the Degree of Corporate Social Media Use" in *International Journal of Market Research*, March 2015, 57 (2): 257-275.

33 Mayfield, *What is Social Media?*

herself archaic, reductant or grossly irrelevant. However, to use ICT in liturgy, discretion and discernment must be of essence.

It is evident that ICT and Catholic Liturgy are complimentary, and this mutual relationship will enhance a deeper appreciation of the Christian worship. Granted that ICT is useful in liturgical worship, it should always be a means to an end and not an end itself. Being physically present at liturgical functions should always be the first choice, except of course, in moments of sickness, old age, pandemics, epidemics, war, emergency, etc. The services of the chief celebrant/liturgist to evolve a digital worship ought to integrate the use of ICT. He/she must discover the link between them. Liturgy is not static and moribund. Liturgy opens new vista. ICT should be studied with its connectivity with worship. This is the link. Liturgical celebration challenges worshippers towards *diakonia* and *koinonia*. In between them, we have "*martes*," that is, witnessing. The liturgical celebration essentially is *anamnesis*. It means that all hope cannot be suspended. In this type, celebration becomes spiritual communion.

ICT offers the Church organs an avalanche of opportunities, with types and forms, to enhance her liturgical celebrations and formation. Undoubtedly, some priests, parishes and chaplaincies have been, over a period of time, applying social media and audio-visual aids in their pastoral ministries. The results one can say have been memorable, wonderful, and great. ICT has been a technology that facilitates information and communication centres essentially on the human person. ICT is person oriented. At the heart of Christian worship is the Person of Christ. In the liturgy, the Church celebrates a Personality, not a theory, or philosophy, or ideology, but a Person, namely Christ. Thus, the search for the nexus is a reality because there is a point of contact between the two, given birth to various types and forms of usage and application.

CHAPTER FOUR

THE USE AND ABUSE OF ICT IN LITURGICAL CELEBRATION TODAY

One of the greatest treasures of our age is the ICT, which is the cheapest and fastest means of providing, compiling, and retrieving information. Evidently, the amount of information available through the internet is enormous and is increasing steadily. In an age where internet is becoming more ubiquitous, Catholic liturgy is another possible area that the ICT can be applied with some useful advantages and efficiency to worshippers. Indeed, the social media are new arrivals in the communication scene, and they have totally changed the way human beings communicated and worshipped God before their arrival. They have their huge advantages and unfortunately there are also some disadvantages. This is the task before this chapter to adjudicate.

Possible Uses of ICT for Catholic Liturgy

A popular novelist called Chinua Achebe in his celebrated novel titled: *Things Fall Apart*, told the story of Unoka, the father of Okonkwo who was woken up one early morning by his debtor, Okoye. Unoka intuitively answered his debtor, I will start by paying my debtors from those that I owe higher amount than those that I am owing the least.[1] In this case, I am beginning this assessment with huge advantages accruing from the ingenuity, revolutionary and ground-breaking creativity of ICT. Admittedly, ICT can be very useful in liturgical celebrations today. It can play important and beneficial roles in the liturgical catechesis for formation and renewal of the worshippers. ICT is a powerful tool for extending liturgical formation and catechesis. Clergy, religious men and women as well as the lay faithful no longer have to rely solely on printed books (such

---

[1] Chinua Achebe, *Things Fall Apart* (London: Heinemann Educational Books, 1973) 5-6.

as liturgical books) and other materials in physical media housed in churches, libraries and available in limited quantities for the formational needs. One can rightly agree with Richard Leonard, in his article titled, "'Light! Camera! Worship! The Cinema and its Challenges to Roman Catholic Worship in Postmodernity," that:

> The way Catholic liturgy is portrayed on the large or small screen directly shapes people's expectations of it. In an increasingly unchurched society, the most regular exposure to liturgical actions which many people have is what they see on television and in film. When they come to our liturgical rites, they bring images of what the ceremonies will look like from the media.[2]

But it is important to always keep in mind that primarily, liturgy is for worship; secondarily, teaching takes place there too. Ordinarily, liturgy provides the basis for human conduct since its fitting celebration, "contains much instruction for the faithful"[3] where values and skills needed for active, full and conscious participation would evolve. At liturgical celebrations, ample opportunities are provided in the introductions, scripture readings, commentaries, sermons, and exhortations for instruction.

Other important areas for instruction and liturgical formation abound, such as prayers and hymns which could serve as supplementary resources for imparting moral and doctrinal truths. Since liturgy has to do with rites, symbols, postures, gestures, ritual duties, and acts of reverence established by religious authority to give honour and glory to God, liturgical celebrations ought always to use means to inculcate liturgical formation. The insight by the reformed liturgy of the Second Vatican Council is quite concise. That liturgy is the source and summit of Christian life.[4] It teaches that with Christian faith, in the divine worship, the faithful's offer and the work of their redemption are all condensed in the liturgy. The faithful uses the liturgy to express the mystery of Christ in their lives and to manifest the

---

2 Richard Leonard, "'Light! Camera! Worship! The Cinema and its Challenges to Roman Catholic Worship in Postmodernity" in Keith Pecklers (ed.), *Liturgy in a Postmodern World* (New York: Continuum, 2003) 27.

3 *Sacrosanctum Concilium* 33.

4 *Sacrosanctum Concilium* 10.

true nature of the Church to the world.[5] Austin Echema rightly affirms that, "Indeed, liturgy can be powerfully effective in informing, forming and transforming its community of participants in Christian faith if it is sacramentally adequate to enable them to express their lives in faith to God and to experience God's life in love to them for the life of the world."[6]

In his Message for the 47th World Communication Day, with the title "Social Networks: Portals of Truth and Faith; New Spaces for Evangelization," Pope Benedict XVI underscores the role of ICT in Christian worship. He notes that: "In the digital world there are social networks which offer our contemporaries opportunities for prayer, meditation and sharing the word of God…thanks to a contact initially made online…elements which are always important in the journey of faith."[7] ICT is also used to share liturgical resources like breviary, homilies, lectionaries, missal, guidelines, etc. which assist Christ's faithful. Other sites also provide scripture verses for meditation or literature for burials, weddings, baptisms and other memorials, a set of prayers from which to select texts for specific needs with meditative pictures and music.

Though, the liturgical correctness is debatable, ipad, as an electronic device is used in accessing the web in networking; hence, some ministers today use it in preaching and giving sermons to their congregation during worship. Smartphones and smart TVs can also be used in accessing the web. Through smartphones and smart TVs, one can get all daily and Sunday readings in one place and can equally adjust to the desired font and whatever prayer. Aides for the preparation of liturgical celebrations are also available on the web and grow in numbers as each Sunday passes. Several broadcasts of liturgical celebrations over the social networks exist. Eternal Word Television Network (EWTN) and other national and local stations (like AIT in Nigeria) and *Lumen Christi* Television (in Lagos, Nigeria) daily broadcast Mass for the participation of the worshippers. Some priests preach online and have online streaming of their liturgical celebrations.

---

5 *Sacrosanctum Concilium* 2.

6 Austin Echema. "Liturgical Pedagogy and Nation-Building" in Ferdinand Nwaigbo *et al.* (eds.) *Theological Education for Human Development and Nation-Building in Africa*. 21st CIWA Theology Week, 22nd to 26th March 2010, 280.

7 Pope Benedict XVI, "Social Networks: Portals of Truth and Faith; New Spaces for Evangelization," Message for the 47th World Communication Day, (Vatican City: Libreria Editrice Vatican).

Others send tracts to various email accounts and websites. Some large churches have satellite branches and websites. There are also telephone services for calls on the internet. There are also video tracts in which preachers use animation and music to win the hearts of internet surfers. Additionally, there are free downloads of CDs that enable internet users to listen to homilies or sermons.

Studies have shown that when pastors and pastoral agents collaborate with worshippers to use ICT tools toward achieving the same goals, it leads to active, conscious and full participation.[8] Experience has shown that many people who demonstrate a more positive attitude toward learning, are better behaved when ICT is used in their learning.[9] Kalaš further expressed that the issues of how ICT can enhance the learning environment are also expressed in literature.[10] Admittedly, research suggests that the value ICT can which add to the learning environments depends on the choices pastoral agents make about which tools to use, when and how to use the tools, alongside their understandings about how these tools can support learning and development in order to recognize how these can be linked to the use of ICT for evangelisation. As indicated above, Mayfield recognizes six forms of social media: social networks (such as *MySpace, Facebook* and *Bebo*); *Blogs* (for thought-provoking homilies and inspirational stories and testimonies can be shared among believers); *Wikis*; *Podcasts* (for sharing pre-recorded homilies and Mass proceedings, among other Church events); *Forums* (for photos (Flickr), bookmarked links (delicious) and videos (YouTube); *Micro blogging* (Twitter is the clear leader in this field).[11]

ICT immediately received high acceptance among the youth and adult populations alike because they are easy to operate. These platforms require minimal technical knowledge to undertake basic tasks such as communication and information exchange and management. Nonetheless, the more complex tasks of building entrepreneurial skills for catechetical

---

8 *Sacrosanctum Concilium* 14.

9 I. Kalaš, *Recognizing the Potentials of ICT in Early Childhood Education*, Russian: UNESCO Institute for Information Technologies in Education from http://iite.unesco.org/pics/publications/files/3214673.pdf. Accessed on 22nd November 2018.

10 Kalaš 2004.

11 Antony Mayfield, *What is Social Media? iCrossing ebook* from https://www.coursehero.com/file/6882077/What-is-Social-Media-iCrossing-ebook/ accessed on 25th August 2022.

formation may require advanced skills. A good example of the power of the new media technology is how Rev. Fr. Dr. George Ehusani, Executive Director, Lux Terra Leadership Foundation in Abuja Archdiocese, Nigeria, is using his Online Sunday Mass to teach the people. According to Clarissa Akjentera, "social networking can be used for communication, publicity, collaboration, reflection, building community and offering mutual support."[12] The potentials of using ICT for developing the learning capacity include that with the use of computers, they can get information about many liturgical subjects and to learn as well.

Obviously, getting information does not necessarily mean significant knowledge. Giving lots of information to passive participants is meaningless. On the other hand, ICTs are highly interactive, and if people take their own decisions, they can become active learners. They are incredibly versatile and malleable to create inventions. The devices consist of many tools and use different representations and data: texts, sounds, animations, images, photographs, diagrams, and any combinations of these processes. ICT can allow people to express themselves, expand their knowledge and information while creating. So, they always change, extend, and review what they have done. ICT can be used to communicate, collaborate, and build teams in small groups or over long distances. According to Kalaš, ICTs offer great potentials which support lifelong learning for all groups of people, including those who have special needs.[13] They can help and support the involvement of people with special needs in learning and play processes, by overcoming some negative influences or impairments, as well as possible barriers that traditional ways of technology may create.[14]

Relatedly, Pope Benedict XVI avers that ICTs have proven instrumental in the spread of literacy, increased socialization, expansion of democratic space and the promotion of dialogue among people. This is because they now foster and strengthen understanding between nations, breathe life into

---

[12] Clarissa V. Akjentera, *The Parish Guide to Social Media: How Social Networking can Recharge your Ministry* (New London: Twenty Third Publications, 2013) 43.

[13] Kalaš 2004.

[14] C. Edwards, & C. Hiler, "A Teacher's Guide to the Exhibit: 'The Hundred Languages of Children'" in *College of Human Environmental Sciences*, University of Kentucky: Lexington, Kentucky, 20.

peaceful dialogues, guaranteeing access to easy and early information.[15] He also enumerates other benefits of social media as: allow bonding of family members across distances, facilitate immediate and easy availability of relevant documents and the dissemination of scientific discoveries and research findings, and provide dynamic forms of learning and communication.[16]

Aberrations on the Use of ICT for Christian Worship

Despite the obvious advantages which ICT usage presents, there are palpable fears that the new platform is also used for dubious reasons, concretised as aberrations in the liturgy. In an era where the miasma of meaningless aberrations looms, the liturgy of the Holy Mother Church is found leaning on a fragile clasp, in imminent danger of collapse. Yes, aberrations on the use of ICT in the liturgy of the Church are gradually becoming common phase. Some devoted Catholics are very uncomfortable with the way the Eucharist is celebrated in many churches in Africa today. The negative influence of ICT is evident in some Catholic parish liturgical celebrations today. As a result, there are some abuses in our liturgy today. The concern here is on what the Church teaches on the subject matter. And one of the ongoing controversies, among some worshippers, for the Church in Africa and beyond, is whether ICT gadgets are still an appropriate means in the Eucharistic liturgy. This came to the fore because of some notable aberrations that worry some worshippers, because of the influx of ICT in liturgical celebrations.

The word "aberration" means "forbidden". Aberration in liturgy means signs and actions that are forbidden within the course of the liturgy. It arises out of some people's inability to adhere to laid down liturgical laws and practices. This is premised on the fact that despite the gift of the new media on the use of ICT to the society and Christian worshippers, they are fraught with shortcomings, and defects. An anonymous dictum holds that "Cellular phone brings one closer to persons who are far. But it takes the person away

---

15 Pope Benedict XVI, *The Media: A Network for Communication, Communion and Cooperation* (Vatican City: Libreria Editrice Vatican, 2006).

16 Pope Benedict XVI, *The Media: A Network for Communication, Communion and Cooperation.*

from the ones sitting next to the user". This same, if care is not taken, can happen to worshippers on the use of ICT.

According to Lukwata, "The mass media are neutral tools that can be misused or manipulated and thus become a disservice to the cause of evangelization."[17] In some places of worshipper today in Africa, the use of ICT in liturgical celebration makes the place of worship to be noisy and destroys the solemn nature of worship. The injection of some background pictures, animation, music, and songs during liturgical celebrations in a manner that the faithful can easily loss sense of the sacred place. The message contained in the screen, projector and songs can generate a noisy atmosphere that is inappropriate for celebration. As such, it degenerates the solemn nature of the liturgy.When ICT is not effectively used, it may constitute distraction to the congregation. In churches where the readings and announcements are projected for instance, usually attention is shifted from the sanctuary to the screen. Equally, in churches where the congregation is being captured and projected on the screen, from time to time, some members of the congregation are distracted as they will be busy positioning themselves, in order to appear well in the screen; instead, of focusing on the worship which is the reason why they have come to Church.

Elsewhere, the writer shares this view that caution be exercised in the use of electronic devices like overhead or screen projectors, banners or PowerPoint displays based on the danger that they can constitute a nuisance and distraction to the worshipping community.[18] This is because they can be very engaging with their power of attraction and can cause people to drift from the essence of the liturgy. Thus, if these devices must be used, then caution and moderation must be the watch word. It is also against liturgical decency and decorum to answer/make call while at the Mass. The cellular phone (GSM) should be switched off or put in silent mode or vibration as a mark of respect for this sacred mystery; better still, one may drop the cellular phone in the house, car, office or any other convenient and secure

---

17 Lukwata 152.

18 Emmanuel C. Anagwo, "ICT in Catholic Worship: Some Pastoral Issues and Implications Today" in Emmanuel Nwaoru (ed.) *Journal of Inculturation Theology* Vol. 14, No.1, 2013, 55.

place before going to the Church for the Eucharistic celebration.[19] Some Churches such as Holy Spirit Catholic Church Onireke, Lagos Archdiocese, Nigeria, and St. James Catholic Church, Eneka, Port Harcourt Diocese, Nigeria, it is strategically captured with sign post at the major entrance doors of the churches: "Switch off your phone please! You are in God's presence." In the bulletin of one of the aforementioned Churches, the back cover has a slot boldly written: "No calls, browsing and chatting inside the Church." Accordingly, the Decree on the Means of Social Communications, *Inter Mirifica*, by the Fathers of the Second Vatican Council, sensitive to the many challenges presented by the modern digital means of social communication, caution that "those who are at the receiving end of the media, especially the young, should learn moderation and discipline in their use of them."[20]

It follows that the various means of social means of communication are meant for man/woman, and not the other way. For instance, problems only arise when we allow ourselves to be overwhelmed, by overusing ICT in worship. Undoubtedly, priests have the responsibility of mentoring and supervising their worshippers especially the young adults in the use of various digital social media. When priests themselves submit to 'digital slavery', the young adults may have very narrow possibility of escaping such slavery when they gather for worship. The Constitution on the Sacred Liturgy is clear on this matter:

> Pastors of souls must, therefore, realise that, when the liturgy is celebrated, something more is required than the laws governing valid and lawful celebration. It is their duty also to ensure that the faithful take part fully aware of what they are doing, actively engaged in the rite and enriched by it.[21]

Today, ICT may constitute itself as nuisance to create the loss of meaning to liturgical proclamation. This includes the *gloria, credo, pater noster, sanctus and agnus Dei*, which are the common of the Mass, accompanied

---

[19] For a detailed study, see Emmanuel C. Anagwo, "Christian Wedding and the Challenge of Liturgical Decorum in Nigeria" in *African Christian Studies*, Vol. 31, No. 3, Sept. 2015, 80.

[20] *Inter Mirifica* 10.

[21] *Sacrosanctum Concilium* 14.

with the allocation of praise to God through Jesus Christ. These parts of the Mass require a sufficient concentration and meditation as they symbolize the proclamation of one's belief and faith in God. They should be rendered with solemnity with the active participation of the worshippers. It is quite unfortunate that some worshippers are now turned into spectators or observers, as ICT gadgets have taken over the rendition as its responsibility. There is the ominous abuse of sacred silence in the liturgical acts of the Mass. Liturgical silence, in some periods of liturgical celebration, should not be compromised.[22] This outstanding norm is no longer the case today. Evidently, interiority and exteriority are indispensable elements of an ascent to God. One notices with dismay that even during penitential rite that should be done in silence, the prayer of the faithful and even the communion, worshippers are distracted from having a quiet time for private prayers. This is largely because the use of ICT gadgets has taken the sacred silence space.

One should be reminded that anytime we surf the internet, use GPS or our mobile phones, we leave traces where we have been or what we have been up to. A number of constraints militate against the optimal use of ICT package for liturgical celebration. Among many, the following are a few: lack of funding to support the purchase of the technology, lack of training among pastoral agents, lack of motivation among pastors and instructors to

---

22 The GIRM 45 clearly re-instates the pivotal role of liturgical silence in worship. It says: "Sacred silence should be observed at the designated times as part of the celebration. Its function depends on the time it occurs in each part of the celebration." It goes further to itemise those moments the liturgical silence is interspaced. First is during the penitential rite whether at Mass or the Liturgy of the Hours. Secondly, after the invitation to pray, it begins with "Let us pray." Third is during the Liturgy of the Word. After the first and second readings and the homily. Fourthly, sacred silence is recommended when the celebrant pronounces the Eucharistic prayer. Fifthly, after Communion, all praise God in silent prayer expressing gratitude to God who has made Himself food to be eaten by mortals. Thus, liturgical silence is strongly recommended since the devout soul restrains the self from talking and attunes the mind and heart to God in prayer. This, however, is not to relegate to the background the irreplaceable role of sacred dance and music as well as ICT during liturgical worship. Indeed, this gesture has its own rightful place to lift the mind and heart to God. Pastors of souls and the faithful must learn to appreciate this gesture and maximise it to the fullest in the quest to worship God (For a detailed study, see Emmanuel C. Anagwo, *Hundred Questions and Answers on the Mass Vol. II*. Onitsha: Laurans Publishers, 2013, 99-100.

adopt ICT as teaching tools.[23] More pungently, the major factors against the use of ICT to advance liturgical development are high cost of the purchase of the gadgets, irregular power supply and under use of such gadgets.

We have nowadays the broadcast of some liturgical celebrations over the social networks from one African nation to another. Consequently, during liturgical celebrations some worshippers especially the youths distract themselves by sending out the homilies and downloading snapshots from the ceremonies to their Facebook, WhatsApp, etc pages. Again, some Catholic youths wrongly prefer to watch Sunday Mass 8.00am at African Independent Television (AIT), *Lumen Christi* Television or Eternal Word Television Network (EWTN) Mass with their ipads, smart TVs, Television sets and other gadgets instead of participating at Mass. They presume that it is the same Mass they have participated. Some of the youths who even attend Mass carry their mobile/cellular phones, ipads and other sophisticated digital gadgets along, making phone calls, browsing and chatting on social media while Holy Mass and para-liturgical activities like Benediction are going on. In recent times, Pope Francis laments that "When the priest celebrating Mass says,

> Let us lift up our hearts, he is not saying, "lift up our cell phone and take a picture. No. It's an awful thing. It makes me so sad when I celebrate (Mass) in the square or in the basilica and I see so many cell phones in the air. And not just by the lay faithful, some priests and bishops, too.[24]

There is no doubt that the media and the usage of modern technology have challenges and can suffer from great abuses. The Fathers of the Second Vatican Council recognized this when they wrote:

---

[23] Akinde Olusola Kunle & Opara Felix Kelechi, "Deployment of Digitized Packages Toward Engineering Education in West African Higher Institutions" in Joseph A. Ilori (ed.) *West African Journal of Higher Education: Christian Higher Education in African Context* (Ilorin: Modern Impressions, 2014) 162.

[24] Pope Francis, "Stop Taking Smartphone Snapshots During Mass, Pope Says" from https://www.ncronline.org/news/vatican/francis-chronicles/stop-taking-smartphone-snapshots-during-mass-pope-says accessed on 25th September 2022.

> The Church recognizes that these media, if properly utilized, can be of great service to mankind, since they greatly contribute to men's entertainment and instruction as well as to the spread and support of the Kingdom of God. The Church recognizes, too, that men can employ these media contrary to the plan of the Creator and to their own loss. Indeed, the Church experiences maternal grief at the harm all too often done to society by their evil use. Hence, this sacred Synod, attentive to the watchful concern manifested by the Supreme Pontiffs and Bishops in a matter of such great importance, judges it to be its duty to treat of the principal questions linked with the media of social communication. It trusts, moreover, that the teaching and regulations it thus sets forth will serve to promote, not only the eternal welfare of Christians, but also the progress of all mankind. [25]

With the regard to smartphone, as one of the gadgets of ICT, in Nigeria, Rita Okonoboh observes that it is changing Christian worship in dramatic ways; smartphone was banned in several churches initially with such inscriptions as "Kindly switch off your handset before entering church premises." Amongst others, smartphones are used to transact financial business right inside churches as well as reading scriptural passages.[26] Similarly, a News Agency of Nigeria (NAN) survey conducted on Christians of different denominations in Lagos, Nigeria found out that the smartphone has effectively replaced the use of bibles in churches[27] and has argued that for this reason the use of smartphone in the Church should not be banned.[28]

---

[25] *Inter Mirifica* 2.

[26] Rita Okonoboh, "Digital Christianity! Smartphones, smart pews, the changing phase of worship" in *The Nigerian Tribune* (22nd October, 2017). from https://tribuneonlineng.com/digital-christianity-smart-phones-smart-pews-changing-phase-worship/. Accessed on 23rd October 2022.

[27] News Agency of Nigeria (NAN), "Using Bible apps on phone during church worship: Some say it is youth culture." In *The Vanguard* from https://www.vanguardngr.com/2018/09/using-bible-apps-on-phone-during-church-worship-some-say-its-youth-culture/ Accessed 20th August 2022.

[28] Ejike Kanife, "Why switching off phones during worship might not be the best policy for the Catholic Church in Nigeria" from https://technext.ng/2020/02/07/why-switching-off-phones-during-worship-might-not-be-the-best-policy-for-the-nigerian-Catholic-church/ Accessed 20th August 2022.

In our age of social media, these abuses and aberrations confront us the more. In Africa today, some people have grown cold of these social media platforms because of the problems associated with the dissemination of ICT, while some others clamour for social media regulation or its total obliteration. Although for some, the words "social media" elicit feelings of anxiety, angst, foreboding, danger and despondency. For some people, they spell excitement, innovation, opportunity and hope. They represent the double edges of a sword, capable of cutting any or both ways. For others still, social media represent a disease to be avoided, to some a cure to be embraced, an ecstatic expression of both freedom and slavery. It is alleged that some people are affected emotionally and psychologically from such damages done in these social media platforms. It is claimed that in them, some people are bullied, character assassination take place, fake news spread, hate speeches are made, scammers are found, to mention but a few. Of course, as anyone can imagine, the Church herself has not been spared from such bullies and online attacks. In the guise of the freedom of information and speech, such online users claim that they are expressing themselves because it gives them some sense of security, or should we say, of facelessness, something they could not dare to do or say physically. Concerning such abuses, the Council Fathers warned:

> Those who make use of the media of communications, especially the young, should take steps to accustom themselves to moderation and self-control in their regard. They should, moreover, endeavour to deepen their understanding of what they see, hear or read. They should discuss these matters with their teachers and experts and learn to pass sound judgements on them.[29]

Implications for the Church in Africa

Despite the abuse, misuse, and overuse, when ICT is put to use in the liturgy and rightly so, it enhances active participation and can be used to reach out both to those who are physically present and those who are taking part in the liturgy from a distance. This is not in the sense of replacing physical presence, but in the sense of attending a spiritual exercise. While using ICT,

---

[29] *Inter Mirifica* 10.

the Church in Africa must rise to the challenge of evolving a perfect, smooth, and effective transmission of liturgical formation to the faithful by connecting, collaborating, and creating the new social media with them. Beyond using the power point presentation of homilies, talks, video sound and animation of some Church's documentaries, every station, parish, and diocese should also create effective platform such as Facebook, YouTube, WhatsApp, Linkedln, Pinterest, Google, Skype and Blog to effectively communicate God's message to the people who spend some of their time in surfing internet. It is true that almost all the dioceses in Africa have websites, but many parishes in Africa do not have website, or better still functioning websites, Twitter and Facebook accounts to upload spiritual materials for the benefits of the parishioners. It will be very beneficial for our parishes to harness the talents of the faithful to embark upon building and facilitating ICT gadgets by posting articles, seminars, and sermons with the aim of informing and forming them. The Church in Africa stands to gain more if the worshippers are prepared well for the use of ICT for liturgical formation. This is true because some worshippers are already on the fast lane with the ICT gadgets, as they browse through them on daily bases.

But the various means of social means of communication are meant for man/woman, and not the other way. For instance, problems only arise when we allow ourselves to be taken charge of, using ICT in worship. Undoubtedly, priests have the responsibility of mentoring and supervising their worshippers, especially the youth, in the use of various digital social media. When priests themselves submit to 'digital slavery', the youth may have very narrow possibility of escaping such slavery when they gather for worship. Liturgical principles guide the use of social means of communication to bear fruits of active participation. Liturgical norms and prescriptions acknowledge modern communication gadgets but emphasize that whatever must be used on the altar be strictly and exclusively blessed and dedicated for the service. In this regard, youths have a duty to enquire from the priests on the responsible use of various digital social media. As it were, forming the youth along the use of modern social media has become a primary task of pastors of souls in an ever-changing digital world. Expressing this concern about unguided youth at the 45th World Communication Day in 2011, Pope Benedict XVI opines that young people particularly are experiencing this change in communication. Yet with all the anxieties, challenges and creativity typical of those open with enthusiasm and curiosity to new experiences in life, their ever-greater involvement in the public digital forum, created by the so-called social networks, helps to establish new forms of interpersonal relations. It influences self-awareness invariably poses questions not only of how to act properly, but also about the authenticity of one's own being. Therefore, entering cyberspace can be a sign of an authentic search for personal encounter and development with others. This is especially when attention is paid to avoiding dangers such as enclosing oneself in a sort of parallel existence, or excessive exposure to the virtual space.[30]

To combat these abuses and aberrations, there is need for the Church to continually discover the advantages on the use of ICT, and work to reach her 'little ones' online with engaging and informative content. Accordingly, Ihejirika noted that:

> ... the need for content that is informative appears to be the dominant need expressed by users of church social communication network."[31] It presupposes that the Church's contents online should be relevant to the local community and related to their growth in faith. It should be rich in content, such content which connects more with the psych of the online users yet maintaining the spirit of the mission of the Church. Yes, "effective use of the mass media in evangelization implies that the content must be packaged in such a way as to communicate the Gospel values.[32]

To reflect the Gospel values, pastoral agents in Africa involved in the mass and social media must have the purpose of conversion and not of a mere online presence, as their ultimate goal.

Evaluation

This chapter underscored the fact that ICT has been blowing winds of both positive and negative changes into various areas of our life on earth. The waves occasioned by these winds of change have constantly rippled into

---

30 Pope Benedict XVI, "Truth, Proclamation and Authenticity of Life in the Digital Age" 2011.
31 Ihejirika 78.
32 Ihejirika 124.

many global institutions and organizations to help advance the ease of doing business with one another. It has also promoted the course of interaction and unity among faith communities around the world. The Church has had her share of this wave. Like other Institutions, she has used the opportunity provided by ICT to promote e-worship. Her online availability is reckoned by many people as a great blessing for our generation, but some others will agree that this blessing does not go without challenges. However, those challenges, leading to aberrations, falsification, and abuse, can easily be mitigated when they are properly used for the right purpose and with the right intention. Catholic faithful who by their active use of the internet see the advantages therein have continued to appreciate the Church's efforts so far. Additionally, they advocate that these social media platforms within the internet space be annexed more by her in bringing Good News to the countless number of her faithful online.

In the spirit of the digital revolution, any action or practice in liturgy contrary to the given liturgical norm is considered an abuse. Such an unacceptable action (abuse) is extraneous to the nature of the liturgy. Nonetheless, the new media offers new platforms for formation notwithstanding, ICT has however posed great challenges to liturgical norms and ethos. Uniquely, the chapter notes the possible errors on the use of ICT, indeed snares, in which participants are apt to get themselves tangled even when they are in good faith. For active participation to evolve, celebrant and participant should be concerned about what tomorrow would be. Preparing worshippers on the responsible use of ICT for liturgical formation will give them access to a sensory-rich world of information made more attractive with full-colour, graphics, video, and stereo sound, will ensure that their positive prospects are well harnessed and maximised and at the same time, narrowing the liturgical challenges they present against liturgical principles, especially against distractions and exclusivity of liturgical objects for worship alone.

CHAPTER FIVE

LITURGICAL EXEGESIS OF ICT IN THE LIGHT OF *INTER MIRIFICA* 13

In recent times, ICT, as one of means of social communication, has been recognized to occupy a pride of place in the Church's life. Indeed, liturgy which is the soul of this life of the Church's is vivified by the application of ICT with which the liturgy is celebrated. Various documents have been issued to serve as manuals or instrumental guide on ICT in the Church. This chapter examines the major text on which this study is based, namely, the Second Vatican Council's interdisciplinary document titled: *Inter Mirifica* (Decree on the Media of Social Communications) 13.[1] It is also supported by the lessons emerging from its theological and spiritual analyses with biblical foundations, patristic and magisterial teachings as well as some contemporary views on the status of ICT in the Catholic liturgy.

Background to the Document

As a decisive turn in the Church's communication apostolate, the decree on social communication, designated as *Inter Mirifica* (translated as "Among the Wonderful"), was one of the very first two documents promulgated by the Second Vatican Council on 4th December 1963; the other being *Sacrosanctum Concilium* (translated as "Sacred Council") on liturgy. Admittedly, *Inter Mirifica* is not the Church's first document on the means of social communication. Before its publication, there had been others such as *Vigilanti Cura* by Pius XI in 1936 and *Miranda Prorsus* by Pius XII in 1957. Nonetheless, the novelty of *Inter Mirifica* lies in the fact that it is the first document on communication to come out of an Ecumenical Council. Besides, it was not part of the initial matters to be discussed at the Council; yet providentially, noticing the importance of the new means of

---

1 *Inter Mirifica (Decree on the Means of Social Communication*), in Austin Flannery (ed.), *Vatican Council II* (Dublin: Dominican Publications, 1987) 13.

communication to the mission of the Church, the Council Fathers gave it the second place in the final document, following that on the Sacred Liturgy. Hence, after a long discussion on liturgical matters the Council Fathers turned to the proposed schema on social communication, a document with some 114 paragraphs. At the beginning of Council's preparations after Pope John XXIII's announcement in June 1959 such a document was not foreseen. Only during deliberations, especially on the "modern means of the apostolate" and the erection of a special commission through the *Motu Proprio Supreno Dei Nutu*, that a proposal to draft a document for discussion was made.

The draft document of *Inter Mirifica* in the hands of the Council Fathers had an introduction (nos.1-5), then, a first part on the doctrine of the Church (6-33) with subdivisions on the rights and obligations of the Church, moral norms to be followed and the obligations of the individual and the state. A second section dealt with the apostolate of the Church in the field (34-48) and a third part on the discipline and the ecclesiastical order (49-63). In its fourth section the document considered the different means of communication individually (64-105) like the press (49-63), film (84-94), radio and television (95-105)[2] and other means of social communication (106-111). The following conclusion (112-114) is basically contained in the present *Inter Mirifica*.

Accordingly, this proposal was discussed only for a little more than three sessions within the Council Hall from November 23 to 27 1962 with all

---

2 In the original draft and the final aspect in the means of social communication was the television, which, at that time, was a novelty. It was anchored on the transmission of visual images in the scanning disk already set by Paul Nipkow in the 1880s, Television finally emerged in the 1960s to be rated a central position in many homes. At the early stage, two required ingredients for the TV were photoelectric sensing material and a technique for encoding pictures for transmission through radio waves. With the complex nature of the technology needed to float the TV at this early stage, it was seen by *Inter Mirifica* as the "last word" in the means of communication, as the preparatory document alludes. Nonetheless, in the words of Emmanuel B. Olusola, "the present realities in cyber-technology and hyper-information point to the contrary. Many of the things that the TV does can now be accomplished through computer and internet" (Emmanuel B. Olusola, "The Church and Communication in an E-Age: The Matrix of *Inter Mirifica*" in *African Ecclesial Review* (AFER): *ICT & Evangelization ~ Christianity in the Digital Culture*, Vol. 57, Nos. 3 & 4 Sep./Dec. 2015, 175).

together some 43 interventions. One of the interventions was a written report by then Auxiliary Bishop Karol Woytyla, later Pope John Paul II (now Saint), who proposed to also consider the importance of culture for communication. This was concern he later as pope developed further in establishing a Pontifical Council of Culture at the Vatican.

From the discussion of the document, it revealed not only quite a diversity of opinions but also a level of understanding of social communication which cannot always be called professional. The concern of the bishops was captured and quite some of them felt not being sufficiently prepared and qualified at that time for an extensive document on the subject. Since the proposal was handled at the beginning of the Council, further theological perspective which surfaced in later council document in principle but to reduce it to the essentials and asked for a more extensive pastoral instruction to be published at a later stage.

In the final version of *Inter Mirifica*, it has 24 paragraphs only. The decree, however, received 503 of the highest number of "No" votes in the whole Second Vatican Council. Between this decision on 23rd November 1962 and the final promulgation on 4th December 1963, there were a growing number of voices proposing to retract or rewrite the document. This developed so far that some Council Fathers distributed leaflets against *Inter Mirifica* in the proposed form at the steps of St. Peter's Basilica where the Council sessions took place. Many professionals in communications felt that the proposed text would not be up to the standard of an Ecumenical Council and the reality of modern communications despite the Council Fathers having approved the first text already in principle and judged it as being "worth a council teaching." Beside the reduction to 24 paragraphs the document was also reduced in its ranks from a constitution to a decree.

Scholars like Emmanuel B. Olusola would rather hold that, "It was then upgraded to a Council Decree between the first and second plenary sessions of the Second Vatican Council."[3] For him, the importance of this upgrading was justified by other aspects of this document on the means of social communication to enjoy much attention at an ecumenical council. No wonder, the document gave birth to the use of the term "Social Communications" as opposed to others such as diffusion techniques and mass media, which were previously used. Additionally, the publication of

---

3 Olusola, "The Church and Communication in an E-Age: The Matrix of *Inter Mirifica*" 175.

Inter Mirifica publicized the World Day of Communications to an international event. On this day, the Holy Father gives a special message based on the signs of the times in the communication sector. This ecclesiastical document called the establishment of an office at the Vatican for the instruments of social communications. The fruit of this was immediately seen in the release of *Communio et Progressio*, which sought to broaden the injunctions of *Inter Mirifica*. Besides, *Inter Mirifica* also called for training of Church personnel in the bid to meet the challenges of the times on communication.[4] Undoubtedly, *Inter Mirifica* remains a trailblazer and watershed with the *magna charta* (great chart) in the Church's communication apostolate. Other documents merely broadened and enlarged guidelines of the Church's improved involvement in communication. Considering the importance of *Inter Mirifica*, this study gives preference to this Second Vatican Council's interdisciplinary document to navigate through the nexus between ICT and Catholic Liturgy.

Overview of the *Inter Mirifica*

Inter Mirifica is the teaching of the Catholic Church in the development on media education for the faithful. It has a preamble, two chapters and twenty-four paragraphs. The preamble serves as an introduction to the entire document. It links the current document to the tradition and the theology of the Church to reiterate that media of communication are good for the society but ought to be subject to the norms of morality.

Chapter one is titled: "On the Teaching of the Church". The decree affirms that men in society have a "right to information," because such right is derived from the fact that the prompt publication of affairs and events enables everyone to contribute more effectively to the common good and advance the welfare of the entire civil society.

Chapter two is titled: On the Pastoral Activity of the Church". It underscores the fact that the Church, for her part, must make use of the media to advance morality and religion. A Catholic press should be promoted with the clear aim of forming, supporting, and advancing public opinion in accord with natural laws and Catholic teaching. To facilitate such

---

4 Olusola, "The Church and Communication in an E-Age: The Matrix of *Inter Mirifica*" 175.

development, the Council proposes that laymen ought to be afforded technical, doctrinal, and moral teaching provided in professional institutes but trained in the Christian spirit.

The concluding sections of the Decree then focused on the organizations of the apostolate. It begins with an office for educational and religious films tentatively to be set up by the Holy See in 1948. In 1952, it extended its competence to all films, in 1954 to films, radio and television; and in 1959 Pope St. John XXIII gave it a new direction in his *motu proprio* titled: *Boni Pastoris*. The Council requested the Holy Father to include the press as well as to staff his office with professionals from every country, including some laymen and women. Pope St. Paul VI granted the request of the Council by his *motu proprio* titled: *In fructibus multis* published on 2nd April 1964, and the recruiting of the international staff.[5]

Presentation of the Text of the *Inter Mirifica* 13

The text of *Inter Mirifica* 13 is chapter II of the document. And because Latin is the official language of the Catholic Church, the text shall first be rendered in Latin:

> *Omnes Ecclesiae filii communi animo consilioque conentur ut instrumenta -communicationis socialis, nulla interposita mora et maxima adhibita industria, efficaciter in multiplicibus apostolates operibus, prout rerum et temporum adiuncta exposcent, usurpentur, noxia incepta praecurrentes, illis praesertim in regionibus quarum moralis et religiosus progressus urgentiorem navitatem exquirit.*
>
> *Sacri ergo Pastores suum munus in hac provincia, cum eorumdem ordinario praedicationis officio arcte conexum, explore properent; laici quoque, qui in his instrumentis adhibendis partes habent, Christo testimonium reddere satagent, imprimis suis cuiusque muneribus perite et apostolico animo perfungentes, immo, pro sua parte, technicis, oeconomicis, cultus artisque facultatibus actioni pastorali Ecclesiae directe auxiliatricem praestantem operam.*[6]

---

5 Herbert Vorgrimler (ed.), *Commentary on the Documents of Vatican II, Vol. 1,* (New York: Herder and Herder,1966) 104.

6 *Paulus Episcopus Servus Servorum Dei Una Cum Sacrosancti Concilii Patribus ad Perpetuam Rei Memoriam, Decretum De Instrumentis Communicationis Socialis,*

It reads in English as follows:

> All the members of the Church should make a concerted effort to ensure that the means of communication are put at the service of the multiple forms of the apostolate without delay and are as energetically as possible, where and when they are needed. They should forestall projects likely to prove harmful, especially in those regions where moral and religious progress would require their intervention more urgently.
>
> Pastors of souls should be particularly zealous in the field since it is closely linked with the task of preaching the Gospel. Laymen who work professionally in these media should endeavour to bear witness to Christ: first of all, by doing their work competently and in the apostolic spirit, secondly by collaborating directly, each one according to his ability, in the pastoral activity of the Church, making a technical, economic, cultural or artistic contribution.[7]

Analysis of the Text of *Inter Mirifica* 13

The text is divided into four parts for the sake of clarity and orderliness, and in accordance with the method of liturgical exegesis.

Part One:

All the members...they are needed.

The opening statement of the text is a condensed sentence that summarizes the basic message of the text under study. In their introductory remarks on the Means of Social Communication, the Fathers of the Second Vatican Council observed that the social media is the chief among all the inventions which mankind made from creation with the help of God. From the beginning, we must technically underscore that beyond the term 'social media,' we have also 'digital/virtual social media.' The difference is that

---

Inter Mirifica from https://www.vatican.va/archive/hist_councils/ii_vatican_council/documents/vat-ii_decree_19631204_inter-mirifica_lt.html accessed on 10th September 2022.

7 *Inter Mirifica* 13.

'social media' is a generic term that refers to all means of social communication, including everyday verbal expressions. When such everyday expressions are passed on by means of a software or hardware, we may speak of the latter too as 'digital/virtual social media,' which constitute only an aspect of social media, just as the everyday expressions themselves. Downloading this document of social communication in the world of today, one can understand that it will also be referring to the digital social media, which gives credence to the context of our study on ICT. One aspect of Information/Communication Technology that has experienced great innovative expansion is the digital social media.

Admittedly, as one of the creations and inventions of humanity which is their nature, digital social media can reach and influence not merely single individuals but the very masses and even the whole of human society. Examples abound with such galaxies of communication gadgets like E-mail, Facebook, WhatsApp, Goggle, SMS, Telex, Telegram, Telephone, Mobile Phone, etc. The Church knows that if these media are properly used, they can be of great benefit to mankind and these means of communication can also help to propagate the kingdom of God in the hearts of men/women. Nonetheless, the Church is not unaware that use of these media can also be detrimental for the salvation of mankind when they are not properly directed and used.

In this section, therefore, the Council Fathers held that all the members of the Church should put in very great effort to ensure that the means of communication are put at the service of the Church. Accordingly, it focuses on the concerted effort to be made by all the members of the Church to ensure that the means of communication are effectively used in various spheres of life including liturgy. This is because it stated, "where and when they are needed". Liturgy cannot be excluded; after all, it is the source and summit of Christian life and spirituality. The reformed liturgy of the Second Vatican Council affirms that the sacrifice of the Eucharist should be the principal expression of our faith and all devotions should spring from the Eucharist and lead back to the Eucharist.[8] The Catholic liturgy has always maintained that the Eucharist is the *culmen et fons* (summit and source/fountain) of other sacraments as well as other celebrations of the

---

[8] SC10; See also *Lumen Gentium* 11 and *The Catechism of the Catholic Church* (CCC) (Nairobi: Pauline Publications in Africa, 1995)1324.

Church.[9] All the sacraments are oriented towards the Eucharist. All tends towards the Eucharist to arrive at the supreme goal. In other words, the Eucharistic celebration brings to culmination the celebration of any other sacrament.

Similarly, all Church's activities and celebrations tilt towards the Eucharistic liturgy and the Eucharistic liturgy in turn brings Christians together and nourishes them. When there is no Eucharist, there is no life and a sublime faith-experience. In this regard, *The Catechism of the Catholic Church* teaches that the Eucharist nourishes the faith-experience of Christians.[10] Hilary Odili Okeke rightly corroborates: "Christian faith and Christian worship meet in the paschal mystery in a very intimate way."[11] The prelate further states that the passion, death, resurrection, and the expectation of the Second Coming of Christ formed, as it were, the hallmark of Christian worship. The faithful congregate in the Eucharistic celebration on weekly and daily bases to celebrate this unique sacrifice, in order to boost the mystery of their faith.

Doctrinally, the beginning of Christian life and spirituality should anchor on *Credo* (I believe). The biblical axiom concurs: "faith is the assurance of things hoped for, the conviction of things not seen" (Heb 11:1). Writing on the need to recover a culture that is genuinely Catholic, Arland K. Nichols laments that: "surveys of Catholic reveal that a majority do not live in accord with, or simply do not know, their Catholic faith."[12] Indeed, culpable ignorance of faith is the stark reality and one of the banes of Catholicism in the 21st century Christianity. Some worshippers do not understand that they are stakeholders to communicate this faith with the mystery that goes within Mass (*intram missam*) and outside Mass (*extra missam*). Pope Benedict XVI therefore observes that:

> Thanks to the remarkable development of the communications media, the word "participation" has taken on a broader meaning in

9 *Sacrosanctum Concilium* 10.

10 CCC 1367.

11 Hilary Odili Okeke, *Let us Celebrate the Mystery of Faith* (Onitsha: Goodmark Prints Production, 2005) 9.

12 Arland K. Nichols, "The Year of Faith: Recovering a Culture that is Genuinely Catholic" in *Homiletic & Pastoral Review* (http://www.hprweb.com/ accessed on 10th February 2013.

recent decades. We all gladly acknowledge that the media have also opened up new possibilities for the celebration of the Eucharist. This requires a specific preparation and a keen sense of responsibility on the part of pastoral workers in the sector. When Mass is broadcast on television, it inevitably tends to set an example. Particular care should therefore be taken to ensure that, in addition to taking place in suitable and well-appointed locations, the celebration respects the liturgical norms in force.[13]

Part Two:

They should forestall…intervention more urgently.

Having emphasized the point that where and when they are needed, this section focuses on the possible errors, abuses and aberrations that may go against moral and religious integrity. This is because though the social means of communication has contributed a lot to the development of the human person and the society, it has also been criticized as providing questionable contents to the audience. For one thing, the power of media has led to highly controversial questions since we experience this effect in our daily lives today. It influences the growth of the economy, our culture, religion, and our living standards. It is however important to note that the benefits are double-edged sword with some being detrimental and others been beneficial. Some areas of media influence hold a great deal of hope that should be encouraged for an effective Christian witnessing in the African society today.

Despite its positive influence, social media is a two-edged sword that can cut in two directions because it has exposed the Catholic faith and morals to some dangers in the African society and beyond. Media must be used morally as it applies to those who watch, read, or listen to it as well as those who produce and regulate it. This is because media can be a hindrance if they become a way to avoid listening to others, to evade physical contact, to fill up every moment of silence and rest, relegating the fact that 'silence is an integral element of communication; in its absence, words rich in

---

[13] Pope Benedict XVI, *Post-Synodal Apostolic Exhortation Sacramentum Caritatis (The Sacrament of Charity*) [Nairobi: Paulines Publications, 2007) 57.

content cannot exist.' Gradually, it is breaking family ties and eroding communal values. It appears to be easier and comfortable to communicate with those located thousands of miles away from people while it is very difficult to facilitate an interpersonal communication. Besides, it is a culture of 'commodification' and constant unthinking consumption. The cyberspace, for Joachin Ozonze, "creates a space for the symbolic and imaginary reorganization of one's existence without any impact on the course of real life."[14] A very thin line is drawn between the imaginary and the real. It is a culture that aims at teaching people to be consuming subjects rather than being critical minded individuals. Often, the users mediate their identity and relation to others through the mere consumption of goods and images without deep, critical, and independent thinking despite the availability of array of information. So, creativity and depth of thoughts are deficient.

The negative impact and influence of the media on the Catholic worship also portend dangerous omen. The Catholic faithful, for instance, have been influenced and infected with their mode of catechesis, preaching, dressing, worshipping, and teaching, and they try to import all these methods into the Catholic mode of worship. One should be very careful since these trends can swim against moral and religious teachings especially in the proclamation of the Gospel. The reason is not far-fetched as people now live in a life immersed in technology and this has become part of the culture for digital natives and one unfamiliar to many ministers. Some of the faithful are still ill equipped to handle the complexities that come with this cyberspace.

Part Three:

Pastors of souls...preaching the Gospel.

This section investigates on the role of the pastors of souls in the field of social communication with the preaching of the Gospel. Pastors of souls should particularly be zealous in this field since it is linked with the task of preaching the Gospel. Consequently, the pastor, as the minister of the

---

[14] Joachin Ozonze, "Learning to Live with Children of the Media Culture" in *The Chronicle Magazine* 21 (December 2016 - December 2017) 18.

Eucharistic liturgy for example, is to plan what he will preach during the homily because the Word of God is always anew and needs to make sense to the people gathered at a particular time and place (see Heb 4:12). Also, the pastor needs to look at the rubrics and the Eucharistic texts of the celebration. Nothing should be left to chances or taken for granted. To maintain the flow of the celebration, the priest needs to plan and prepare very well, gathering and working with the various liturgical planning team. The priest is the true coordinator, animator and collaborator in the eucharistic celebration and he must cultivate the attributes that make for good human relations, namely, respect for others, concern for their welfare, generosity, openness, truthfulness, ability to listen, ability to engage in dialogue, ability to take advice and correction, able to delegate assignments, trust, humility and pastoral charity to the people.[15] Since it is the obligation of the Church to announce the Gospel, pastors of souls must announce the Good News employing the means of social communication. The Code of 1983 rightly states: "In exercising their office the pastors of the Church, availing themselves of a right which belongs to the Church, are to make an ample use of the means of social communication."[16]

Evidently, pastors have been using the means of social communication since the beginning of the world to spread the Good News to the nations. They have been addressing the problems and challenges facing these means from one period to the other. They have been part of the development from one stage to the other, availing themselves to the use of these means. The document under study tasks the pastors to use all the means of social communication within their environment, most particularly in Africa to ease their burden in spreading the Gospel of Christ in the 21st century Christianity. It follows that pastors of souls must communicate the Word of God in this new reality of the digital age. The accessibility of technologies in the new digital age demands greater consciousness on the part of the ministers and all whose aim is to execute the command of our Lord Jesus Christ: "go into the world and proclaim the Good News to all nations" (Mark 16:5).

---

15 Patrick C. Chibuko, "Active Participation in the Liturgy: Towards the Revival of Christian Culture" in *Bigard Theological Studies,* Vol. 26, No 2, 2006, 54.

16 *The Code of Canon Law* (Bangalore: Theological Publications in India, 2001) Canon 823 § 1.

St. Paul collaborates this understanding when he affirms: "Woe to me if I do not preach the Gospel" (1 Cor 9:16). So, the Church of today must find bearing in the current shift from our cultural way of communication technologies for its digital limitless capacity especially in our world, where people are susceptible to the digital age, and its apparent social networks, creating deeper forms of relationship across greater distances-which initially serves as communication barrier between groups and families. For this to be very possible, pastors of souls must themselves be properly formed to be positively internet savvy, because they are ordained to lead in liturgical celebration, where they employ the use of cybermedia. The e-priest of the 21st century cannot live and act like a person of the last century.

In this regard, worshippers have a duty to enquire from the priests on the responsible use of various digital social media. As it were, forming worshippers along the use of modern social media has become a primary task of pastors of souls in an ever-changing digital world. Expressing this concern about unguided youth at the 45th World Communication Day in 2011, Pope Benedict XVI opines:

> Young people in particular are experiencing this change in communication, with all the anxieties, challenges and creativity typical of those open with enthusiasm and curiosity to new experiences in life. Their ever-greater involvement in the public digital forum, created by the so-called social networks, helps to establish new forms of interpersonal relations, influences self-awareness and therefore inevitably poses questions not only of how to act properly, but also about the authenticity of one's own being. Entering cyberspace can be a sign of an authentic search for personal encounter with others, provided that attention is paid to avoiding dangers such as enclosing oneself in a sort of parallel existence, or excessive exposure to the virtual world.[17]

Part Four:

Laymen who work...or artistic contribution.

---

[17] Pope Benedict XVI, "Truth, Proclamation and Authenticity of Life in the Digital Age" 2011.

This section underpins the fact that professional laymen and women in the media industry should be co-opted as they will use the means also to bear witness to Christ. The technical term is tagged as collaboration which is an invitation to the people of God (the clergy and the lay men and women) to work together in ministry to build and share the vision and mission of the Church. Collaboration means teamwork, people working together as a body. Accordingly, Austin Echema avers that, collaboration is the "coming together of two people or groups that are different, but who, for a common purpose, must put aside their differences in order to achieve a common goal."[18] In collaboration, teamwork is always the answer in all spheres of managerial life, including village and family living. Collaboration involves consultation, obedience, span of control, decentralisation, submissiveness to a higher superior and so on. It can be used in every sphere of human endeavour, be it in civil or ecclesiastical.[19] In the ecclesiastical usage, it is often used with the addition of the word *ministry*, giving rise to the nomenclature: collaborative ministry. The word *ministry* means office, duties, and functions of a minister. It is employed to imply the identification, release and union of all baptized persons.[20] As a collaborative ministry with the ordained ministers, the lay faithful who by baptism are incorporated into Christ, are placed in the People of God, and in their own way share the priestly, prophetic and kingly office of Christ in the Church, and to the best of their ability carry on the mission of Christ among the Christian people in the Church and in the world.[21] Collaboration in liturgical celebration expresses the ability to engage in dialogue, ability to delegate functions and responsibilities, basic trust and charity towards everyone.[22]

As such, in collaboration, laymen and women who work in these media should endeavour to bear witness to Christ first of all by doing their work

---

18 Austin Echema, *Priests and Laity Collaboration in the Post-modern Church*, (Owerri: Assumpta Press, 2011) 25.

19 Emmanuel C. Anagwo, *New Trends of Fundraising in Christian Worship: The Nigerian Pastoral Experience* (Berlin: Peter Lang International Publisher, 2022) 148-149.

20 Loughlan Sofield & Carrol Juliano, *Collaborative Ministry: Skills and Guidelines*, (Notre Dame: Ave Marie Press, 1987) 11.

21 *Lumen Gentium* 31.

22 Patrick C. Chibuko, "The Priest as Sole Administrator, A Hindrance to Effective Ministry: A Liturgical Perspective" in Ignatius M.C. Obinwa (ed.) *Collaborative Ministry in the Context of Inculturation*, (Enugu: SNAAP Press, 2006) 309.

competently and with an apostolic spirit. The key term here is 'witness'. As a Christian religious term, 'witness' means 'a person who testifies for Christ or the Christian faith by his/her actions or words; formerly especially for martyr'.[23] John Mckenzie observes that the English word 'witness' derives from the Greek word, martyrs, and the cognates (*martyria, martyrion*). He further states that witness "...is never an impersonal marshalling of facts but always remains a personal attestation...The witness consists in the communion of a person to the truth which he attests. The supreme commitment of a person to truth is the commitment of his/her life. This is implied in Rev 2:15, and 17:6".[24]

This immediately defines the idea of Christian witnessing as could be differentiated from the court-room legalistic idea of witnessing in modern day formal jurisprudence. Christian witnessing involves personal commitment to attest to Truth per excellence, the Christ Jesus. It is supreme commitment: to Christ, to attest that Christ is the Truth, the Way and the Life (John 14:6). It could be in the form of martyrdom: it could be seen *via* evangelical and missionary enterprises as preaching the Word of God, charity work, apostleship through the pen, apologetic endeavours, all geared towards making Christ known round the world (Matt 28:19). All choices and decisions about the media should be anchored on moral principles.

In fact, the next number (14) further gives us various instances how Christian witnessing can be achieved by professional laymen and women. For a responsible press to be achieved, the production and screening of films which provide wholesome entertainment should be done by screening films that are cultural and artistic, especially films destined for the young. Similarly, decent radio and television programmes should be effectively supported especially those suited to the family. This is premised on the fact that with the robust developments in communication witnessed today, the highest authorities of the Church have come to see engagement in the media as a priority in the scale of preference. Accordingly, Pope Paul VI rightly warns that:

---

23 Lesley Brown (ed.), *The New Shorter Oxford English Dictionary*, Vols. (Oxford: Clarendom Press, 1993) 3706-3707.

24 John I. Mckenzie, *Dictionary of the Bible* (London: Macmillan Publication, 1976) 935.

> The Church would feel guilty before God if she did not avail of those powerful instruments which human skill is constantly developing and perfecting. With their aid she may preach upon the 'housetops' the message which has been entrusted to her.[25]

In this way, professional media practitioners should be trained at once and should acquire the competence needed to use these media for the apostolate. The text reinstates that we have an obligation to sustain and assist Catholic newspapers, periodicals and film projects and it would be shameful if the Church cannot uphold the Word of God due to the technical difficulties which the media presents and by their cost. The influences of the means of social communication extends beyond national frontiers, making individual citizens of the world today. Undoubtedly, the Church urgently needs pastoral agents who are enthusiastic in employing the modern means of communication in sharing the faith.

Emergent Themes from the Liturgical Exegesis

From the liturgical exegetical study of the text, it has brought about the emergence of four themes such as: the means of social communication to be at the service of the Church, the Church to ensure that the integrity of moral and religious progress is not compromised, pastors of souls to be zealous in using these media for preaching the Gospel, and the laity to use the media to bear witness to Christ. The Fathers of the Second Vatican Council maintain that the use of the media of communication in the direct service of the apostolate; "all members of the Church" are to collaborate "with one accord" in this task; but the task is envisaged as that of the "pastors of the Church", which laymen and women must directly support "with their economic, cultural and artistic ability."[26] It is based on the assumption that social communications make people to conscious in all that happens in the society and the Church and take part when their opinion is required for the upliftment and promotion of the world at large and the

---

[25] Pope Paul VI, Apostolic Exhortation on *Evangelii Nuntiandi* (Evangelization in the Modern World) in http://w2.vatican.va/content/paul-vi/en/apost_exhortations/documents/hf_p-vi_exh_19751208_evangelii-nuntiandi.html accessed on 17th April 2022.

[26] Vorgrimler 102.

Church in particular. These emergent themes shall be developed along the theological underpinnings on the use of ICT at the Catholic liturgy.

Biblical Foundations on the Use of ICT at the Liturgy

Both the Old and New Testaments of the Holy Bible have passages that deal with liturgical celebration. According to Pope Gregory the Great, "Holy Scripture by the manner of its language transcends every science, because in one and the same sentence, while it describes a fact, it reveals a mystery."[27] The written Word of God in the Scripture plays a significant role in the liturgy. Jovian P. Lang rightly described liturgy as "Bible in action."[28] For Scripture is central to our understanding of the liturgy, just as it is central to the life of the Church, for it is in the sacred liturgy that the two sources of divine revelation (*scriptura et traditio*) are most obviously evident and most frequently experienced by most Catholics. Without the liturgy, uncelebrated Word of God in the Bible, so to speak, can be regarded as "a dead letter." A dead letter is of no consequence. It has no vital force. In the liturgy, its vivacity and liveliness are celebrated, dramatized, and concretized. That is why every aspect of liturgical rite is informed and formed on the Bible as the guiding principle. Whereas there may not be an explicit mention of the word ICT in the Bible, the act of visual, communication and teachings in the Bible served as what the ICT communicates today. Accordingly, several passages in the Old Testaments and New Testaments have explicitly and implicitly addressed the matter under study.

Old Testament (OT)

In the OT, God communicated with and continues to communicate Himself to humanity. He communicated with man/woman in various ways that human being was accustomed to. For instance, God communicated face to face with Adam and Eve (Gen 3:8) in the form of an angel to Abraham (Gen

---

[27] Pope Gregory the Great, "Interpreting the Scriptures Continued" from https://prezi.com/efe37lioghms/interpreting-the-scriptures-continued/ accessed on 28th September 2022.

[28] Jovian P. Lang, "Bible and Liturgy" in *Dictionary of the Liturgy* (New York: Catholic Book Publishing, 1989) 64.

18:1-3) in dreams and visions to Joseph (Gen 37:5), through a burning bush to Moses (Exod 3:1-9), through the sound of a voice and appearance of a dove for the witnesses of Jesus' baptism (Matt 3:13-17) and through tongues of fire to the Apostles. In such instances of communication by God, he used different methods or media (burning bush, dreams, visions, sound, voice, tongues of fire, etc.) that were appropriate at the time and based on the needs of different hearers of the message. Simply put, God uses different "media" to communicate with mankind.[29]

The concept and process of communication of God to human beings, in OT, appear to be on various phases through creation, words, messengers, dreams, etc. God is transcendent and inaccessible Being, dwelling in the heavens (Gen 28:12-13). Yet, He progressively reveals and unfolds His eternal plan of salvation to humanity, as He calls the Church into being and requires the loving response of assent and obedience. Hidden God, shrouded in the Holy of Holies and even in theophanies (Exod 20:21; Deut 4:11) can be known through reasoning from creation, though that did not lead them to knowledge of God, expressed through worship and moral commitment. With the Israelites of old, God communicated through His creation (Ps 18:2-5; 103). This is because it seen as subservient to His will and directly controlled by Him. Hence, every phenomenon of creation, such as a timely wind (Exod 14:21), calamities like famine (2 Sam 21), a storm (Ps 28), etc, were viewed as God's acts of communication to the people.

Additionally, through creation, God communicates Himself to the people as He reveals Himself through his word. Some biblical passages abound in this regard (Amos 3:7; Isa 45:19; Num 12:6; Deut 18:15-18; Dan 2: 47; Sir 42:19) affirm to God's will to communicate Himself to His people by a wide variety of terms and expressions:

> God uncovers or reveals (*gãlâ*) some truth or quality (in *qal* or *piel*) or Himself (*niphal*); He makes Himself known (*niphal* of *yãda*) or causes another to know (*hiphil*); He appears (is seen- *niphal* of *rã'â*) or makes someone to see a fact, His glory, a vision (*hiphil*); He causes someone to hear his word, voice, judgement (hiphil of šãma); He announces (*higgid*); He speaks (*dibbêr*); He says (*'ãmar*); His word (*dãbar*) comes to the prophets. The *niphil* of the

[29] Mike Mazzalongo, "The Use of Media in Ministry: Communicating the Message" from https://bibletalk.tv/media-in-ministry accessed on 20th August 2022.

> verb often has some divine force or quality as subject, such as word, glory, arm or salvation.[30]

The initiative is always taken by God, acting as a person to communicate Himself to His people. It was forbidden to communicate with God through necromancy, divination and other forms of magic (Deut 18:9-14).

It is equally important to note that God communicates through prophetic word. Though his messengers, He makes His plan and secrets known to the people of Israel. The word of God as spoken by the prophets has a dynamic reality (Isa 40:6-8; 55:10-11). The prophets usually address the people with this formula: "The word of the Lord came to N..." (Isa 38 4; Jer 28:12). This expression demonstrates their conviction that they are communicating the message of the Lord. As people who have experienced the holiness, personality and will of God in an inexpressible way (Isa 6; Jer 1; Ezk 1-2), setting them apart from their people, they look at the concrete historical situation of their nations and pronounce God's blessings and judgement on them.[31]

Besides, through dreams, God communicates with His people. In the OT, as in the Ancient Near East, dreams, especially those experienced by kings and priests, are regularly understood to have message from God. They can be direct communication or symbolic ones that need interpretation. In a dream, God warned Abimelech, King od Gerar, of the impending death when he wanted to take Sarah, the wife of Abraham, whom Abraham had referred to as his sister (Gen 20:30). Another direct communication was the warning to Laban against harming Jacob because of his flight (Gen 31:24). Betty J. Lillie rightly observes that "the direct communication came in the words of God, and reiteration of patriarchal promise emphasized the continuity of God's presence with the chosen people."[32] Dreams that have divine content usually occur at the sanctuaries. Example of such dream include Joseph at Bethel (Gen 28:12ff); Samuel at Shiloh (1 Sam 3:1ff); and Solomon at Gibeon (1 Kgs 3:4-15). Consequently, the OT provides a

30 Joseph Jensen, "Revelation, Concept of (in the Bible)," in *New Catholic Encyclopedia* 12 (Washington DC: Jack Heraty, 2003) 436-437.

31 Jensen 437.

32 Betty J. Lillie, "Dreams" in Caroll Stuhlmueller, Dianne Bergant, Demetrius Dumm, *et al.* (eds.), *The Collegeville Pastoral Dictionary of Biblical Theology* (Bangalore: Theological Publications, 2011) 226.

variety of rich resources and insights for adequate communication that dovetail into NT era.

New Testament (NT)

As Jesus Christ was about to ascend to his Father, he gave all Christians a mandate: "Therefore go and make disciples of all nations, baptizing them in the name of the Father, and of the Son and of the Holy Spirit, and teaching them to obey all that I have commanded you" (Matt 28:19-20). This missionary mandate, otherwise called "the Great Commission," was given by Jesus Christ, over two thousand years of her existence now, to the apostles and by extension the subsequent followers, to go and preach the Gospel to the whole world. As they disseminate this Good News, they should embrace the culture of the people they were sent to evangelize, especially, the cultures that are in harmony with the Gospel message. Part one of *Communio et Progressio,* a Pastoral Instruction of the Roman Catholic Church, issued by the Pontifical Council for Social Communications on 23rd May 1971, prepared in accordance with the Second Vatican Council's 1963 Decree, *Inter Mirifica,* states that:

> While He was on earth, Christ revealed Himself as the perfect communicator. Through His 'Incarnation', He utterly identified Himself with those who were to receive His communication and He gave His message not only in words but in the whole manner of His life. He spoke from within, that is to say, out of the press of His people. He preached the Divine Message without fear or compromise. He adjusted to His people's way of talking and their patterns and thought. And He spoke out of the predicament of their time.[33]

Admittedly, Jesus Christ is described as the perfect communicator because He understood and employed the cultural realities of the people to communicate His message about the Kingdom of God. The apostles followed the example of Christ by sharing the Good News where people spent their time. For instance, Peter preached the Gospel in a public place

---

[33] *Inter Mirifica* 11.

and thousands responded with their conversion. (Acts 2: 14-42). The Apostle Paul preached the Gospel at the centre of culture and influence in Greece and influential people responded. Before then, he (Paul) first received his initial education in Tarsus, and probably became familiar with the pagan culture, since his acquaintance with the Gentile writers is clearly shown in his speeches and writings (Acts 17:28; 1 Cor 15:33; Tit 1:12). One of the most natural careers for the youths to follow as at that time was that of a merchant but it was decided that he should go to college and become a rabbi, that is, a minister, a teacher, and a lawyer, all in one. According to Jewish customs and traditions, he learned a trade before preparing for the sacred profession. He acquired the trade of tent making from goats' haircloth, a trade from his own labour (Acts 18:3; 2 Cor 11:8; 2 Thess 3:8). His preliminary education having been completed, Saul was sent, when he was about thirteen years old, to the great Jewish school of sacred learning at Jerusalem as a student of the law. It was here that he became a pupil of the celebrated rabbi called Gamaliel. The Gamaliel referred to in the scriptures, was the first of the famous rabbis of that name. He was a descendant of Hillel and was considered an expert in the law.

Despite belonging to the party of the Pharisee, Gamaliel was a freethinking person (Acts 5:34) and an admirer of Greek wisdom. Apostle Luke wrote that Saul studied under Gamaliel, in Jerusalem: "I am verily a man which am a Jew, born in Tarsus, a city in Cilicia, yet brought up in this city at the feet of Gamaliel…" (Acts 22:3). This is where Saul spent many years in an elaborate study of the scriptures and of the many questions, concerning them with which the rabbis exercised themselves. During these years of diligent study, he lived "in all good conscience," unstained by the vices of that great city. Admittedly, young Saul was preparing for a rabbinical career, for on completing his education and training, he emerged as a strong zealot of pharisaic traditions and persecutor of the Christian faith.

Patristic Insights on ICT

The Church Fathers (otherwise called Early Fathers, Christian Fathers or Fathers of the Church) were ancient and influential Christian theologians and writers who established the intellectual and doctrinal foundations of Christianity. The historical period in which they worked became known as the patristic era and spans appropriately from the late first to mid-8th centuries, flourishing in particular during the 4th and 5th centuries, when Christianity was in the process of establishing itself as the state Church of the Roman empire. In traditional dogmatic theology, authors considered Church Fathers as authoritative and a somewhat with restrictive definition. Nonetheless, in the academic field of patristic, the study of the Church Fathers, has extended the scope of the term, and there is no definitive list.

During the early years of Christianity, many of the Church Leaders or "Fathers" wrote down admonitions and instructions on what it is meant to be a follower of Jesus as well as what liturgical ceremonies should be followed as a believer in these early Christian communities. One of these Apostolic Fathers, whose identity is unknown, wrote such a document titled, *The Teaching of the (Twelve) Apostles*, or as it is commonly referred to today-*The Didache*. This document, composed sometime between 70 and 150 CE in Syria or Egypt, presents to its readers a message of instruction regarding liturgy, personal behaviour and eschatological application and belief. The liturgical or common ceremonial practices of the Church are thoroughly detailed in this document as are the admonishments towards individual holiness in specific and common circumstances. *The Didache* ended by synthesizing these two factors (public manner *versus* personal integrity) and shows their connection and grand purposes.

The impact and value of this document to its original readers and even to modern-day Christian believers is monumental. *The Didache* highlights in a concise way the pragmatic constructs of the Christian Church. Nonetheless, it still cleverly and successfully melds the functionality of Christianity with its spiritual side. In his *Patrology* series, Johannes Quasten states that: "Scholars, constantly drawn to its precious contents, have gained repeated inspiration and enlightenment from this little book."[34] Kurt Niederwimmer writes that: "The whole composition is unpretentious as literature, nourished by praxis and intended for immediate application."[35] Whereas in *The Apostolic Fathers*, it proclaims that the *Didache* is "one of

---

[34] Johannes Quasten, *Patrology. Christian Classics*, 1986, 30.

[35] Kurt Niederwimmer, *The Didache (Hermenia and Historical Commentary on the Bible)*, (New York: Fortress Press, 1998) 3.

the most fascinating yet perplexing documents to emerge from the early church."[36]

Accordingly, the importance of *The Didache* should not be dismissed merely because of its size or exclusion from the Scriptures. As many other theological works written at the time, its usage was at times questioned, and a general opinion of it emerged as it being non-canonical. Theologian and monk, Tyrannius Rufus (340-410 C.) specifically makes reference to *The Didache* and remarked that it would have been "read in the Churches, but not appealed to for the confirmation of doctrine."[37] Athanasius of Alexandra (296-373 C.) avers that this document was "appointed by the Fathers to be read by those who newly joined us, and who wished for instruction in the word of godliness."[38] Eusebius Pamphilus, in his *Ecclesiastical History*, also notes of *The Didache* as not being in the Canon of scripture. Accordingly, it provides to the modern-day reader an understanding of the influence of this work had on the early church despite its lack of canonical authority. It also shows that Christianity, like the Jewish faith, had its own unique ceremonies of religious value.

Magisterial Views on ICT

The Church must raise its concerns like digital divide (information rich and information poor). It underscores that individuals, groups and nations must have access to the new technology to share in the promised benefits of globalization and development. When *Sacrosanctum Concilium* speaks of liturgy under "signs that are perceivable to the senses,"[39] digital mediated signs had not yet flooded the world. In the sixty years since the Constitution on the Sacred Liturgy, however, profound cultural changes have taken place in whose wake pixels, visual literacy and digital materiality have begun to dominate the cultural imaginary. This development has put pressure on the desire contained in *Sacrosanctum Concilium* for a simplification of rites.[40]

---

[36] J. B. Lightfoot & J. R. Harmer, *The Apostolic Fathers* (New York: Apocryphile Press, 2004) 145.

[37] Philip Schaff, *Nicene and Post-Nicene Fathers Series 2, Volume 3*, CCEL, 2009, 558.

[38] Schaff 552.

[39] *Sacrosanctum Concilium* 7.

[40] *Sacrosanctum Concilium* 34.

Undoubtedly, ICT has been compared to a medieval cathedral[41] and Christians with regard to parallels between online modes of engagement and offline gestures towards the transcendent. Whether one finds these claims convincing or not, online liturgical practices are material practices as are all offline liturgies.

The kinds of materiality involved in the two realms differ at significant points. Whereas in both offline and online worship, a human body is the core materiality, the human body in online worship is interfacing with an internet-accessing device without necessarily being physically co-present to other worshippers. There is more to the realm of digital *signa sensibilia* (sensible/perceptible sign). While *Sacrosanctum Concilium* is heralded for broadening the exercise of liturgical authority,[42] this broadening pale compared to the unprecedented levelling of traditional *loci* (place) of authority in ICT. This online reality is related to broader cultural changes in the experience of authority in a network-based society, especially to the move toward increasing decentralization while at the same time, more interconnected living. Liturgical experience has been generated in all directions through a multiplication of voices rather than through a simple replacement of traditional *loci* (place) of liturgical authority.

The Church's interest in the internet is a particular expression of her longstanding interest in the media of social communication. Accordingly, the Church's communication remains a mission and an essential part of the proclamation of the kingdom. Like any other media, even when condemning dangerous abuses, the Church has taken a fundamentally positive approach to the internet and ICT. In this way, quoting Pope Pius XII's 1957 Encyclical Letter, *Miranda Prorsus*, the Pastoral Instruction on the Means of Social Communication, *Communio et Progressio*, published in 1971, underlined that point: "The Church sees these media as 'gifts of God' which, in accordance with his providential design, unite men in brotherhood and so help them to cooperate with his plan for their salvation."[43]

---

41 Andrew Dewdney & Peter Ride (eds.), *The New Media Handbook, Media Practice* (New York: Routledge, 2006) 293.

42 *Sacrosanctum Concilium* 22.

43 Joseph Migga Kizza, *Ethical and Social Issues in the Information Age* (New York: Springer Media, 2003) 13.

Ever since the publication of the decree *Inter Mirifica* in 1963 by the Second Vatican Council, the Church has done much to encourage and facilitate the use of emerging means of social communications, in order to advance in its teaching along with the technological advancements in the digital media. Admittedly, no one who takes postmodernity seriously underestimates how important the ICT are in relation to every part of the people's lives. Pope St. John Paul II rightly notes that: "The impact of the media can hardly be exaggerated. For many the experience of living is to a great extent an experience of the media."[44] In 1995, the Pontiff (Pope St. John Paul II), speaking to African missionaries, stressed the importance of the various means of social communication, emphasizing that the world has become a global village due to digital revolution and application. He referred to the "world of communications as the first *Areopagus* of the modern age" that unifies humanity, turning it into a 'global village,' and further observed that "the younger generation is growing up in a world conditioned by the mass media."[45]

Similarly, Pope Benedict XVI observed that, "Technological advances in the media have in certain respects conquered time and space, making communication between people, even when separated by vast distances, both instantaneous and direct," which provides potential "for service of the common good and constitutes a patrimony to safeguard and promote."[46] The Church has closely monitored the phenomenal changes in technology, all the time being cautious in order not to be overwhelmed by the ingenuity and creativity as well as the unquenchable enthusiasm of the users. Down the memory lane, Popes (1965-2023) have been very proactive in providing directions to the Church and the world at large especially on the best way to search for the nexus between ICT and Liturgy in the light of emerging media technologies. We all gladly acknowledge that the media have also

---

44 Pope John Paul II, *Proclaiming Christ*, (Vatican City: Libreria Editrice Vatican) 9 & 13.

45 Pope John Paul II, *Redemptoris Missio*, (Vatican City: Libreria Editrice Vatican, 1990) no. 37.

46 Pope Benedict XVI, *The Media: A Network for Communication, Communion and Cooperation*, 40th World Communication Day, 2006, (Vatican City: Libreria Editrice Vatican, 2006) 2.

opened new possibilities for the celebration of the Eucharist.[47] This requires a specific preparation and a keen sense of responsibility on the part of pastoral workers in the sector. When Mass is broadcast on television, it inevitably tends to set an example. Care should therefore be taken to ensure that, in addition to taking place in suitable and well-appointed locations, the celebration respects the liturgical norms in force.[48]

In the light of the above guidelines, the universal Church has made efforts to use the new social media as well as teach the faithful about the kind of connectivity among peoples engendered by the digital media. It offers the Christian worship an opportunity to similarly unite people with one another and with Christ. The importance of social media in preaching, catechesis and dissemination of Church teachings cannot be over-emphasized. Championing the cause of this mission, Vatican officials also make use of social media platforms to disseminate other documents and the various declarations of the universal Church. Evidently, every frontier of the field of new evangelization has portals of the Apostolic See visible. Accordingly, many of the faithful are actively making progressive use of the different social media platforms by publishing opinions, homilies, articles and official Church documents and messages.

Pope Benedict XVI acknowledges this trend of the new media as a powerful resource for priestly ministry in the service of the World, but cautions that: "priests present in the world of digital communications should be less notable for their media savvy than for their priestly heart, their closeness to Christ."[49] Priests stand at the threshold of a new era, as new technologies create deeper forms of relationship across greater distances, they are called to respond pastorally by putting the media ever more effectively at the service of the Word: "Priests are thus challenged to proclaim the Gospel by employing the latest generation of audio-visual resources (images, videos, animated features, blogs, websites) which

---

47 See Pontifical Council for Social Communications, Pastoral Instruction on Social Communications on the Twentieth Anniversary of "*Communio et Progressio*" *Aetatis Novae* (22nd February 1992): AAS 84 (1992), 447-468.

48 Pope Benedict XVI, *Post-Synodal Apostolic Exhortation Sacramentum Caritatis* 57.

49 Pope Benedict XVI, *The Priest and Pastoral Ministry in a Digital World: New Media at the Service of the Word*. 44th World Communication Day, 2010.

alongside traditional means, can open up broad new vistas for dialogue, evangelisation and catechesis."[50]

In his address titled, "Bringing Christ to the Digital Continent," Pope Francis instructed that the world of social communications, more and more, has become a "living environment" for many, a web where people communicate with each other, expanding the boundaries of their knowledge and relationships." The goal in communications is ultimately to dialogue with today's men and women, who sometimes feel let down by "Christianity that to them appears sterile." In today's globalized age, the Pontiff stressed, there is a "growing sense" of isolation, an inability to connect with others that impede people from building meaningful relationships. It is crucial to know how to dialogue with others, in the environments created by technology and social networks, "in such a way as to reveal a presence that listens, converses, and encourages."[51]

The Pontiff further encouraged the Church thus: "Do not be afraid to be this presence, expressing your Christian identity as you become citizens of this environment. A Church that follows this path learns how to walk with everybody! Through both social communications and personal contact, the Church is called to "warm the hearts of men and women" who he said was "made up of real men and women who bring with them their hopes, their suffering, and their pursuit of what is true, beautiful and good." "We need to descend into the darkest night without being overcome and disorientated; we need to listen to the dreams, without being seduced; to share their disappointments, without becoming despondent; to sympathize with those whose lives are falling apart, without losing our own strength and identity."[52]

Liturgical Sources on ICT

Admittedly, the liturgy of the Church does not exist for the sake of human beings but for God; although, it has the pedagogical power to inculcate doctrinal and moral truths. Participants in the liturgy are led to realize that

---

[50] Pope Benedict XVI, *The Priest and Pastoral Ministry in a Digital World*... 1.

[51] Pope Francis Addresses Plenary Assembly of the Pontifical Council for Social Communications, *Bringing Christ to the Digital Continent By Junno Arocho Esteves,* Vatican City, 23rd September, 2013 (Zenit.org).

[52] Pope Francis, *Bringing Christ to the Digital Continent.*

bodily movements, gestures and material objects which it employs offer "great opportunities of expression, of knowledge, and of spiritual experience... and capable of presenting a truth more strongly and convincingly than can the mere word of mouth."[53] The Church's liturgy is pedagogical. The cult of the Church is purely the affair of God in Christ Jesus. It is not a means to an end but an end itself. Though its main essence is the worship of God in and through Jesus Christ; however, it has the power to inform, form and educate the minds of the faithful. Though the antiphons, readings, homily and exhortations and creed are more didactic; yet, through its symbols, prayers and euchologies, the faithful are drawn into a deepened experience about God, humanity, and creation.

For instance, in the *Book of Blessing*, Chapter 19 on "Order for the Blessing of Centres of Social Communication" clearly states that the Church pays particular attention to the technological developments that have an important influence on the human spirit. Of great interest are those organs of communication that have the power to affect not only individuals but whole populations, even all of human society. These include the press, the cinema, radio, television, and the like and are designated by the general term "media of social communication." The provision of a blessing for the buildings and equipment for these media is one way in which the Church exercises its vigilance for the right use of the media.[54] Meanwhile, the present celebration, of the Book of Blessing, admonishes that the rite has reference both to the community whose interests the new building and media will serve, particularly to those who will work in the building and use the media to communicate news, ideas, and other forms of information.[55] It enjoins that the blessing may not be celebrated without the presence both of the community involved, or at least a group of its representatives, and of the management and staff of the facilities to be blessed.[56]

In Christian tradition, Eucharistic liturgy has always been considered as a key place where the challenges and prospects affecting Christianity are properly located. Liturgy is a place where the divine and the human meet.

---

[53] Romano Guardini, *The Spirit of the Liturgy* (New York: Crossroad Publishing Co., 1998) 60.

[54] *The Roman Ritual* 357.

[55] *The Roman Ritual* 357.

[56] *The Roman Ritual* 357.

God appears through grace and human beings appear through worship. And it is achieved through the exercise of the priestly office of Jesus Christ, the action of Christ the priest and of his Body the Church and, therefore, demands only what is most suitable to its proper and sublime character. There is always the danger to misconstrue liturgical celebration as what begins and ends 'during' worship. The angle of the preparation, formation and attitude that constitutes the 'before, during and after,' as the totality of celebration is left hanging. It has always been the cherished tradition of the Church that, *lex credendi* (norm of belief), *lex orandi* (norm of prayer) and *lex vivendi* (norm of living) should complement and enrich one another. Their mutual relationship is displayed in such a way that the people's belief system determines how they pray and ultimately the life that ensues from the prayers or worship. This explains why *Ite Missa est* (Go forth, the Mass is ended) encompasses the lived life that flows from the Eucharistic celebration that has just taken place from where the participants are sent forth to the world. The formation and information garnered in the liturgy should dovetail into the socio-communitarian living are easily side-tracked by some worshippers.[57] After all, the Church does not exist for worship alone; there is need for interaction between individual members. On the level of practicality and personal persuasion, the contemporary liturgical celebrations will unite and transform participants into instruments to fight against abuse in digital worship. The era of dichotomizing worship from life should be thrown overboard. Holistic life must avoid compartmentalization. The contemporary liturgical assembly needs to embark on aggressive formation and information programmes to facilitate proper celebration that will promote Eucharistic responsibility.

By virtue of the dismissal mandate at every Eucharistic celebration, this sense of responsibility is revealed as an integral part of the Church's mission. Eucharistic liturgy is a great teacher. Those who actively participate learn how to be in relationship with God, neighbour and the rest of the created order. Eucharistic responsibility emboldens Christians to learn about the demands their liturgical participation places upon them and the vocation to exercise legitimate and responsible use of ICT. This is with the view of using any media of social communication by humanity for the greater glory of God. One of the vernacular translations which supplement

---

57 Austin Echema, "Liturgy: A Teaching in Action" in *Journal of Inculturation Theology*, October, Vol. 5 (2003) 141.

the juridical dismissal formula with missionary mandate *Ite Missa Est* (Go and announce the Gospel of the Lord) is the *vade mecum* (Go-with-me) from the eucharistic celebration. Every eucharistic liturgy calls to mind this command to leave the venue and go announce the goodness of God, celebrated at the Eucharistic worship to the people. Interestingly, ICT is a gift of God to the whole world, the world to which He has created and gave humanity the command to have dominion. ICT is the symbol of God who communicates, and He is the communication per excellence. It can be used to communicate the message of God and Christ to the world. The Church sees the web as a missionary territory with people in need of salvation. She uses the ICT as a modern pulpit to reach out the people in the cyberspace. Indeed, it has become the fastest means of communication that could be deployed to reach out millions of people in the shortest possible time. Liturgy challenges participants to use this means to preach the goodness of God they have celebrated at the Eucharistic liturgy.

Views of the Contemporary Theologians on ICT

The contemporary media revolution is certainly a welcome development in the world of communication technology. Accordingly, a good number of renowned scholars have commented on the use of ICT at Christian worship. They identify the importance of the proper means of social communication to promote evangelization in the Church. As ICT provides ample opportunities that could be addictive and obsessive to people, there is an urgent need from the side of the Church and the civil society to make people aware of the dangers of the abuse and overuse of it. Indeed, the Church must encourage media's right development and right use for the sake of human development, justice, and peace, for building up the society at the local, national and community levels in the light of the common good and in a spirit of solidarity. Studies in ICT recognise that the new "virtual" communities are no longer defined by geographic or even semiotic (ethnic/religious/linguistic) boundaries. Instead, communities are being constructed in cyberspace on the basis of common interests, transcending boundaries of class, nation, race, gender and language.

Carlos Errazuriz emphasizes the importance of social media in preaching, catechesis, and dissemination of Church teaching.[58] Describing how social media affects the Christian thoughts and actions, Spadaro notes that "cyber theology focuses on virtual church, mission, discipleship and the use of social media and academic sources online. It explores how our thoughts and actions affect Christianity and its theology and then looks at how technology can strengthen them."[59] Cybertheology seeks to redefine the way we transact, connect, and communicate. Notably, it seeks to have a positive influence on the way we perceive reality and God. The digital age with its prolific use of the internet and associated application has affected every facet of human life. With half of the world's population having access to the internet, this technology is not only having an impact on the way people work and spend their leisure time but is also changing the way they maintain their religious and spiritual life.

Expressing his feelings about social networking among young adults, Helmith Rolfes says: "I have yet to find a student who has not indicated that something is happening that is making a difference in how the student feels about himself or herself and relationships with the world *via* those who visit their site and engage in animated, extensive, and revealing conversations. As people are beginning to move away from mainstream TV programmes and towards reality shows, YouTube, MYSpace and Facebook create a personal engagement with the virtual reality that adds a new dimension to their lives."[60] He further expresses the view that they cannot provide answers to all questions facing socialization. According to him,

> Social networking sites can create and maintain relationships that would not have existed otherwise. But can they sustain relationships? Are these expanding e-socialization sites only a way to avoid dealing with people's Facebook? Is it possible that our youth, in particular, can lose the limited interpersonal communi-

---

[58] Carlos Errazuriz, "*Title IV, The Means of Social Commentary on the Code of Canon Law, Vol. III*, no. 1, 296-297.

[59] Antonio Spadaro, *Cybertheology: Thinking Christianity in the Era of the Internet* (New York: Fordham University Press, 2014) 11-12.

[60] Helmuth Rolfes, *Communicatio Socialis Challenge of Ministry in the Church* (Kassel: Kassel University Press, 2007) 132.

cation skills they currently have by our ignoring, encouraging, or affirming their time in these "places"?

Thomas Stransky offers an avalanche of suggestions on how Catholics and non-Catholics can achieve institutional and personal cooperation. He states that:

> Interconfessional institutes subject to conditions of time and place, the institutes and centres just referred to many be conducted either by Catholics or by several confessions simultaneously. Joint institutes are particularly useful where churches or ecclesial communities need to examine certain questions together (for example, mission work, dealings with non-Christian religions, questions about atheism and unbelief, the use of media of social communication, architecture, and sacred art and in the province of theology, explanation of Holy Scripture, salvation history, pastoral theology, etc., which if they are properly resolved can very much advance Christian unity. The setting up and administration of these institutes should normally be entrusted to those who conduct them, saving the rights of competent ecclesiastical authority.

In his article, "Social Media and Mission-Based Marketing Approach for New Evangelization in the Digital Age", Kenneth Inaku Egere pointed out that Church representatives especially after the establishment of the *Propaganda Fide* in 1622 and subsequent establishment of *L'Osservatore Romano* and Radio Vatican have made tremendous use of the traditional Mass Media in her mission of evangelization. Recently, when digital technology such as the World Wide Web (www) and the internet facilities created in the 1990s came into existence, the Church did not exclude herself from membership of this digital world. In the business world, advertisers have realized the globalization of business that has caused many people to make their purchases right from their bedrooms with just a click in their digital technology. This new technology has created new platforms and ways on how products can be advertised so that the target audience may be reached.[61] Today, we have different fora, blogs, and groups where communities are created with common interests. In the virtual world of cyberspace, we get into various kinds of activities and relationships, which need to be guided by various theological, ethical and liturgical strands and principles.

The Church, and indeed, the contemporary society are living through an epochal age. As digital residents, some today refused to migrate into the digital age; hence, they are the digital fugitives. Many of us make effort to explore the opportunities and threats; hence, they are the digital immigrants. While our young people born since 1980, who are versatile with modern technological toys and tools, are digital natives. We must collaborate and co-operate, in order to instruct and communicate the designs of God to His children in this New Era of Evangelization. Patrick Chukwudezie Chibuko, in his article titled: "Information and Communication Technology (ICT) in the Liturgical life of Christians Today: An Anglophone West African Response" states that there is the functional relationship between the liturgy and the Information Communication Technology (ICT) on the human person and the larger society. As ICT is person oriented; in the liturgy, the Church celebrates a Personality, namely Christ, not as a theory, philosophy, ideology or figment of imagination. What liturgy recalls in celebration, ICT records and preserves for posterity in gadgets. He notes that ICT simply facilitates the celebration of the re-enactment and the preservation of the memories of the mystery celebrated for the present and posterity. It is not surprising that ICT qualifies as a perfect partner with liturgy only to an end and not the end itself especially when applied with utmost caution, decorum, reverence, discretion and diligence.[62]

Peter Eshioke Egielewa, in his article titled: "The Perception of Smartphones among Catholic Faithful: A Study of Selected Parishes in Edo State, Nigeria," empirically analyses the perception on the use of smartphones by Catholic faithful. He discusses how smartphones have increasingly become a common feature in Catholic parishes during Masses

[61] Inaku Kenneth Egere, "Social Media and Mission-Based Marketing Approach for New Evangelization in the Digital Age" in *African Ecclesial Review* (AFER), Vol. 57, Nos. 3 & 4, Sep./Dec. 2015, 186-205.

[62] Patrick C. Chibuko, "Information and Communication Technology (ICT) in the Liturgical Life of Christians Today: An Anglophone West African Response" in *Journal of Inculturation Theology*, Vol. 16, No.2, 2019, 140-155.

and other liturgical celebrations. Exiting from the era of analogue, the Church is giving way to this new trend, the digital age. Unfortunately, while priests perceive the smartphones in the church and personal Christian life more positively, some lay faithful perceive them negatively. Proposing them as an invaluable tool, the Church cannot afford to lose; hence, he recommends some form of regulations and guidelines of smartphones both at the parish and diocesan levels.[63]

The article titled: "Church and Mass Media: Harnessing Opportunities for Evangelization in Eastern Africa," by John Lukwata, posits that evangelization involves communicating the Gospel of the Kingdom of God, as embodied in the person of Jesus Christ, using languages and media that are accessible to the people with the main goal being human salvation. He argues that radio and television, which represent the civilization of the word and the image, respectively, are important tools that the Church should use to spread the Good News of God across. According to Lukwata, Africa has witnessed a liberation of airwaves which has led to a proliferation of both public and private audio-visual means of mass communication. Therefore, the Church should – with the guidance of the Gospel and the Holy Spirit - harness these media to proclaim the message of Christ from "the housetops" of Africa.[64]

Aidan Msafiri took the discussion of e-Church in Africa to another level that could be regarded as being too ambitious. In his article, "Globalization of Concern: Opportunities and Risks of Using Cyberspace to Spearhead Evangelization in Tanzania," he argues that the Church can take a bolder step towards what he refers as "smart evangelization". The ultimate advantage is to link the Church in Africa to cyberspace where African churches would be linked to a *global cyber church; with an e-church, an e-congregation or e-sheep and e-shepherds*, the *Homo sapiens* zooming away towards an anonymous *homo cybercus*.[65] One may not be far from the assertion that this bogus roadmap towards the technological connectivity

---

63 Peter Eshioke Egielewa, "The Perception of Smartphones among Catholic Faithful: A Study of Selected Parishes in Edo State, Nigeria" in Emmanuel C. Anagwo (ed.), *Journal of Inculturation Theology*, Vol. 17, No.2, 2020, 257-290.

64 Lukwata 151-152.

65 Aidan Msafiri, "Globalization of Concern: Opportunities and Risks of Using Cyberspace to Spearhead Evangelization in Tanzania," in John Lukwata (ed.), *Search for New Paradigms of Evangelization in the 21st Century* (Nairobi: CUEA Press, 34-49.

will not be realizable for the Church in Africa, at least in recent times, since connectivity is a very big challenge.

Theology of ICT in Christian Worship

Theology is a systematic articulation of faith in God as a guide for all who are in search for God. Theology exposes the meaning and understanding of God to inform, form and transform the recipients of its message. Without theology, our understanding of the theological finding is bound to be incomplete. The purpose of liturgy is to contribute to theology that possesses faith and doctrine. It is not of theology which exists on the cult but of cult of the theology, that is, liturgy of service of theology (theology without liturgy is incomplete). Liturgy is theology in celebration. Theology is impossible without the import of liturgy. Liturgy is the living principle of theology. It is in the liturgy that the source of faith becomes a living organism. Liturgy determines the purpose of theology. It is a way of life.

From the view of St. Anselm, theology is 'faith seeking understanding.' It seeks to comprehend the reality, meaning, significance, and approach of the Church's worship to ICT. The use of ICT, as one of the mass media technologies, expresses the foundation of our theological beliefs and practices. In theology, the Church is designated as a communicating community. The nature of communication in the Church is communion, communitarian and dialogical. Each of these three aspects intertwines, leads to and confirms the others. In the creation account where the dialogical God, in communion with other persons in the Trinitarian community, communicates His essence in the assertion,

> God said, 'Let us make man in our own image, in the likeness of ourselves, and let them be masters of the fish of the sea, the birds of heaven, the cattle, all the wild animals and all the creatures that creep along the ground' (Gen 1:26).

Theology explains how God, as the giver of this wonderful gift to humanity, is the first communicator and the perfect communicator. In creating human beings in his image and likeness (Gen 1:26), God gave them also the capacity and need to establish the reciprocity and dialogue between human beings and all pages of the scripture to deepen the events, the crises and the reconstruction of this dialogue.

According to the new dispensation, Jesus Christ becomes the incarnation, that is, self-communication of God which leads finally through the Paschal Mystery to a new dimension of God's self-communication. Thus, the Paschal events "are the time of the new beginning of the self-communication of the Triune God to humanity in the Holy Spirit through the work of Christ, the Redeemer. This new beginning is the redemption of the world: 'God so loved the world, that he has given his only Son' (John 3:16).[66]

From oral tradition, the NT provides a good theological foundation anchored from examples of Christ and the disciples sharing the Good News where people spend their time. Christ participated actively in the synagogal liturgy and read the scroll like others. During His inaugural speech, He opened the scroll, after reading, the whole eyes were fixed on Him. He elicited such attention involving the body, soul and spirit that when He finished addressing them, they gave a rapturous ovation by saying that nobody has read and spoken like this before. They marvelled at the wisdom and the spirit moving in Him (Luke 4:16-22). For Ajay Varghese, Jesus' method of communication is summed up thus: (1) Ability to listen to others (Jam 1:19); (2) Ability to think deeply before speaking (Eccl 5:2); (3) Ability to exercise restraint in situations that provoke anger (Col 4:6). Jesus Christ was an orator to be able to convert large crowds in his sermons but above that, he was not used to long speeches or lengthy sermons. Jesus' Sermon on the Mount lasted no longer than seven minutes.[67]

In the words of John Edappilly "Jesus, the Messiah, the Son of God, was the decisive and final form of God's communication to man."[68] Indeed, Jesus' method of communication can summarily be captured in the instruction to His disciples when He gave them the challenge to go out and preach in Luke 10: 5-9: Whatever house you enter, first say, 'peace to this

---

[66] Pope John Paul II, Encyclical Letter, *Dominium et Vivificantem* (On the Holy Spirit), (Vatican City: Libreria Editrice Vatican) 23.

[67] Ajay Varghese, "Jesus' Methods of Communication" from http://ajayvarghese.blogspot.com/2007/06/jesus-methods-of-communication.html accessed on 22nd August 2022.

[68] John Edappilly, *The Emerging Electronic Church: A Theological Critique on the Church Encountering Computer, Television, and Cyber World* (Bangalore: Asian Trading Corporation, 2003) 61.

house!' And if anyone is there who shares in peace, your peace will rest on that person; but if not, it will return to you. Remain in the same house, eating and drinking whatever they provide, for the labourer deserves to be paid. Do not move about from house to house. Whenever you enter a town and its people welcome you, eat what is set before you; cure the sick who are there, and say to them, 'The kingdom of God has come near to you.'[69]

Admittedly, Jesus is the specific order of importance in His strategy of communicating the Gospel message, which includes four steps: declare peace, eat with people, pray for their healing and declare the kingdom.[70] The above steps showed that Jesus emphasized a communication strategy to blend communication of the Gospel message through interpersonal involvement, relationship building, and group ministry experiences. The effectiveness of Jesus' communication was in His ability to live among the ordinary people, eat with them, be their friend, care about their problems and ultimately be their Saviour. Similarly, Apostle Paul's preaching in Greece had a significant impact on the culture of the people such that many turned to Him and accepted the content of his message.[71]

From written tradition, there was a time in liturgical history, with the invention of the printing press, worship aids changed from hand-lettered scrolls to bound books. These bound (sacred writings and liturgical books) are supposed to be signs and symbols of heavenly things and so truly worthy, dignified and beautiful[72] that "will lead the faithful to a greater reverence for the Word of God and for sacred realities."[73] It is also a known fact that we are now in a digital age. The world of digital communication, with its avalanche of great and many opportunities, makes us appreciate more Paul's exclamation: "Woe to me if I do not preach the Gospel" (1 Cor 9:16).

---

[69] For a detailed study, see Egielewa 258-259.

[70] Alan Tippett, *Missiology*. Pasadena: William Carey Library (1987).

[71] Christian Bolu, "The Church in the Contemporary World: Information and Communication Technology in Church Communication for Growth: A Case Study" in *Journal of Media and Communication Studies*, *4*(4), 2012, 80-94.

[72] *General Instruction of the Roman Missal* (GIRM), (Nairobi: Paulines Publications Africa, 2003), no. 349.

[73] *Liturgiam Authenticam* no. 120 in http://www.usccb.org/about/divine-worship/policies/guidelines-for-the-publication-of-liturgical-books.cfm accessed 10th February 2017.

Indeed, ICTs have constituted great effective factors in the digitalization of the nations. They have come to stay for good with their numerous benefits such as being able to circulate information from one place to another in a short period in a twinkle of an eye. One achieves that by simply pressing and manipulating the right buttons. As this age has witnessed great innovations and inventions, these advancements in science and technology have impacted the *modus operandi* (mode of operation) in Christian worship. Antonio Spadaro notes that applied theology uses its own theological instruments to respond to the demands of communication.[74] The challenges and prospects abound as the Fathers of the Second Vatican Council rightly put it in the Decree on the Means of Social Communication, *Communio et Progressio*: "the constant improvement in the media puts them at the disposal of more and more people who in their daily lives make increasing use of them. More than ever before, the way men live, and think is profoundly affected by the means of communication."[75] The Church's openness to the use of mass media is unmistakeable. For instance, *Communio et Progressio* as a Church document indicates the basis for the Church's use of the media: "The Church is in duty bound to communicate her belief and her life publicly because Christ has communicated it and because men and women have a right to know."[76]

Furthermore, Pope Paul VI reiterated that the "Church would feel guilty before the Lord if she did not utilize these powerful means that human skill is daily rendering more perfect. It is through them that she proclaims from the house tops the message of which she is the depository."[77] Communication theology is really the continuation of the task of communicating God in His revelation and incarnation as well as how to fulfil that mission today. The Church needs to be increasingly present in the media so as to make them not only a tool for the spread of the Gospel but also for educating the peoples for liturgical formation.

---

[74] Antonio Spadaro, *Cybertheology: Thinking Christianity in the Era of the Internet*, Trans. By Maria Way (New York: Fordham University Press, 2014) 11.

[75] *Communio et Progressio* 1.

[76] *Communio et Progressio* 122.

[77] Pope Paul VI, Apostolic Exhortation on *Evangelii Nuntiandi* (Evangelization in the Modern World) in http://w2.vatican.va/content/paul-vi/en/apost_exhortations/documents/hf_p-vi_exh_19751208_evangelii-nuntiandi.html accessed on 17th April 2022.

The Spirituality of ICT

Spirituality covers a lot of terms previously used to express Christian lifestyle and spiritual exercises. Before now, some schools of thought hold the wrong assumption that Christian spirituality has nothing to do with communication especially Mass Media. Due to lack of the recognition and promotion of this vital course, a lot of spiritual good for human communication are yet to be realized. Addressing this *lacuna*, the section discusses the issue from the liturgical perspective and how this spirituality can be promoted through mass communication. Assuredly, the Church has always provided the template for assessing the spirituality of anything or being. It is a participation in the mysterious communion of life with God. Here, our focus is the spirituality of ICT in Christian worship.

Understandably, besides the educational value, suitable liturgical and spiritual formation can also be given to the faithful in a such a way that the proper use of ICT will not only enhances the beauty of the celebration, but also be an excellent example for the faithful, thereby bringing the whole lots of spiritual benefits with digital worship. Authentic suited ICT complaint liturgy fosters active and fruitful participation and geared toward the building up of the assembly. Active participation is one of the basic themes in the reformed liturgy of the Second Vatican Council.[78] It is a means toward the achievement of the transformation and development of a true Christian spirit. It demands the people's entrance into the very mystery of God with the totality of their being to become part of the event being celebrated. The participation should be full, conscious and active. To participate fully means that the assembly is to come to the liturgy as human beings with all the faculties that make them human- body, soul and spirit. It implies using all the human senses and dimensions that are available to the faithful to take part in the liturgy.

ICT should assist the faithful to express and share the gift of faith that is within them. The theologian, Tom Beaudoin rightly states that: "Cyberspace underlines our finitude," "reflects our desire for the infinite, the divine." Seeking such fullness signifies, then, working in a field "in which spirituality and technology intersect."[79] Digital worship helps

---

78 SC 14.

79 Tom Beaudoin, *Virtual Faith: The Irreverent Spiritual Quest of Generation X* (San Francisco: Jossey-Bass, 1998) 87.

parishioners and chaplaincy members to commune better during the Mass and if and only if the media team prepares very well when the choice of the liturgical seasons, scriptural readings and liturgical actions of the celebrations are strictly adhered to. And the saying goes: "it is the modern cat that knows how best to hunt the modern rat."

The Church today needs the guidance of the Holy Spirit to effectively bring a resounding success to the spirituality of the ICT. Unless we invoke the aid of the Holy Spirit, we only discover that our worship cannot be heard by God. The Holy Spirit is the sanctifier who clears the way for a contact with the Divine. Just like the ICT gadgets to be used, the proper wordings and management of gadgets are selected by the Holy Spirit to bring success to our prayer/worship (Rom 8:26). This action is achieved only when we invoke the presence of the Holy Spirit. That is why the earliest teaching of the Church advises us to begin our prayer by saying, "Come Holy Spirit and fill the hearts of the faithful…."

When this doctrine is imbibed, it goes a long way to add meaning to liturgical life especially as the Pope Benedict XVI in his Encyclical Letter *Spe Salvi* brings out, "*Lex orandi, lex sperandi*", calling prayer "a school of hope".[80] When the Holy Spirit accompanies the use of ICT at worship and liturgical prayers, the result is superb as the Holy Spirit speaks for us in the words we cannot utter (Rom 8:26-27). Surely, digital worship made with the above tit bits and more stand to be heard by God. Accordingly, liturgy is also the action of the Holy Spirit, the Teacher and Sanctifier of the faithful. CCC further likened the Holy Spirit, whose presence and activity in the liturgy, to the electric current that activates and energizes the whole system and is certainly the live wire of the liturgy. In the liturgy, the Holy Spirit, "prepares the Church to encounter of the assembly. By his transforming power, he makes the mystery of Christ present here and now. Finally, the Spirit of communion unites the Church to the life and mission of Christ."[81]

Applying the analogy of a pencil to ICT can illustrate our point on this groundswell of interest on how ICT can best be harnessed to improve the efficiency and effectiveness of the Catholic liturgy. It is a proverbial story

---

80 Pope Benedict XVI, Encyclical Letter *Spe Salvi* (Vatican City: Libreria Editrice Vaticana, 2007).

81 *The Catechism of the Catholic Church* [henceforth CCC] (Nairobi: Paulines Publications, 2001) nr. 1092.

or better still, the analogy given to a pencil by a pencil maker. Once, the pencil maker took each pencil aside, just before putting it into a box. "There are five things you need to know before I send you into the world," he told each one. "Always remember them and never forget, and you will become the best pencil you can be."

- You will be able to do many great things, but only if you allow yourself to be held in someone's hand.
- You will experience a painful sharpening from time to time, but you will need it to become a better pencil.
- You will be able to correct mistakes you will make.
- The most important part of you will always be what is inside.
- On every surface on which you are used, you must leave your mark. No matter what the condition, you must continue to write.
- The pencil understood and promised to remember and went into the box with a genuine sense of purpose in its heart.

Now, replacing the pencil with ICT gadgets, always remember the advice and never forget it, and it can become the best instruments that can be used to worship God through evangelization, catechesis and formation.

- ICT can be used to do many great things, but only if it is to be at the service of God and the Church. Accordingly, ICT must also allow other human beings to access the many gifts, talents, and potentialities therein.
- ICT will experience a painful sharpening from time to time by going through guidelines and principles of liturgical norms. They need each sharpening to make them fitting instruments for worship.
- Genuine users of ICT will be able to correct some of the mistakes and abuses against the applications. Be wise and grow with them.
- The most important part of ICT will always be what is inside, the potentialities to be channelled towards active, conscious and full participation of the faithful.
- On every surface on which ICT is used, it must leave its mark. No matter the situation of abuses and aberrations, ICT can still be turned around at the service of God in everything it is used for. ICT can be used to make God visible in the world. If we

> understand the message of the Pencil Maker and remember these things, ICT can be used fittingly to achieve a lot in this digital era especially in relationship with our Maker, God.

A celebrated Latin adage holds that: "*Sancta sancte tractadanda sunt*" (Holy things must be handled holily). Among other things, the expression challenges those who handle sacred things like the priests and the media crew to live above board. This explains the simple reason why people expect all stakeholders at worship to exhibit qualities that befit the ministers around the holy of holies (sanctuary) since "those who live around glass houses do not throw stones." It is also a unique way of ensuring that things used in liturgy are spiritually oriented. They should be at the service of liturgy. The liturgy is the public worship of the Church. So, all gadgets of ICT to be used in the worship must conform to the Holy Spirit and not the way of carnality (worldliness).

Nonetheless, to reach this stage, those who participate in the liturgical celebration should do so with the best for-m of preparation. The reformed liturgy of the Second Vatican Council reminds worshippers that for the liturgy to produce its full effects, "it is necessary that the faithful come to it with proper dispositions, that their minds should be attuned to their voices, and that they should cooperate with divine grace lest they receive it in vain."[82] It must be traditionally carried out worthily, in a dignified, devout and attentive manner (*digne, attente et devote*). Everything that has to do with the liturgical prayer must manifest the faith of the Church in the Most Holy Eucharist.[83] As the slogan of what the Church believes goes: "*lex credendi, lex celebrandi, lex vivendi*" (what the Church believes, she celebrates, and she lives out). The spirituality of ICT at worship can, therefore, progressively help to enhance the beauty and prayerfulness of the liturgical celebrations. The collective assistance of all stakeholders is however needed to develop this digital spirituality, with general dexterity and professionalism that relate to the celebration of liturgy.

---

82 *Sacrosanctum Concilium* 11.

83 Hilary Odili Okeke, *Let us Celebrate the Faith* (Onitsha: Goodmark Prints Production Inc, 2005) 68.

Evaluation

This liturgical exegesis chapter employed the Second Vatican Council's *Inter Mirifica* (Decree on the Media of Social Communications) 13 to navigate on the theological insights on the use of ICT at the service for Christian worship. It deeply expressed the Church's position in the previous century, in which new avenues of social communication were uncovered. Such means included the press, movies, television, radio, etc. Nonetheless, a lot have happened in the development of the media, both in the secular and religious settings. Today, not only are individuals, or the masses affected, the entire human society has been engrossed by many new social media of the present century. While the Church so much cherishes its indispensable values in the service of the contemporary man, she is not unaware of other diverse impacts that the media creates.

The fruits of the exegesis portend that the use of these means to announce is the Good News of salvation to all men and women of whom God loves, for the liturgical formation and for pastoral activity, to instruct and direct the faithful how to use these means of social communication in a way that will ensure their own salvation and perfection and that of all mankind, and to teach the faithful especially the professionals to have a human and Christian spirit in the use of instruments of ICT. Unarguably, the Catholic Church is doing something already, heeding the clarion call in *Inter Mirifica* that the Church has right to use the means of social communication to spread the teaching of the Gospel,[84] as some parishes are already using info-technology gadgets to preach the Good News. This is a welcome development. But more efforts can still be made at Catholic worship. Admittedly, the bishops, priests, religious men and women, and indeed, all those directly connected with the care of souls should make conscious effort, in the spirit of collaborative ministry, to assist the faithful to build up their Catholic faith through proper catechesis and mass media education. Remarkable success would be achieved if pastors and pastoral agents entrusted with assisting the faithful would be more dedicated.

More often than not, these worshippers are desirous to learn about their faith and related affairs, but it would seem that those who are charged with the responsibility are either not aware of their need or are not willing to help them. Liturgical worship provides a veritable platform to always be

[84] *Inter Mirifica* 3.

available and sensitive to their needs. They should stoop down to their level so as to chart and encourage them through the positive use of ICT which they are digital natives. The faithful are known for their appreciation of what they want. Directing them towards a dignified and fitting use of ICT for worshippers and liturgical formation remain an outstanding feat to explore with rich content drawn from all the teachings of the Church, tradition, and liturgical sources. In this way, the growing and developing ones, among them, will be formed after the mind of Christ and the Church.

The liturgical exegesis could be summed up as an invitation and a challenge. It is an invitation for the faithful to examine themselves individually and collectively. As a challenge, this calls for more attention to the local church on how to use the ICT, like salt and light of the world (Matt 5:13-16), to add flavour to the earth and be the light to the world. The next chapter will explore on how the Church in Africa is called to justify the hopes of the universal Church on her by using ICT during Christian worship to bear fruits of authentic and convincing Christian living and witnessing. This is because the digital culture is rich with abundant fruits to press, and the Christian is called to undertake the work of mediating between the worship and digital culture.

Chapter Six

The Future Of The Digital Worship for The Church In Africa

This chapter anchors the writer's contribution to the recent debate on evolving a digital worship. In the digital era, ICT has become an indispensable tool for human communication in general and the Church's social communication, in particular. Development of African Catholicism, taking cognizance of the handicaps of the past, should chart the way for future consideration. This new *magna charta* (great chart) should be homely and dynamic in order to integrate the African way of celebrating worship. It should be *anamnetic*, so that the people could picture the Paschal Mystery of Christ. It should also be pedagogical for easier understanding. This new African digital worship should also be transformative since the people should be touched by the Word of God. It should be oriented towards missionary endeavours and be compatible with ICT for easy documentation, preservation, and replay. This is the focus of this chapter to expound more on this mantra.

E-Worship in African Liturgical Practices Today

The advent of the digital age is often compared to another epoch of seismic upheaval related to decisive advances in communication technologies.[1] Undoubtedly, the time for worshippers to ward off uncertainty and build their future has arrived. Abraham Lincoln is often famously credited to have said that: "The best way to predict your future is to create it."[2] ICT has come to stay! The rapid development of technology in the media is surely one of

---

1 Terese Berger, @ *Worship Liturgical Practices in Digital Worlds* (New York: Routledge, 2018) 117.

2 Abraham Lincoln, ""The Best way to Predict your Future is to Create it" from https://www.wanderlustworker.com/the-best-way-to-predict-the-future-is-to-create-it/ accessed on 26th September, 2022.

the signs of progress today. As the world today is growing more conscious of digital worship, it resonates louder than ever in the comity of technological advancement. Churches in Africa must now make haste to improve their ICT complaint indices and register themselves online for the countless number of her members online. To effectively achieve this feat, she should furnish her children with resources of how to make efficient and effective use of them. Jacob Dankasa avers that, "effective use of the social media will generate great benefits to the ministry of the Church in Africa."[3] Admittedly, media is a veritable tool for the dissemination of the Gospel message. The Church then must embrace as well as annex them for the everyday life and work of mission.

A survey conducted by the writer shows that from Johannesburg to Lagos, Cairo to Dakar, Kinshasa to Kigali, Nairobi to Accra, etc., the debate on how Africa worship should respond to the digital revolution is raging and imminent. Since it is clear now that ICT and Liturgy can have mutually beneficial relationships, the Church should entrench the new media in more of its activities, pastoral strategies, and liturgical events. After all, we live in times of great change in the society and in the Church. A million-dollar question, begging for an answer is: "What kind of liturgies are we proposing for the future?" The reformed liturgy of the Second Vatican Council recommends the kind of worship that suits the joys of hopes of the people. It must deal with innovation and creativity. Again, how are we to hold firm and authentically express our love of God liturgically with ICT, recognizing the need to follow certain guidelines and set limits? To the extent the Church is using ICT, it follows, then, that Catholic worship is not static or moribund. Since the liturgical life of the Church is constantly evolving, she believes that "*liturgia semper reformanda est*" (liturgy is always in need of reformation). The Church responds and reacts always to history and signs of the times. Accordingly, the Church, while keeping to its authentic ancient tradition, following the spirit of the liturgy, projects models for liturgical celebrations that will elicit active, full and conscious participation. The reality of active participation in the liturgy is such that it leads to the maximum engagement of the entire component of the human person, the entire human person make-up: the body, soul, or mind and spirit, the human

---

3 Jacob Z. Dankasa, *Technology for Ministry: Best Practices for Evangelization on Social Media and internet in Africa* (Nairobi: Pauline Publications Africa, 2017) 12.

faculties, imaginations and emotions. When rightly used, the relevance of ICT in Catholic worship is predicated on the idea of promoting active participation in the liturgy with modern gadgets and facilities. The admonition of Emmanuel Olusola is very apt:

> The fact that many Churches in Nigeria (Africa) today mostly use the PowerPoint projectors in Church activities is a step in the right direction. However, the architectural designs of most of these Churches do not allow for good use of such means of communication. This means that, going forward, the construction of Church buildings must take cognizance of factors such as the acoustics of sound production and sitting arrangement that give everyone in the congregation the opportunity to view the projected content in front. This will improve participation in Church activities. For example, the projection of the lyrics to songs will enable the congregation to join the choir in the singing. Projecting the readings will similarly enhance participation.[4]

We must, however, take great care that the use of ICT, which by its nature is a wonder of development today, does not become a source of distraction and hindrance to full, conscious participation of the faithful due to failure to follow humbly and obediently the liturgical norms set out by the Church for the use of mass communication and technology. The ICT should not be used to imply passivity and impede gestures like concentration, meditation, silent moments, as such, hindering active participation of all. To be persons who use ICT to celebrate with faith, the faithful must first know the content of faith. Knowledge of the content of faith and is essential for giving one's own assent, for adhering fully with intellect and will to what the Church proposes.

It follows that there should be proper catechesis to deepen the faith of the worshipping community on ICT as a tool to worship God and not the goal. Some Catholic worshippers know very little about core elements of the divine worship they participate in on daily, weekly, monthly, and yearly bases. This book enjoins pastors to utilize every available opportunity to

---

4 Emmanuel B. Olusola, "Digital Church and E-Culture in the New Media Age: The Spectrum of Nigeria" in *African Ecclesial Review (AFER): ICT & Evangelization ~ Christianity in the Digital Culture*, Vol. 57, Nos. 3 & 4, Sept./Dec. 2015, 220.

stress on the good use of ICT for Catholic worship through homilies, seminars, workshops, etc. Priests have to carry out their role effectively and lovingly and help the faithful to come to Mass not expecting to be entertained by the use of ICT or to be given 'something', but to encounter the presence of Christ, as they bring themselves as offering unto God. Pope Francis avers that, "the sacramental character of faith finds its highest expression in the Eucharist. This is an encounter with the Lord Jesus Christ truly present in the greatest act of His love, the life-giving gift of Himself." Essentially, one thing is to use ICT and another thing is to link the spiritual dimension of them when used in liturgical worship. Whenever the spiritual dimension is neglected, it backfires with attendant passivity in worship as one loses the spiritual unction that should characterize the liturgical space for effective and efficacious response from God.

Evidently, ICT has become the wonder of development today and is becoming the fastest means of communication that could easily reach millions of people in the shortest time. As we discussed earlier, it should be used to disseminate liturgical catechesis. The people of God could be reached through these avenues on liturgical information and formation. All Catholics who are media practitioners should be co-opted to join the crusade. They should be given adequate catechesis of the Church for proper guidance in their professional duties. They should have a common body to oversee their affairs. This body should be represented in a diocesan committee on social communication when they are formed. This diocesan organ should be charged with the responsibility of transmitting religious matters through the radio, television, and newspaper. The members of the committee should include priests who are specialists in Mass Communication along with other Catholic faithful who are media practitioners and other specialists in their various professional calling. Moreover, a permanent place could be provided for the agents of ICT to render their services during worship since ICT plays an important role in liturgical ceremonies. In this way, they will not constitute a nuisance or object of distraction or even irritate the liturgical assembly by blocking their views in the cause of their coverage of the liturgical event.

The media education will help to increase their understanding of the impact of social communications on individual and community levels and would help them acquire a manner of communicating that speaks to the sensibilities and interests of people in a media culture. Today, this includes training in the use of the Internet during worship. They can also profit from websites offering theological updating, pastoral suggestions, and liturgical courses. In agreement with Olusola, this study advocates training in the media and information technology to the extent that the Church's liturgy will not only resonate with Christ's faithful but that a media-oriented mode of worship will enhance active, full and conscious participation at our liturgical celebrations.[5] With ICT, those who preach and make known the Word of life can reach, with words, sounds and images, individuals and whole communities on every continent. This enables the creation of new areas of knowledge and dialogue, enabling one to propose and carry out programmes for communion. Ihejirika states that if used wisely, with the help of experts in technology and the culture of communion, the info-tech media can thus become, for priests and all pastoral agents, valid and effective instruments of true and profound evangelization and communion. This will extend the work of evangelization since the faithful will be enabled to "express in their lives and manifests to others the mystery of Christ and the real nature of the true Church."[6]

Some Key ICT Pastoral Issues for Consideration[7]

Salus animarum suprema lex (Salvation of soul is the supreme law) is an outstanding pastoral principle for liturgical action. It means that saving soul is an essential thing to be considered always. Christian worship both expresses and shapes our faith. Therefore, some pastoral concerns make decisions on whether in a particular circumstance or concrete situation ICT expresses the faith of the community in this place or at this age. Worship must be ICT-faith oriented to enable the people to enter the liturgy and pray

---

5 Emmanuel B. Olusola, "The Christian Liturgy in the Age of Info-Technology: Prospects and Challenges" in Luke Ijezie et al (eds.) *Theology and Liturgy in the Life of the Church Proceedings of the 26th Annual Conference of the Catholic Theological Association of Nigeria* (CATHAN) 2012, 270.

6 Ihejirika 79.

7 Insights used to address some of the issues on ICT are influenced by the collection of writings by Legionary of Christ Father Edward McNamara, professor of liturgy and dean of theology at the *Regina Apostolorum* University of "Zenit: The World Seen From Rome" on his online column dedicated to incisive and scholarly answers to the liturgical questions (See Permalink: http://www.zenit.org/article-3563 5?l=english).

as they should. Some specific pastoral issues that concern the faithful on the liturgical guidelines and set limits for the use of ICT gadgets in Catholic worship are hereunder examined:

Banners, Overhead/Screen Projectors and PowerPoint Displays

It is gradually creeping in that all over the world, more and more Churches in the 'first class urban cities' are using banners, screen projectors and power point displays to show the Mass intentions, hymns, readings, announcements, etc. Except for some African countries like Sierra Leone[8] and Cameroon[9], many African Catholic Churches are not left out in this frenzy effect of e-worship. For instance, it is a common practice for some Churches in Kenya[10] and Ghana to project hymns, readings, and responses during Mass.[11] In some places in Nigeria like Abuja, Lagos, Port Harcourt, and Aba,[12] it is also becoming the common practice for some parishes and

---

[8] There is no parish in Sierra Leone that uses projectors for Mass; although, it is used in most Protestant Churches and Evangelical Fellowships. Catholic Churches there are yet to reach this digital worship stage.

[9] The use of screen projectors for Mass is not a common practice in Cameroon. For instance, in the diocese of Buea where the writer has visited, they do not have such. The same is applicable to other dioceses in Cameroon.

[10] Only a few churches use projectors for Mass in Kenya. Among them are Sacred Heart Cathedral, Eldoret, Holy Family Basilica, Nairobi, in the Cathedral Church in Mombasa.

[11] A random roll call of the Ghanaian Catholic Churches where screen projectors are used include St. Thomas Aquinas Catholic University of Ghana, Legon-Archdiocese of Accra, St. Joseph Parish, Bechem-Goaso Diocese, Corpus Christi Parish, new Tafo-Archidocese of Kumasi, St. Anthony Parish, Ejisu-Konongo-Mampong Diocese, St. Francis de Sales Cathedral, Cape Coast-Archdiocese of Cape Coast.

[12] The roll call of parishes where the screen projectors are mounted and used in Nigeria include Our Lady Queen of Nigeria Pro-Cathedral, Garki-Abuja, Catholic Church of Assumption Asokoro-Abuja, *Lux Terra* Catholic Chaplaincy Apo-Abuja, *Regina Pacis* Secondary School Chaplaincy Garki-Abuja, *Gaudium et Spes* Institute Chaplaincy Asokoro-Abuja; Holy Cross Cathedral, Lagos, Our Lady of Lourdes Catholic Church, Coker, St. Denis Catholic Church, Bariga, St. Mary's Catholic Church, Ajegunle, St. Matthew's Catholic Church, Amukoko, Our Lady of Queen of Nigeria Catholic Church, Ojuelegba; *Corpus et Sanguis Christi* Cathedral, Port Harcourt, Christ the King Parish, Port Harcourt, Our Lady of the Holy Rosary

chaplaincies to use them during Sunday Masses and festive occasions such as Holy Week ceremonies, priestly ordinations, Chrism Mass, funeral Masses, to mention but a few. As already quoted above, one of the general principles on liturgical artwork in "Built of Living Stones" states that,

> ...artworks consisting of technological and interactive media, such as video and other electronically fabricated images, may also be appropriate for sacred purposes. Subject to the same criteria of suitability as other sacred art, technologically produced works of art can point toward sacred realities even though they do not possess the more enduring form, colour, texture, weight, and density found in more traditionally sacred art.[13]

Another reason usually adduced by the proponents of this audio-visual aid technology is that when the contents are presented to the congregation, it helps to facilitate their understanding of the Mass better. And to a large extent, it facilitates the active, conscious and full participation of the liturgical assembly. According to Edward McNamara, it has also made it cheaper as the parish does not have to invest in hundreds of weekly bulletins or expensive missal.[14]

But the danger is that they can constitute a nuisance and distraction to the worshipping community because they cause the people to drift away from the essence of the Eucharistic liturgy. Sometime ago, this writer attended a Holy Mass at a nearby parish in Nigeria. During the homily, the projection was focused on the different locations of the faithful. It was observed that people were busy adjusting themselves in order 'to package themselves better' once they are being beamed. At another instance, the picture of the parish priest who was not even in the Mass was projected throughout the homily! Imagine if the text of the Eucharistic Prayer should be projected in

---

Catholic Chaplaincy, Port Harcourt, St. Jude's Catholic Parish, Rumuokoro-Port Harcourt; St. Joseph's Catholic Parish, Aba; to mention but a few.

13 US Bishops' Document on Church Art and Architecture, "Built of Living Stones" nr. 163 in http://www.usccb.org/liturgy/livingstonesind.shtml, accessed on 23rd August 2022.

14 Edward McNamara, "Follow-up: On Banners, Overhead Projectors and PowerPoint Displays" 8th June 2010 in http://www.zenit.org/article-29678?l=english accessed on 20th August 2022.

the screen during Mass, it will inevitably turn attention away from the altar and toward the screen.[15]

The issue at stake is that since the use of overhead projectors and power points must be made, they should be moderated. A Latin expression holds, "*Virtu in medio stat*" (Virtue stands in the middle). It means that as we use them in Catholic worship, their excesses must be controlled. For instance, the screen should not be in front of the presbyter and never behind the altar as they are means to an end and not the end itself, they are used only as aid to liturgical participation. To avoid irreverence, they are just tools, and should never take the place of proper celebration of the liturgy which must never be influenced or limited by their use. They can, however, be mounted at any other place that may enhance liturgical participation such as the two aerial wings (extreme) of the Church (left and right) with four column pews, front and middle roll.

Pre-Recorded and Televised Masses

Another related salient pastoral issue to the ICT compliance hype is the pre-recorded Mass aired on the TV and Radio stations. It is not uncommon that some Churches air pre-recorded Masses. For instance, the Catholic Institute of West Africa, Port Harcourt, Nigeria has *Oremus* aired by 5.00am daily and 'live' transmission of the 8.00am Holy Mass every second Sunday of the month on African Independent Television (AIT), a private independent station in Nigeria. We must make a point that broadcasting such is no real substitute for an actual celebration. Rather a televised/recorded Mass is a spiritual blessing for those home bound, sick and aged; and can also be a means of evangelization since one cannot rule out the effect it has on those who participate in it. The above merits constitute the possible widespread benefits of televised Masses.

In any case, whenever a pre-recorded Mass is to be done, it is strongly recommended to take place in churches or oratories with a genuine congregation present, thus retaining the feeling of the support of a congregation for those unable to attend. In the absence of the congregation, it would be best to ensure the presence of at least one person who could

15 Emmanuel C. Anagwo, "ICT in the Catholic Worship: Some Pastoral Issues and Implications Today" in *Journal of Inculturation Theology*, Vol. 14, No.1, 2013, 56.

give the responses and especially on a Sunday. It is only when this fails that the priest may resort to celebrating alone and responding the parts of the congregation for the benefits of the listeners/watchers who may be following from their homes, offices, or hospital's closed-circuit TV system (wards).

About the televised Masses, there is no doubt that some people have apathy for them. For such people, by their very nature, television and cinema induce mental passivity and polarize attention and thus are more likely to impede rather than enhance active participation at Mass which consists in much more than merely seeing the action on the altar. But the writer agrees with McNamara that watching a televised Mass especially the Holy Father's Midnight Mass or indeed any televised Mass is a commendable spiritual exercise; above all, for those unable to attend Mass, but also for any Catholic faithful who desires to unite heart, mind, and soul in prayer together with the Pope and the Church.[16]

Traditionally, among Catholic faithful, when someone follows a televised Mass, it cannot, strictly speaking, fulfil the festive obligation. However, it remains a source of spiritual comfort and growth to those legitimately impeded and dispensed from attending Mass due to age, infirmity, distance or some other just cause. For those who have attended Mass also, but followed a televised Mass, it can be a source of spiritual nourishment. In any case, since we appreciate the merits of televised/recorded Mass, there is no comparison to the actual physical presence at Mass.

Live Streaming Programme

This is the pastoral situation when a particular liturgical celebration is being telecast live as the event or celebration is going on. This varies from situation at hand. Sometimes, it could be a recorded for a particular occasion or most times, it is aired as the programme is happening live. By so doing, there is no direct connection between the celebration and those who are watching at different locations. In the case of the Holy Eucharist, communion is received spiritually and even the responses to the different parts of the Mass may not be in the same way it is being aired. Live

---

[16] Edward McNamara, "Follow-up: On Banners, Overhead Projectors and PowerPoint Displays" accessed on 8th June 2022.

streaming is good but given the chance or opportunity after the programme, one can still find time to attend Mass, so as to receive holy communion. The aged, infirmed and sick people can prayerfully sit at home to attend the live-streaming programme. Peter O. Ezekoka copiously notes that:

> Live streaming is yet another strong way of building an online community of e-worshippers. Being one of the great resources that these media platforms provide, its great merit is that online viewers and worshippers are able to follow their pastors and Mass online at the exact time of the Physical Worship, and not on their time. That means they get ready as they would for physical participation. In it, the Church can easily target content at people who are more likely to convert and become followers after. This is the veritable way of building an online community of worshippers. Of course, live streaming should be done bearing in mind the local regulations of Dioceses and the Government since it has data protection concerns.[17]

Since live-streaming of the worship is the situation where a minister celebrates the Eucharistic liturgy in person with a congregation whereas people can watch it though streaming at the convenience of their homes, offices, cars, markets, schools, etc., it has its rules guiding it. For instance, during pandemics or epidemics such as the COVID-19 pandemic, it was "a given faculty" during the "trying time of the COVID-19, since the Church respects civil authorities and obeys her rules and regulations for the safety and health of the worshippers.

The divine worship which involves people as seen at the Last Supper is a worship of communion. It is a communion of pilgrim who with one voice lift up their prayers and petitions to God our loving Father. The Church is a holy place and everything or events have their places, so also the worship. Going to Church to worship involves the journey of faith of the pilgrim people who will gather and call upon God. Here, active, conscious and fruitful participation is encouraged. Nonetheless, live streaming of worship

---

17 Peter Onyekachi Ezekoka, "ICT as an Agent for e-worship in Nigeria" in Emmanuel C. Anagwo & Kelechi Anyanwu (eds.), *Theory and Praxis of Sacred Liturgy in Nigeria: A Festschrift in Honour of Most Rev. Prof. Augustine Ndubueze Echema* (Umuahia: Sons Digital Press, 2021) 434.

will eradicate this fraternal gathering that depicts the spirituality of the early Christians who did everything in common. Pope Benedict XVI advises that,

> …with regard to the value of taking part in Mass via the communication media, those who hear or view these broadcasts should be aware that, under normal circumstances, they do not fulfil the obligation of attending Mass. Virtual images can represent reality, but they do not actually reproduce it. While it is most praiseworthy that the elderly and the sick participate in Sunday Mass through radio and television, the same cannot be said of those who think that such broadcasts dispense them from going to Church and sharing in the Eucharistic assembly in the living Church.[18]

An Ipad at the Gospel Reading

By ipad we mean a line of tablet computers designed by Apple Inc. It runs with Apple's iOS. It is very informative that the first ipad was released on 3rd April 2010 and has more than four generations of ipad. The user interface is built around the device's multi-touch screen, including a virtual keyboard. Beyond using it to record video, take photos, play music, perform internet functions such as web-browsing and emailing, it has other functions like games, reference, GPS navigation, social networking, to mention but a few. It enables one to download and install applications.[19] Evidently, the use of tablets, smartphones and ipads are becoming more useful and powerful means to communicate. Some worshippers are increasingly using technology to enhance their life of faith and opportunities for prayer, meditation and sharing the word of God.[20]

With respect to the issue of using an ipad for the reading of the Gospel by the priest/deacon/bishop, the universal Church has no official

---

18 Pope Benedict XVI, *Post-Synodal Apostolic Exhortation Sacramentum Caritatis (The Sacrament of Charity)* [Nairobi: Paulines Publications, 2007) 57.

19 "What does ipad stand for/" from http://www.abbreviations.com/IPAD. Accessed on 1st April 2021.

20 Emmanuel C. Anagwo "Ipad at the Service of Liturgical Formation of the Youth" in Luke Ijezie *et al.* (eds.) *Youth Formation & Globalisation in the Nigerian Context", Proceedings of the 32nd Annual Conference of the Catholic Theological Association of Nigeria* (CATHAN) 2017, 422.

pronouncement to the use of electronic tablets in the liturgy. Hence, no direct mention of it was made by the *General Instruction of the Roman Missal*, although there is a related liturgical legislation and norm to that effect. Even though, as McNamara mentioned, one Cardinal celebrating in his Cathedral was seen publicly using ipad, that does not constitute the official ratification by the universal Church. If anything, he further states, "In contrast, recent statement from the bishops of New Zealand said that tablets should not be used for Mass and other public rituals."[21]

One may argue that the liturgical books, like any other books, are essentially used to conserve and transmit information. In the same way, the electronic tablets like ipads do the same function even with some added advantages. For instance, a tablet can contain all the ritual books in one place and allows the celebrant to switch the text from one language to another whenever there is need to do so as well as enlarge to the size or change to font of their comfort level. It can also help in the singing of unfamiliar hymns as the congregation reads from them.

Nonetheless, the reasons for refraining from the use of ipad at the Gospel reading are anchored on some liturgical principles.[22] Among them is that it has always been the cherished tradition of the Church to reserve the objects used in the liturgy exclusively for the sacred functions. This accounts why these objects are blessed and set apart from other uses. In this sense, one does not use a blessed chalice for domestic purposes, nor would a priest wear his alb, stole and chasuble to move round the town. It is not a question of impracticality, but because sacred objects, linens and vessels are exclusively reserved for sacred rites. It presupposes that the books used in the liturgical celebrations are usually blessed and reserved for sacred function. They are also printed and beautifully bound and adorned to designate this holy use. Conversely, by the nature of electronic tablets, they are capable of multiple functions. The same ipad used to proclaim the

---

21 Edward McNamara, "Using an Ipad at the Gospel" in http://www.zenit.org/article-34958?l=english accessed on 8th June 2022.

22 However, it can be allowed for a talk in the Church or Parish Hall to the congregation by the priest or lay faithful. In recent times, precisely on 30th August 2022, it was beautifully used by Mrs. Mojisola Akpojiyobvi during their Parish Annual Family Week Celebration at Our Lady Queen of Apostles Catholic Church Ilupeju, Lagos Archdiocese, Nigeria on the theme "Family Love: Wonderful and Fragile."

Gospel, may shortly be used to browse and respond to e-mails, surf the web or download home video or pornographic films.

The related liturgical legislation expressed above comes from the *General Instruction of the Roman Missal* which specifies that only the Book of the Gospel, and not the lectionary, can be carried in the entrance procession and placed upon the altar.[23] We can easily deduce that the norm precludes carrying a multiuse tablet in a procession, laying it upon the altar, reverencing and incensing it. However, if we are to think loud, we may speculate that maybe in the future, somebody may develop a tablet/ipad specifically for liturgical use with an appropriate design and no other programme may be installed. Surely, in that case the debate on whether to use the ipad may change the calculus.

Furthermore, granted that ipads and other electronic media are becoming more and more reliable and user-friendly, there is the possibility of malfunction or operator error.[24] If this should fail in the course of reading or proclamation of the Gospel, how will such a disaster be rescued? This practical reason presents another possible 'loose reason' to discourage the use of ipad for Gospel reading at Mass. Of course, there might be special exceptions even to this, for instance, to use these gadgets to pray the breviary especially for those with eye challenge or when a priest has no access to a missal especially while travelling. It is impossible to foresee all possible situations. This book believes, however, that we should insist on the guiding principle that whatever is to be used in the liturgy must be blessed and designated for sacred use in specific time, place and function. In this sense, the use of ipad for Gospel reading should not be

---

23 *General Instruction of the Roman Missal* (GIRM), (Nairobi: Paulines Publications Africa, 2003) 120d.

24 We often witness the use of the public address system/microphone where the battery might have gone low, dropping or light/total black out or pressing wrong key. A life-experience was once recounted about the visit of an early missionary bishop to a remote African village Church. The parish priest prepared the people very well. Among his preparations was to inform them that in the second response to the Holy Mass, in the old translation of the Roman Missal, they are to respond, "And also with you." On this fateful day, the bishop started the Mass by making the sign of the cross. But he discovered the microphone was dropping (that is not functioning well). So, he turned to the parish priest and said: "I think something is wrong with this microphone" Unfortunately, the microphone picked the statement and the people responded: "And also with you."

accommodated or promoted until such a time we have an ipad exclusively reserved for worship.

Slide Show at Homilies

Another important issue for consideration is the use of slide show at homilies. By slide, we mean to cause something to move smoothly along an even, polished, or slippery surface. Here the different stages of the homily are showcased in this slide for the people to watch. It has given rise to the fact that nowadays, there seems to be a shift from the spirit of the liturgy to technical, mechanical, and ritualistic performance during homilies. This has raised eyebrow to the authenticity of such practices whether there are guidelines for slide shows during homily at Mass. It is pertinent to underscore that the most recent norms regarding the homily are found in the Instruction *Redemptionis Sacramentum* (*On Certain Matters to be Observed or to be Avoided Regarding the Most Holy Eucharist*).[25] We have two norms that would help to address this issue emanating from the use of slide show at homilies: Firstly, the document notes that:

> The homily, which is given in the course of the celebration of Holy Mass and is a part of the Liturgy itself, 'should ordinarily be given by the Priest celebrant himself. He may entrust it to a concelebrating Priest or occasionally, according to circumstances, to a Deacon, but never to a layperson. In particular cases and for a just cause, the homily may even be given by a Bishop or a Priest who is present at the celebration but cannot concelebrate.[26]

Secondly, it copiously observes that:

> Particular care is to be taken so that the homily is firmly based upon the mysteries of salvation expounding the mysteries of the Faith and the norms of Christian life from the biblical readings and liturgical texts throughout the course of the liturgical year and

---

[25] Congregation for Divine Worship and the Discipline of the Sacraments, *Redemptionis Sacramentum* (*On Certain Matters to be Observed or to be Avoided Regarding the Most Holy Eucharist*), (Okpuno: Fides Communications, 2004).

[26] *Redemptionis Sacramentum* 64.

> providing commentary on the texts of the Ordinary or the Proper of the Mass, or of some other rite of the Church. All interpretations of Sacred Scripture are to be referred to Christ himself as the one upon whom the entire economy of salvation hinges, though this should be done considering the specific context of the liturgical celebration. In the homily to be given, care is to be taken so that the light of Christ may shine upon life's events. Even so, this is to be done so as not to obscure the true and unadulterated word of God: for instance, treating only of politics or profane subjects or drawing upon notions derived from contemporary pseudo-religious currents as a source.[27]

It follows from the above statements that the priest or deacon who gives the homily must be physically present. A homily is more than just a slide show, video tape or text that is shown or read (especially as read by a layperson). It is closer to a conversation, a personal communication in which the ordained minister explains God's word and exhorts the faithful to live in accordance with what they have heard. The use of tapes or videos cannot replace the homily. This point is corroborated in a statement of the Pontifical Council for Social Communications on *The Church and Internet*. It writes: "Virtual reality is no substitute for the Real Presence of Christ in the Eucharist, the sacramental reality of the other sacraments on the Internet; and even the religious experiences possible there by the grace of God are insufficient apart from the real-world interaction with the other persons."[28] The personal element is very relevant to the efficacy of the communication itself. In the same manner, the proper place for appeal or fundraising is preferably after the post-communion prayer. Elsewhere, we argue that,

> Fundraising within Mass (*intra missa*) should not or never be after homily, but after post-communion prayer or final blessing, so that the order of Mass is not structurally disrupted and to avoid the temptation of distraction, and even for people to eat or drink because the worship was too long. Maybe a dinner party can be

27 *Redemptionis Sacramentum* 67.

28 Pontifical Council for Social Communications, *The Church and Internet* in www.vatican.va/.../rc_pc_pccs_200202228_church-internet-en.html accessed on 12th August 2022, 9.

organized in the parish hall or any other convenient gathering environment.[29]

In exceptional cases, however, some priests may effectively integrate in a direct appeal with the themes of the liturgy during the homily. Common sense of time judgment demands from the priest if a taped appeal/fundraising is to be made, the homily should be shortened in order to accommodate it. In that way, the Mass will not unnecessarily be long. However, if a bishop has tape or video clip that will replace the homily in his diocese, the only way to justify it to look at it as merely a modern version of a pastoral letter. These letters, which the bishop addresses to the whole diocese as its pastor, usually deal with matters of particular concern. It is because of this important value they are sometimes read in place of the homily. For now, there is no specific norm regarding the use of slide shows or presentations to substitute the homily. So, the same argument to enforce the value of interpersonal communication and personal contact in homily can also stand against slide shows and presentations because images produced can induce a passivity that distracts from the core message being transmitted by the words. The tradition of the Church favours hearing which comes through preaching which has a privileged practice in the Church. While the homily may not be the best place for the use of such media as DVD's and slide presentation, they can be useful for evangelization and catechesis in the context of continual Christian formation. Preferably, a day or later time may be fixed for that, or the pastor could invite the faithful to wait behind a few minutes after Mass to view a video or presentation on some topical issues of pastoral or spiritual concern rather than disrupting the order of Mass.

iBreviary as the Prayer of the Church

iBreviary is another issue that demands pastoral consideration. By iBreviary we mean the portable breviary, accessed on android, smartphone or ipad. One can use it to pray with the full text of the Liturgy of the Hours

[29] Emmanuel C. Anagwo, "Fundraising in Worship: Implications for the Church in Nigeria" in Frederick Wanjala (ed.), *African Christian Studies,* Vol. 31, No. 3, Sept. 2015, 71.

in some languages (for instance, in English, German, Latin, Igbo, Yoruba or Hausa). It can be downloaded online. One can pray online with it or put iBreviary in one's website or blog. Visitors to one's blog can have an opportunity to pray on one's site and to spread the beauty of Catholic Prayer. With the added advantage for a person with eye challenge, as the font can be enlarged to suit the convenience of their comfort level, iBreviary does not require installation of any additional software within one's website.[30]

Although the word Breviary, which is now abandoned although habitual in use in the Latin Church (as *breviarum*), was literally an abridgement and yielded its true meaning only when given its full form, namely, *breviarum officii*. In the Middle Ages, this name was given to a book which brought together for convenience in the celebration or recitation of all the parts which make up the office which had previously been scattered in several different books. The Eastern Churches give the name *Horologion* to the book which is the basis of their daily office.

Ordinarily, Breviary, (otherwise called Liturgy of the Hours, Divine Office, Divine Duty, Divine Hours, Prayer of the Hours, Canonical Hours, etc) is the official public prayer of the Church which consists of hymns, Psalms, spiritual and Biblical readings, and prayers. It is shaped by the liturgical year which has the Paschal Mystery of Christ at its centre and as its source. Since the Liturgy of the Hours embodies the common action of Christ and His Church, it is therefore an important aspect of the total liturgy, for here the Lord is present and active in the Scriptural readings and the members are united with Him through the praying Church. The reformed liturgy of the Second Vatican Council elaborates this understanding that Christ continues his priestly ministry through the agency of his Church, not only by celebrating the Eucharist, but also in other ways, especially by praying the Divine Office. The Breviary is the very prayer of Christ Himself, together with His Mystical Body, the Church, publicly praising God. In it, Christ himself "continues his priestly work through his Church."[31] Through it the people of God (clergy, religious, and lay people) participate in and exercise the royal priesthood of the baptized according to their own place in the Church and the circumstances of their lives. Through

---

30 The sites for downloading ibreviary include: https://www.ibreviary.org., www.ibr eviary.org/en/ , www.kaiserdom.virtuell.de/, to mention but a few.

31 *Sacrosanctum Concilium* 83.

the celebration of the Liturgy of the Hours, the Paschal Mystery of Christ, which we celebrate in the Eucharist especially at the Sunday assembly, permeates, transfigures, and sanctifies the time of each day.

Whereas some Christians generally realised that the Eucharist is the celebration of the whole Christian community, many of them, clergy, religious and laity, have not yet come to the full awareness that the same is true of the Liturgy of the Hours. In effect, for many centuries, the Church had, at least, on the practical level, almost completely lost sight of the Liturgy of the Hours as a public act of worship of the whole Christian community. In the minds and psyche of most priests, religious and laity alike, it became the exclusive and principally private prerogative of the clergy and religious, a peculiar form of prayer, one with which the laity has nothing to do. This is a wrong perception of the intent of the Liturgy of the Hours. In his 2010 Post-Synodal Apostolic Exhortation on the Word of God (*Verbum Domini)*, Pope Benedict XVI makes a heartfelt appeal that "this prayer becomes more widespread among the People of God, particularly the recitation of Morning Prayer and Evening Prayer. This could only lead to greater familiarity with the word of God on the part of the faithful…To this end I recommend that wherever possible, parishes and religious communities promote this prayer with the participation of the lay faithful."[32]

Very significantly, this Exhortation re-echoes the appeal made by the Second Vatican Council: “The laity, too, are encouraged to recite the divine office, either with the priests, or among themselves, or even individually.”[33] There is no doubt that the *General Instruction on the Liturgy of the Hours* (GILH) views the promotion of the involvement of the laity as fundamental to the entire reform of the Liturgy of the Hours and has made it one of its principal recommendations. The Church desires the participation of the faithful not as something to be merely tolerated, or as some peripheral, devotional support to the worship of the clergy, but quite to the contrary, their involvement is seen as an exercise of their rightful role and obligation in the official worship of the Body of Christ, the Church, by reason of their

---

[32] Pope Benedict XVI, Post-Synodal Apostolic Exhortation on *Verbum Domini* “the Word of God” [Henceforth VD] (Vaticana: Libreria Editrice, 2010) 67.

[33] *Sacrosanctum Concilium* 10, see 88, 94.

baptism.[34]

If there is also an honest assessment of what has happened since the promulgation of the revised Liturgy of the Hours in 1970 till date, it would seem to lead one to admit that the desire of the Council Fathers and that of Pope Paul VI and Pope Benedict XVI has not been very much realised as it concerns the laity. The pastoral-liturgical challenge that this situation poses remains ever present and urgent. This can simply be stated as follows: "How can we better promote the celebration of the Liturgy of the Hours so as to achieve a fuller integration of the lay faithful and ensure their more active participation in it in our African parishes and religious communities?" Through the iBreviary, the Church imitates and extends on earth this priestly action, essentially one of praise and at the present time one of propitiation and ministration which Jesus Christ is exercising in glory. The actualization of the priesthood of Jesus Christ, brought about by the liturgy, is the basis of the sanctifying efficacy of the rites of the Church's public worship. In the spirit of the future of the African Catholicism, the writer recommends that one or some sites of ibreviary can be downloaded and accessed on android, smartphone or ipad: My Catholic Prayers, *Laudete*, Breviary, *Universalis*-Liturgical Horarum, Breviary online, Magnificat, Divine Office RC Calendars, Prayers, to mention but a few.

Concelebrants Snapping Pictures at Mass

Another important issue becoming a rampant experience is to behold these days of ICT influence that some concelebrants use ipads, video cameras, smart/android phones, etc. to take pictures at Masses especially during festive occasions like priestly ordinations, religious professions (first or final), silver/golden/diamond jubilee of marriage anniversaries, etc. The danger is to think that because everybody is doing that it is proper. To assess the propriety of this action, we need to know something about a concelebrant. A concelebrant, in a strict sense, is a priest/bishop who officiates at the Holy Mass but is not the chief celebrant (otherwise called the president or presider) at the Eucharistic liturgy. He collaborates with the chief celebrant but because one person must preside at a time, he joins him

34 "The General Instruction on the Liturgy of the Hours" (GILH) in *The Divine Office: The Liturgy of the Hours According to the Roman Rite* (London: The Talbot Press, 1974) no.22, xxxii.

to celebrate the Eucharist as a concelebrant. In a loose sense, every baptized participant in the celebration of the Eucharistic liturgy is a concelebrant joining in the common mystery of faith. Our usage in this context, however, is the strict meaning of the word, as it pertains to the clergy.

The minister who celebrates the Holy Mass is doing that *in nomini et persona Christi capitis* (in the name and person of Christ the head). As such, it demands complete and undivided attention from the minister who officiates whether as the chief celebrant or the concelebrant. As the Mass is the highest form of prayer, the priest must stop at nothing to align himself with Christ whom he represents in the celebration of the Mass. Imagine a bizarre scenario where the chief celebrant brings out his camera and cell phone to take photographs or to answer calls. It is not only absurd, but it is a breach of liturgical etiquette![35] The concelebrant should not take photographs or answer phone calls, granted that there is no law to that effect since it was never contemplated that a concelebrant will do so. The guiding principle is for the priest not to do anything he will not do if he is celebrating with a congregation. It gives the clue that as a concelebrant his unalloyed attention is still needed in the celebration. It must be carried out in a dignified, devout and attentive manner (*digne, attente et devote*).[36] No form of distraction should be allowed or tolerated. That accounts for why the teaching of the Church, which never contemplated that a concelebrant should be involved in this practice of taking photographs during Mass, had already warned that,

> Great care should be taken to ensure that liturgical celebrations, especially the Mass, are not disturbed or interrupted by the taking of photographs. Where there is a good reason for taking them, the greatest discretion should be used, and the norms laid down by the local Ordinary should be observed.[37]

It means that those who are appointed or commissioned (media men and women) to take photographs must not constitute a nuisance to the celebration. In some dioceses, great care is taken to ensure the orderly application following the diocesan regulation for liturgical decorum to be

---

[35] Anagwo, "ICT in the Catholic Worship…" 63.

[36] Okeke, *Let us Celebrate the Mystery of Faith* 68.

[37] Congregation of Rites, *Eucharisticum Mysterium* (1967) 23.

maintained especially during diocesan functions like ordination, religious profession, etc. Similarly, a concelebrant can delegate somebody (outside the sanctuary) to snap the pictures because it is against liturgical decency and decorum to engage in such acts when one is presiding or concelebrating in such a sacred mystery.[38]

Functioning Public Address/Sound System

With good acoustics of sound production, there is such a meritorious benefit and strength with the proper celebration of the Word of God. This explains the fact that any place where the Word of God is powerfully proclaimed and preached, using a functional public address system, enriched with nourishing fruits of deep prayerful reflections, with local idiomatic expressions, poetic forms, proverbs and wisdom thought, ladened with good liturgical and cultural music to help in digesting the Word and Signs, the situation is always quite different and memorable.[39] Such a celebration is usually full and the Christian living is exalted. The people take up responsibilities to solve socio-politico-economic problems because they are now fully armed with Christian values and these of course, lead to reverence to the Word of God, the sacrament of the Eucharist being celebrated with a view to authentic Christian living and witnessing.[40]

Admittedly, good public and sound system in the Church can contribute towards the digital worship for the Church in Africa today. The era of managing the sarcastic analogy of Catholic microphone (with the usual hitting of the microphone) unlike the Pentecostal microphone (audibly clear and distinct) is indeed a necessity to meet the demand of digital revolution. Nonetheless, one of the challenges in celebrating the liturgy is when the Church's sound system is not properly set up to project his voice. The digital age has opened the dire necessity of good acoustics to reach out to many people in a liturgical space especially because of online worship. It is to the advantage of the worshipping community to employ the services of

[38] Emmanuel C. Anagwo, *Hundred Questions and Answers on the Mass Vol. II* (Onitsha: Laurans Publishers, 2013) 17-19.

[39] Emmanuel C. Anagwo, *Celebration of the Word of God: A Liturgical Enquiry* (Berlin: Peter Lang International Publisher, 2020) 146-147.

[40] Chibuko, *Paschal Mystery of Christ, Foundation for Liturgical Inculturation in Africa* 19.

a technician who is a good sound engineer to aid in the choice and location of sound systems within the Church.

It is, therefore, very necessary that this should be considered at the point of constructing the Church. Periodic maintenance of the public address system is highly recommended for an optimal service to evolve. Stabilizers should be provided to ensure adequate light supply and avoidance of damage to the public address system. "The experience of COVID-19 pandemic era has shown that neglect on this aspect of Church Building has colossal consequence to the dissemination and celebration of the eucharistic liturgy."[41]

Evaluation

This chapter underscores that the Church in Africa should consider advancing digital worship in an effort to consolidating knowledge and resources about e-worship and the modern media. After all, a famous quotation from Cardinal John Henry Newman once said: "To live is to change and to be perfect is to have changed often."[42] Since the use of ICT gadgets are in continuous evolution, the Church in Africa is called to evolve with them and must assume prophetic role in them. As the Church in our modern world, the responsibility falls on each one to help steer the Church through this era. To use the Pope's words in his Pentecost message to priests of the Diocese of Rome, "we are called to proclaim and prophesy the future, like the sentinel announcing the dawn that brings in a new day (see Isa 21:11)."[43] That future is now, and that dawn that brings in a new day could be the electronic space. Undoubtedly, a change of mentality is imperative to evolve a digital evolution. The Church will need to study how ICT functions and see how each of these forms of social media operates and find ways to utilize them in evangelisation, celebration, and worship.

---

41 Anagwo, "Adopting New Ways of Celebrating the Word of God in a Pandemic Era" 34.

42 Cardinal John Henry Newman, "On the Development of Ideas" from https://www.newmanreader.org/works/development/chapter1.html accessed on 20th September 2022.

43 Pope Francis, *Letter to Priests of the Diocese of Rome: Prophets of a New Future,* 31st May 2020 [Published in L'*Osservatore Romano*, 5th June 2020, no. 23, 5 & 8.

Accordingly, the continent, rather than bemoan the past, should chart a new course for the future, that is ICT savvy complaint, do her research and findings and come up with ICT complementary procedures that take into consideration the African concerns. This is not in any way a push for an independent Church but downloading the universal principles for the Church in Africa. It presupposes that the Church's contents online should be relevant to the local community and related to their growth in faith. It should be rich in content, such content which connects more with the psych of the online users; yet, maintaining the spirit of the mission of the Church. Yes, "effective use of the mass media in evangelization implies that the content must be packaged in such a way as to communicate the Gospel values."[44] To reflect the Gospel values, pastoral agents involved in the mass and social media must have the purpose of conversion and not of a mere online presence. Hence, this blueprint is made with the view to enhancing the evangelization mission for the Church in Africa and renewing the vigour with which they carry out pastoral care of Christ's faithful with ICT. Since "only the best is good enough for God," they have to ensure the growth of the faith and its practice among the people.

[44] Ihejirika 124.

CHAPTER SEVEN

PRACTICAL RECOMMENDATIONS AND CONCLUSION

This chapter sums up the whole study in a precise manner since the subject matter has gained much currency now than ever, no thanks to the wrong application of ICT in Christian worship today, even in the highly placed Catholic Churches. Some worshippers watch with dismay what is happening and remain unsure of what to do, when to use, how to use and why it must be used. This book systematically addresses the issues by presenting and analysing matters arising under review. It concludes with practical recommendations, resulting from the discussions and findings.

Recommendations for Digital Worship

The value of ICT in liturgical celebrations cannot be over-emphasized. It is quite obvious that the nexus between ICT and liturgy is quite revealing and rewarding. While using the mass and social media, the Church in Africa must rise to the challenge of evolving a perfect, smooth and effective transmission of liturgical celebration and formation by connecting, collaborating and creating the new social media with worshippers. She needs "to enter the modern media marketplace where, these days, we have unashamedly to compete with other groups for minds, hearts and values."[1] Nonetheless, there is need to check the aberrations and abuses that are trying to destroy the solemn nature of the liturgy. The following recommendations are made:

[1] Richard Leonard, "'Light! Camera! Worship! The Cinema and its Challenges to Roman Catholic Worship in Postmodernity" in Keith Pecklers (ed.), *Liturgy in a Postmodern World* (New York: Continuum, 2003) 30.

Proper Training of the Ministers to be ICT Complaints Savvy

The pope and the bishops, as the pastors of the Church, are those alone who have authority for spiritual, juridical and disciplinary decisions about the Church's liturgical practice and formation. Priests, as their collaborators, must seek to explain, guide and deepen the understanding of the deposit of faith by way of liturgical formation. While some forms of these technologies may constitute distractions, there is broad consensus that, if properly harnessed, the adoption of ICT for liturgical celebration and formation is advantageous in a number of ways through connecting, collaborating and creating social media with the worshippers. As the impact of the digital culture of the 21st century dawns on the Christian assembly, the use of ICT is inevitable. For Stella B. Esirah, "in our world today, we cannot downplay the importance of Information and Communications Technology (ICT)."[2] However, the Church insists that in carrying out various ministries in the Church, the ministers must be properly trained. They do not simply teach, they are critical personalities who nurse and nurture the faithful to understand Christian faith, the world and to understand themselves. Evidence shows that for pastors and pastoral agents, their liturgical ministry and skills are the most important factor for active, conscious and full liturgical participation. Hence, those chosen to function require appropriate formation for the role they are called upon to play in the Church.

Ongoing Formation of Priests, ICT Directors and the Lay Faithful

Knowledge is power. Pope Benedict XVI rightly notes that, "Knowledge of the content of faith is essential for giving one's assent; that is to say, for adhering full of intellect and will to what the Church proposes."[3] Having developed a positive attitude towards the digital world, the stakeholders will be better equipped to dialogue with the opponents of such innovations as to offer good alternatives to those who go against Christian values. Formation is a continuous process which should not be stopped after a fixed period.

---

2 Stella B. Esirah, "Ministry in a Digital World: The Media at the Service of the Word of God" in *Koinonia*, Vol. 7, No.3, June 2016, 47.

3 Pope Benedict XVI, "Truth, Proclamation and Authenticity of Life in the Digital Age," on 45th World Communications Day, 2011.

As liturgy grows like a living organism, so also should liturgical formation continue if the Church continues to offer praise to God with ICT. Priests, ICT directors and the lay faithful should be invited for seminars as need arises, in particular, to educate them on how to maintain and use ICT that is being threatened by the use and overuse of digital worship. They should be made to understand that the Catholic liturgy is unique in her way of celebration. Her worship is guided by liturgical norms and principles. Accordingly, they must be informed and formed on the acceptable ways of worshipping with ICT to avoid the danger that constitutes distractions. Liturgical norms and prescriptions acknowledge modern communication gadgets but emphasize that whatever must be used on the altar be strictly and exclusively blessed and dedicated for the service. Thus, the use of ipad, iphone, galaxy, etc cannot replace Lectionary, Book of Responsorial Psalms/Songs, Book of the Gospel, etc. So liturgical ministers, both major and minor, must always use proper book designated for their functions to proclaim the Word of God; although, beyond personal use, modern technology can be used to magnify their voice and visibility, especially in the case of physical impairment.

Need for Substantial Fund for the Procurement and Maintenance of ICT

To contend with the present challenges of ICT, there is also need for substantial fund to be generated for the maintenance of ICT materials and personnel. Participants also are often found complaining about the cost of participating in online worship, especially on the excessive data usage, the lack of appropriate gadgets, and the poor network situation of their local area. While these challenges might not be reckoned as a great challenge for worshippers from some other parts of the Africa, it continues to pose as an obstacle to active participation of e-worshippers. To mitigate against this challenge at the parish level, elsewhere the writer proposes that:

> There must also be a good budget for maintenance culture of the ICT and training of personnel, priests, deacons, religious men and women, and lay pastoral workers who ought to be e-worship

> compliant. It will be most ideal to include this in the annual parish budget.[4]

It presupposes that there must also be a good budget for servicing ICT gadgets. 'A stitch in time saves nine' applies very well to any ICT. It will be most ideal to include regular maintenance of ICT in the annual parish budget. Good communication costs time, money, and energy. No resources should be considered too big to be committed to setting up state of art communication ICT gadgets.[5] In this way, they will be able to connect, collaborate and create with the worshippers.

Parish Pastoral Plan to Adequately Integrate ICT

The liturgical celebration is not meant to be a haphazard affair, or an enterprise dotted with makeshift or rescue operation.[6] The worship of God is an expression of the faith and love of God. The worship of God must be worship "in spirit and in truth" (John 4:24). Thus, the celebration of the liturgy requires great care and attention to fine-tune the details of the planning and execution by the liturgical planning team. Imagine the scenario of a military funeral, at which the honour guard slowly, silently, carefully and respectfully folds the Nigerian flag to give to the bereaved family. At that instant, for somebody with a patriotic inclination, it is a tremendously moving experience to behold. Here we see the outward execution of a ritual powerfully inciting our interior understanding of what is happening.[7] Similarly, in the Eucharistic liturgy, we become participants in Christ's Passion, from the Last Supper to the Immolation on the Cross. The physical reverence should palpably speak to our inner disposition and

---

4 Emmanuel C. Anagwo, "ICT in the Catholic Worship: Some Pastoral Issues and Implications Today" in *Journal of Inculturation Theology*, Vol 14, No.1, 2013, 67.

5 Anagwo, "ICT in the Catholic Worship: Some Pastoral Issues and Implications Today" 67.

6 See Emmanuel C. Anagwo, *Active Participation in the Eucharistic Celebration* (Port Harcourt: University of Port Harcourt Press, 2013) 106.

7 See Thomas Aquinas Pickett, "Active Participation: Historical Continuity in the Church's Worship and Teaching" in https://www.academia.edu/11688578/Active_Participation_Historical_Continuity_in_the_Churchs_Worship_and_Teaching accessed on 22nd September 2022.

augment its attention and love, if those charged with liturgical planning are able to discharge their work creditably well.

Accordingly, the parish pastoral plan should adequately integrate ICT into the liturgical formation and catechesis to be actively involved in the interactive cyberspace communities. The parish pastoral council should install ICT gadgets (overhead projectors, video tape, CGs and other such equipment towards parish liturgical formation) in the hall or parish buildings and encourage their use by the pastors and pastoral agents by providing technical assistants to put them through whenever they encounter difficulties in the application. We urge pastors and pastoral agents to be more involved in the liturgical formation of the young using ICT. This means that they need to be constantly updated in the use of ICT. Training and re-training of pastoral agents should be on continuous basis so as to minimize resistance and enhance adoption of ICT as a tool of evangelization.

Need to Develop a Model Youth Mass

There is the need to develop a model youth Mass, using the new media applications. This will be a separate Sunday Mass for the youth in addition to a day set aside each month for youth Mass (not Sunday Mass), like 'Catholic Women Organization' (CWO) for married Catholic women, every first Saturday in most dioceses of Nigeria and other African countries. Elsewhere we argued that maintaining the basic structure of the Ordinary Form of the Roman Rite of the Catholic Church, a model Youth Mass should involve group participation in an environment that is characterized by warmth, trust, acceptance, and care, so that young people can hear and respond to God's call. Here they are told what patterns to them and what they should know. The Eucharistic celebration should foster the freedom to search and question, to express one's own point of view and to respond in faith to that call. It should provide for real-life application of learning by helping youth to apply their learning to living more faithfully as Catholic youth. It will provide parent education programme and resources, incorporating a family perspective in catechetical and liturgical formation and providing parent-youth and intergenerational catechetical formation. It should also promote Christian attitudes toward human sexuality.[8] After the youth Mass, counselling section can follow to aid those who have psychological problems. Parents and guardians who have problems handling their young ones could also be invited to accompany them.

Re-Orientation in the Seminary

This might be a little more complex, but it will not be out of place to draw our attention to it. It is essential that seminarians take their ICT formation very seriously during their formation years. It has been noticed that some seminary authority and seminarians show laisser-faire attitude to ICT. For instance, up to 2018 and backwards, some seminaries in Nigeria still disallowed the use of laptops and cellphones by students who are being trained to graduate and minister to an ICT savvy and digital generation. When such seminarians graduate without making personal efforts to be attuned to the use of ICT, it might become a challenge to put ICT to effective use in the liturgy as future ministers. Olusola rightly and optimistically states that:

> This kind of thinking points the wrong image of the Church as a relic of the analogue age in a world of that has gone digital. To forestall this, CESACC, in conjunction with the Catholic Secretariat of Nigeria, has over the years organized workshops for formators in the Major Seminaries in Nigeria. In these workshops, Seminarians are urged and trained to incorporate communication studies into their curriculum to make future priests conversant with the modern means of communication prior to ordination.[9]

The Guide to the training of future priests concerning the instruments of social communication, includes theoretical knowledge of the cultural, political, and religious functions and moral trends of media and practical

---

8 For a detailed discussion, see Emmanuel C. Anagwo, "Enhancing Youth Ministry in the Eucharistic Liturgy for Integral Transformation in Africa: Issues, Challenges and Prospects" in Ferdinand Nwaigbo *et al.* (eds.) *Theology and Youth Empowerment for Integral Development of Africa* (25th CIWA Theology Week), 7th– 11th April 2014, 345-346.

9 Olusola, "Digital Church and E-Culture in the New Media Age…" 221-222.

formation in using the tools of social communication. The goals of such a communication formation are to educate the future priests to "impose self-discipline," "train the faithful to exercise discipline" and "use the media in their apostolate." These goals based on three levels of training that are hereby recommended: moral (the receiver of media messages); instrumental (the user of media and specialized (producer); the third level is intended primarily for those who will be engaging fully in communication ministry. Accordingly, it should be recommended that communication studies should be spread through the curriculum from first year philosophical study to last year of theological study. By this, basic studies in ICT will be promoted and inculcated into them. Through all these their level of ICT competency will be determined and coordinated before they go into the pastoral field.

Proper Legislation on the Use of ICT at Worship

The use of ICT in Christian worship should faithfully conform to the principles and norms of divine celebration. In this way, they will have the qualities proper to genuine and wise use of ICT. Stakeholders animated by the Christian spirit should accept that it pertains to their vocation to apply ICT and increase its store of treasures. Efforts have been made by the Church to come up with documents to guide the use of ICT in worship and evangelization. A lot can still be done with respect to implementation of recommendations of the Second Vatican Council, the Pontifical Commissions and the Bishops' Conferences, Papal encyclicals, pastoral letters and decrees in such documents as the *Inter Mirifica*. Accordingly, the Church in Africa should borrow a leaf from the universal Church and adapt an integral approach on the use of ICT during the Catholic liturgy. They should come up with the proper ways of using ICT in liturgical celebrations especially on the need to checkmate the aberrations and abuses that are trying to undermine the essence of Christian liturgy in the name of digital revolution. For instance, we must have a designated place for the agents of the ICT to stay and cover the liturgical ceremony in our parish Church. It may be from the gallery section, at the edge of the front in the Church, etc. but never to block the view of the congregation or constitute distractions to the faithful. There must be known and implementable sanctions to anyone who defaults on the legislation.

Setting up the Media Office at the Parish and Diocesan Levels

A Media Office is to be established and supported in the parish, diocesan levels, secondary schools, and seminaries. Young people could obtain basic knowledge in media literacy. It will be charged with the responsibility of designing websites with the purpose of giving something to those who surf the pages. Web pages and sites must have an inherent quality to form, consolidate and promote public opinion in conformity with the natural law and Catholic liturgical norms to internet visitors. With Gerald Musa, we say that: "The studio can serve as a place where parishes or dioceses record audio and video programmes that could be presented to mass media broadcasting stations; the media centres may take care of the public address systems of the diocese or any parish; a media centre could also serve as a resource centre for the teaching of catechism with multimedia."[10] It would also record and publish news of the liturgical life of the Church and informed comments on it.

Furthermore, to attain an optimal use of ICT in the liturgy, it requires engaging the services of professionals. There may be myriads of them in the ranks of Christ's faithful but not among the clergy who preside over most liturgical celebrations. Simeon Eboh quotes the view of the pastoral instruction, *Communio et Progressio* which states that:

> The active cooperation of Christians who are professionally competent in the field of social communication is one of the contributing factors to human advancement. The excellence which they bring to their professional duty is itself a powerful testimony to Christianity. And moreover, as members of companies or organizations without religious affiliations, they should bring to the fore a Christian point of view on all questions that affect men in society.[11]

The media centre can also serve as a place for basic communication courses that can be offered to school children who are on vacation and adults who

---

[10] Gerald Musa, "Priests in Nigeria and the Use of Social Media" in Emmanuel C. Anagwo (ed.), *Journal of Inculturation Theology*, Vol. 16, No.1, 2019, 127.

[11] Simeon Eboh, *Freedom of Communication and Evangelization in Nigeria* (Lagos: AUP, 1994) 65.

have special interest in communication. Besides, a media centre could offer computer training to those who indicate interest. The Church has much to gain if she trains people in the use of media and on ways to produce media content on print, electronic and social media. The person who has the tools in his hands determines media content. Emmanuel Badejo rightly states that: "It depends on the man who is behind the camera, nor can the pen decide what to write, it depends on the one who is holding the pen."[12] The advantage of a well-trained media literate worshipper is that such a person could transform the face of social media.

Establishment of Diocesan and Parish Ministers of ICT

With the rise of challenges, bordering on the use of ICT in the Catholic liturgy, it is pertinent that dioceses set up Diocesan Committee for ICT (Media Unit), in order to curb excesses and abuses in ICT in the Church. This body is of most valuable assistance to promote ICT together with pastoral liturgical action in the diocese. These committees should consist of persons who are experts in ICT technicalities. They should be those in-charge of the gadgets and media communications in the Church such as microphones, bulletins, brochures, power point displays, slide shows, video cameras, ipads, overhead projectors, parish/diocesan/congregation websites, VCD, pre-recorded and televised Masses, to mention but a few. The media unit has an important role to play in the society and even more in the Church during liturgical celebrations. We must, however, take great care that media communications do not become a sign of distraction and hindrance to active, full and conscious participation of the faithful due to failure to follow humbly and obediently the liturgical norms set out by the Church for the use of mass communication and technology. In planning liturgical celebrations, the members of the station, parish or diocese should be included in the liturgical planning team.[13] At the parish level, the responsibility for effective pastoral celebration in a parish community falls

---

[12] CNA/EWTN News, Evangelize though Family, Social Media, (2nd February, 2017) in https://www.catholicregister.org/home/international/item/24231-nigerian-bishop-evangelize-though-family-social-media accessed 5th September 2022.

[13] Emmanuel C. Anagwo, "Liturgy as Public Work in the Context of the Liturgical Planning Team: Challenges Facing the Theology of Work in Nigeria" in Michael Sasa (ed.), *The Aquinas' Journal*, Vol. 8, June 2016, 199-200.

upon those who exercise major roles in the liturgy. Therefore, the particular maintenance of order, for instance, abuse of ICT during Christian worship, for each liturgical celebration should be directed to the ministers of ICT.

Annual Week of ICT at the Parish and Diocesan Levels Respectively

It is strongly recommended that a Week of ICT could be set out, from the diocesan calendar and celebrated annually in the parishes. For greater emphasis, the grand finale on a Sunday should be earmarked for "ICT Mass Celebration." The liturgical celebration on such a day should have a special rite that can be created specifically for it. In regions where it is customary to have an annual blessing of centres of communication during the Easter season or at some other set-time, celebration of such a blessing should be arranged by use of the chief elements in this present order.[14] The parish (liturgical) assembly could use such a week for to explore the vast opportunities of ICT for virtual worship. Through such, the pastors will accompany their parishioners in their journey of savouring the merits of ICT as they shun the abuses and aberrations that can easily crop up. Notably, these activities can create positive approach towards digital worship. To this end, flyers or banners that expose the dangers of abuse of ICT at worship may be distributed and even mounted in strategic places to corroborate the prior actions. The Church must be champions and seen as such when it comes to promoting the veritable means of ICT for worship.

Increased ICT-Thematic Homilies

The Liturgy of the Word is an indispensable part of the Eucharistic celebration. One essential part of this liturgy is the homily. The homily is the kerygmatic expression of the Word of God in the linguistic currencies familiar to the people. The ministers of the Word have a very significant role to play in promoting the search for the nexus between ICT and Liturgy as a means of promoting digital worship. The pivotal place the homily plays in the liturgy makes it a veritable tool for human transformation. Indeed, what we hear can change or affect our behaviours. Thus, priests and other ministers of the Word should always remember how far this aspect of the

---

[14] *The Roman Ritual* 357.

liturgy could build up a fruitful Christian community. As such, homilists need to increase ICT-thematic homilies in places where that is already taking place. Parishes where there have never been ICT-thematic homilies need to include them. Such homilies should be well-prepared and should reflect the web relationship between ICT and Liturgy.

The intermingling of ICT and Liturgy has become an affirmation of the immanent and the transcendent God who is constantly at work. The scripture (especially readings of the day) also serves as the foundation of such homilies and there are some scriptural passages that focus on human development and progress, for instance, the divine call to increase, multiply and subdue the earth for the sake of humanity (Gen 1:28). As a result of well-prepared, well-delivered homilies, worshippers should leave the Church as ICT complaint savvy, ICT-friendly and digital natives/migrants who should become ICT-evangelists. While the relationship between God and human beings is the focus of homiletics, homilists must promote a relationship that interweaves love between God, human beings and human development. In creating human beings in his image and likeness (Gen 1:26), God gave them also the capacity and need to increase and multiply. Humanity's progress and solidarity should be a major objective of the kerygma. The homily is one very resourceful way of promoting a harmonious relationship between ICT and Catholic worship.

Need for a Periodic ICT-Penitential Service

Humanity's failure in the effort to carry out her duties by using ICT in the service of the liturgy demands that we all seek forgiveness from the abuses which everyone has been guilty at one time or another. God, as the giver of this wonderful gift to humanity, is the first communicator and the perfect communicator. In creating human beings in his image and likeness (Gen 1:26), God gave them also the capacity and need to establish the reciprocity and dialogue between human beings and all pages of the scripture to deepen the events, the crises and the reconstruction of this dialogue. Human attachment and selfishness have driven human beings into wilful exploitation and abuse of ICT to the extent of deifying the ICT gadgets today. People get up from bed and they check first their cellular phones. People do not easily discuss again at meetings or dinner, but they are distracted by their cellular phones. These acts are surely sinful since they wilfully glorify them instead of God. Christians need to acknowledge these sins and humbly confess them at confessions. Usually, the sacrament of reconciliation ought to begin with a penitential service before individual confessions. Dioceses should annually organise and celebrate an ICT-penitential service where people are carried through an examination of conscience considering ICT sins. This activity should boldly be in the diocesan calendar. The bishop, priest or deacon who leads such services should have a list of many ways we sin against the use of ICT and read it out to the people as a guide. It is believed that as the people avail themselves for such services, they will gradually be converted into ICT complaint savvy, reliable and user-friendly people who genuinely use ICT for its positive advantages more.

Composition of the Rite of Celebration of a Digital Liturgy

With liturgy, as the highest form of prayer to God, the highest form of the use of ICT is to ultimately direct all works of human hands to worship God. Since all was made by God and for God, human stewardship finds its fulfilment in channelling every human progress of technology for God. After all, science in its original state is a companion to worship in human beings' attempt to demonstrate his/her wisdom, endowed by God in understanding the realities around him/her. Science and technology are precious resources when placed at the service of humanity and promote their integral development for the benefit of all.[15] By properly using ICT, they should lead humanity to worship God. Indeed, the best place for such worship is in the Eucharistic liturgy. It provides the platform for the self-realisation of all creatures and created things. Consequently, God's injunction that required humanity to have dominion over things of this earth also calls for human beings to use the technology of this world to deepen and enhance cyber devotional space. As such, there is need to have a particular rite for such worship that will be truly digital. It should have its *Collecta* (Opening Prayer), *Super Oblata* (Prayer over the Offering), Preface and *Post communionem* (Prayer after Communion). Liturgists should compose these prayers and those who have done so should seek the

---

15 CCC 2293.

appropriate approvals so that they can soon be in use for the celebration of the Digital-liturgical Mass.

Conclusion

From the foregoing discussion, as evident from the facts and analysis extemporized above, it is established that the relationship that exists between ICT and Catholic Liturgy is a complementary relationship. Both have common features which can be expanded and exploited towards understanding how the former can lead to the latter especially as espoused through *anamnesis*, person and event-based relationship. The book has also discovered that the disadvantages generated by e-worship have, again, brought to the fore the peculiarity of ICT in the Catholic worship, whereby modernity seems to conflict with the age-long traditions of doing things particularly in the area of liturgical patrimony and tradition. However, the Church cannot, because of abuse, relegate to the background many laudable advantages of ICT. After all, *"Abusus non tollit usum"* (Abuse does not destroy use/utility). The Church must advance in her use of ICT in the worship of God. It is a surer way to ensure that the celebration of the goodness of God reaches the ends of the earth. Although we must be careful to distinguish earthly progress clearly from the increase of the kingdom of Christl; nevertheless, such progress is of vital concern to the kingdom of God, insofar as it can contribute to the better ordering of human society. When used well, ICT contributes greatly to active, full, and conscious participation of the faithful which will lead to the socio-communitarian participation. Some pastoral issues and their implications for Catholic worship today were evaluated in terms of harnessing the relevance of ICT.

The idea of a digitalized worship is a welcome development for the Church in Africa. The effort made so far shows that the Africa context and her mode of worship cannot afford to let the present ICT innovations pass without tapping these resources in a way that her members will find resonance with the Catholic liturgy. More efforts can still be expended towards consolidating Christian formation and for pastoral *cum* liturgical activities. Indeed, the bishops, priests, religious men and women, and all those directly connected with the care of souls should make conscious effort to assist the lay faithful to build up their Catholic faith through proper catechesis and mass media. Pope Francis encourages the Church thus:

> Do not be afraid to be this presence, expressing your Christian identity as you become citizens of this environment. A Church that follows this path learns how to walk with everybody! Through both social communications and personal contact, the Church is called to "warm the hearts of men and women" who he said was "made up of real men and women who bring with them their hopes, their suffering, and their pursuit of what is true, beautiful and good." "We need to descend into the darkest night without being overcome and disorientated; we need to listen to the dreams, without being seduced; to share their disappointments, without becoming despondent; to sympathize with those whose lives are falling apart, without losing our own strength and identity.[16]

In conclusion, ICT in the Catholic worship must be given the priority it deserves to move its usage into the next level of e-worship by committing their time and money to improve education in ICT, then more individuals will become ICT literate and eventually be the ones to initiate ICT in their local parishes, chaplaincies and institutions. As such, it will go a long way to address the current challenges to Catholic worship. A celebrated adage says: "it is the modern cat that knows how best to hunt the modern rat." What a glorious prospect lies ahead for Christianizing the world as we recognise the nexus between ICT and Liturgy, whereby we embrace more and more the modern techniques of accessing, connecting, communicating, collaborating and celebrating the worship. It all depends on how effectively those who evangelize through the media blitz are themselves connected with the spiritual dimension of ICT. The challenge of this e-worship which the digitalization of ICT offers to the 21st century African Catholic Christianity must be embraced. Experientially, the emergence of COVID-19 pandemic has now formed part of the challenges of ICT to religious worship. It has reshaped, moderated, and left an indelible mark on humanity. The book demands a radical response by those who read it. Consolidating on the gains in some parts of the continent, the Church in Africa is urged to justify the hopes of the universal Church on her by using ICT at Christian worship in order to bear fruits of authentic and convincing Christian living and witnessing.

---

16 Pope Francis, "Bringing Christ to the Digital Continent..."

BIBLIOGRAPHY

Achebe, Chinua. *Things Fall Apart*. London: Heinemann Educational Books, 197

Agu, Osita. "Uses and Applications of Information and Communication Technologies in Broadcasting", in Ndolo, Ike S. (ed.), *Contemporary Issues in Communication and Society*. Enugu: Rhyce Kerex Publishers, 2011.

Aichner, J. & Jacob, F. “Measuring the Degree of Corporate Social Media Use” in *International Journal of Market Research*, March 2015, 57 (2): 257-275.

Akjentera, Clarissa V. *The Parish Guide to Social Media: How Social Networking can Recharge your Ministry*. New London: Twenty Third Publications, 2013.

Allen, Ronald J. "Preaching on Social Issues" in *Encounter* 59.1-2 (1998) 61-80.

Anagwo, Emmanuel C. *Hundred Questions and Answers on the Mass Vol. II*. Onitsha: Laurans Publishers, 2013.

Anagwo, Emmanuel C. *Active Participation in the Eucharistic Celebration*. Port Harcourt: University of Port Harcourt, 2013.

Anagwo, Emmanuel C. “ICT in the Catholic Worship: Some Pastoral Issues and Implications Today” in Nwaoru, Emmauel (ed.) *Journal of Inculturation Theology*, Vol. 14, No.1, 2013, 50-71.

Anagwo, Emmanuel C. “Enhancing Youth Ministry in the Eucharistic Liturgy for Integral Transformation in Africa: Issues, Challenges and Prospects” in Ferdinand Nwaigbo *et al.* (eds.) *Theology and Youth Empowerment for Integral Development of Africa* (25th CIWA Theology Week), 7th– 11th April 2014, 345-346.

Anagwo, Emmanuel C. "Fundraising in Worship: Implications for the Church in Nigeria" in Wanjala, Frederick (ed.), *African Christian Studies,* Vol. 31, No. 3, Sept. 2015, 61-73.

Anagwo, Emmanuel C. “Christian Wedding and the Challenge of Liturgical Decorum in Nigeria” in *African Christian Studies,* Vol. 31, No. 3, Sept. 2015, 74-89.

Anagwo, Emmanuel C. "Liturgy as Public Work in the Context of the Liturgical Planning Team: Challenges Facing the Theology of Work in Nigeria" in Michael Sasa (ed.), *The Aquinas' Journal*, Vol. 8, June 2016, 199-200.

Anagwo, Emmanuel C. “Preparing the Youth on the Use of ICT for Liturgical Formation: A Challenge for the Church in Nigeria” in *Koinonia*, Vol. 7, No.5, June 2017, 37-55.

Anagwo, Emmanuel C. “Ipad at the Service of Liturgical Formation of the Youth” in Luke Ijezie *et al.* (eds.) *Youth Formation & Globalisation in the Nigerian Context”, Proceedings of the 32nd Annual Conference of the Catholic Theological Association of Nigeria* (CATHAN) 2017, 419-434.

Anagwo, Emmanuel C. “Active Liturgical Participation and Collaborative Ministry in Nigeria" in Ukutegbe, Benedict E., Anagwo, Emmanuel C. & Jamahh, Victor U. (eds.), *Active Participation and the Church in Nigeria, Proceedings of the Annual Conference of the Catholic Liturgists' Association of Nigeria (CALAN)*. Warri: Vinnyl Communications, 2017, 45-71.

Anagwo, Emmanuel C. “The Value of Liturgical Catechesis for Formation and Renewal of Young Adults: Challenges for Utilizing ICT in Nigeria” in *Discovery and Empowering African Youth* (*Jos Studies*), Vol. 26, May 2018, 37-54.

Anagwo, Emmanuel C. *Celebration of the Word of God: A Liturgical Enquiry*. Berlin: Peter Lang International Publisher, 2020.

Anagwo, Emmanuel C. & Umekwe, Peter O. “Enhancing Evangelization and Inculturation through the Print Media in Nigeria” in Anagwo, Emmanuel C. (ed.), *Journal of Inculturation Theology*, Vol. 18, No.2, 2021, 257-273.

Anagwo, Emmanuel C. "Adopting New Ways of Celebrating the Word of God in a Pandemic Era" in Clement Obasi (ed.), *Bigard Theological Studies (BTS)*, January-June 2022, Vol. 42, No.1, 20-37.

Anagwo, Emmanuel C. *New Trends of Fundraising in Christian Worship: The Nigerian Pastoral Experience*. Berlin: Peter Lang International Publisher, 2022.

Anagwo, Emmanuel C. "Sacred Liturgy and COVID-19 Pandemic Era Guidelines and Lessons by the Church in Africa" in *Vidyajyoti Journal of Theological Reflection*, Vol. 86, August 2022, 605-618.

Arinze, Francis. *The Eucharist and Mission*. Onitsha: Invoice Master, 2005.

Badejo, Emmanuel A. "The Role of the Media in Evangelisation: Opportunities and Challenges" in *www.recowacerao.org*. Accessed on 18th October 2021.

Beaudoin, Tom. *Virtual Faith: The Irreverent Spiritual Quest of Generation X*. San Francisco: Jossey-Bass, 1998.

Beninger, J. "Personalization of Mass Media and the Growth of Pseudo-Community," in *Communication Research*, Vol. 14, Issue 3, 1987, 352-371.

Benedict XVI, *The Media: A Network for Communication, Communion and Cooperation,* 40th World Communication Day. Vatican City: Libreria Editrice Vatican, 2006.

Benedict XVI, *Post-Synodal Apostolic Exhortation Sacramentum Caritatis (The Sacrament of Charity*). Nairobi: Paulines Publications, 2007.

Benedict XVI, Encyclical Letter *Spe Salvi.* Vatican City: Libreria Editrice Vaticana, 2007.

Benedict XVI, Post-Synodal Apostolic Exhortation on *Verbum Domini* "the Word of God." Vaticana: Libreria Editrice, 2010.

Benedict XVI, Reflection at the Synod of Bishops on New Evangelization. Vatican City: Libreria Editrice Vatican, 2012.

Benedict XVI, "Social Networks: Portals of Truth and Faith; New Spaces for Evangelization." Message for the 47th World Communication Day. Vatican City: Libreria Editrice Vatican, 2013.

Benedict XVI, "Truth, Proclamation and Authenticity of Life in the Digital Age" in http://www.vatican.va/holy_father_xvi/messages/communications/documents/hf_ben-xvi_mes20110124_45th-world-communication-day_en.html. Accessed 10th January 2022.

Benedict XVI. *Priests and Pastoral Ministry in a Digital World: New Media at the Service of the Word* (44th World Communication Day, 2010) in http://w2.vatican.va>documents>hf-b. Accessed on 8th August 2022.

Benedict XVI, *New Technologies, New Relationships: Promoting a Culture of Respect, Dialogue and Friendship* (43th World Communication Day, 2019) in http://w2.vatican.va>documents>hf-b. Accessed on 8th September 2022.

Berger, Terese. @ *Worship Liturgical Practices in Digital Worlds*, New York: Routledge, 2018.

Bolu, Christian. "The Church in the Contemporary World: Information and Communication Technology in Church Communication for Growth: A Case Study" in *Journal of Media and Communication Studies*, *4*(4), 2012, 80-94.

Brown, Lesley. (ed.), *The New Shorter Oxford English Dictionary*, Vols. Oxford: Clarendom Press, 1993.

Castells, Manuel. *The Internet Galaxy: Reflections on the Internet, Business and Society*. Oxford: Oxford University Press, 2001.

Catholic Bishops' Conference of Nigeria (CBCN) "The Word of God and the Building of the Nigerian Nation" Communiqué at the end of the First Plenary Meeting, Abuja March 2009.

Celestine VI, *The Letters of Pope Celestine VI to all Mankind*, English Edition. Vatican City: Libreria Editrice Vatican, 1948.

Chibuko, Patrick C. "Active Participation in the Liturgy: Towards the Revival of Christian Culture" in Nwatu, Felix (ed.), *Bigard Theological Studies.* Vol. 26, No 2, 2006, 39-56.

Chibuko, Patrick C. "The Priest as Sole Administrator, A Hindrance to Effective Ministry: A Liturgical Perspective" in Obinwa, Ignatius

M.C. (ed.) *Collaborative Ministry in the Context of Inculturation*, (Enugu: SNAAP Press, 2006) 299-314.

Chibuko, Patrick C. "Information and Communication Technology (ICT) in the Liturgical Life of Christians Today: An Anglophone West African Response" in *Journal of Inculturation Theology*, Vol. 16, No.2, 2019, 140-155.

Chibuko, Patrick C. *Dynamics of the Liturgy in the COVID-19 and Post-COVID-19 Pandemic Era: Implications for the Church in Nigeria (1st Inaugural Lecture)*. Port Harcourt: CIWA Publications, 2021.

Chibuko, Patrick C. "Foreword" in Anagwo, Emmanuel C. & Anyanwu, Kelechi (eds.), *Theory and Praxis of Sacred Liturgy in Nigeria: A Festschrift in Honour of Most Rev. Prof. Augustine Ndubueze Echema*, Umuahia: Sons Digital Press, 2021, viii-xvii.

Chiluwa, I. "Community and Social Interaction in Digital Religious Discourse in Nigeria, Ghana and Cameroon," in *Journal of Religion, Media & Digital Culture*, Vol. 2, Issue 1, 2013, 11-13.

Chupungco, Anscar J. *Handbook for Liturgical Studies; Fundamental Liturgy*, Vol. II. Collegeville, Minnesota: Liturgical Press, 1998, 339-340.

CNA/EWTN News, Evangelize though Family, Social Media, (2nd February, 2017) in https://www.catholicregister.org/home/international/item/24231-nigerian-bishop-evangelize-though-family-social-media. Accessed 5th September 2022.

Commentary on Eusebius' Ecclesiastical History 3.39 from https://biblicalscholarship.wordpress.com/2020/01/03/commentary-on-eusebius-ecclesiastical-history-3-39/. Accessed on 15th September 2022.

Congregation for Catholic Education, *Ratio Fundamentalis Institutionis Sacerdotalis*, 2. Rome: Vatican Polyglot Press, 1970.

Congregation for Divine Worship and the Discipline of the Sacraments, *Redemptionis Sacramentum* (*On Certain Matters to be Observed or to be Avoided Regarding the Most Holy Eucharist*). Okpuno: Fides Communications, 2004.

Dankasa, Jacob Z. *Technology for Ministry: Best Practices for Evangelization on Social Media and internet in Africa*. Nairobi: Pauline Publications Africa, 2017.

Dewdney, Andrew & Ride, Peter (eds.), *The New Media Handbook, Media Practice*. New York: Routledge, 2006.

Earey, M. *Liturgical Formation and Education of the People of God in Worship-shaped Life.* Ruth Meyers and Paul Gibson (eds). London: Canterbury Press, 2010.

Edappilly, John. *The Emerging Electronic Church: A Theological Critique on the Church Encountering Computer, Television, and Cyber World.* Bangalore: Asian Trading Corporation, 2003.

Eboh, Simeon. *Freedom of Communication and Evangelization in*

Nigeria. Lagos: AUP, 1994.

Echema, Austin. "The Sacrament of Reconciliation: Implications of the New Term" in *Journal of Inculturation Theology*, Vol. 4, April 1997, 32-44.

Echema, Austin. "Liturgy: A Teaching in Action" in *Journal of Inculturation Theology*, October, Vol. 5 (2003) 141-155.

Echema. Austin. "Liturgical Pedagogy and Nation-Building" in Ferdinand Nwaigbo *et al.* (eds.) *Theological Education for Human Development and Nation-Building in Africa*. 21st CIWA Theology Week, 22nd to 26th March 2010, 273-295.

Echema, Austin. *Priests and Laity Collaboration in the Post-modern Church*. Owerri: Assumpta Press, 2011.

Edwards, C. & Hiler, C. "A Teacher's Guide to the Exhibit: 'The Hundred Languages of Children'" in *College of Human Environmental Sciences*, University of Kentucky: Lexington, Kentucky, 20.

Egere, Inaku K. "Social Media and Mission-Based Marketing Approach for New Evangelization in the Digital Age" in *African Ecclesial Review* (AFER), Vol. 57, Nos. 3 & 4, Sep./Dec. 2015, 186-205.

Egielewa, Peter Eshioke. "The Perception of Smartphones among Catholic Faithful: A Study of Selected Parishes in Edo State, Nigeria" in Anagwo, Emmanuel C. (ed.), *Journal of Inculturation Theology*, Vol. 17, No.2, 2020, 257-290.

Errazuriz, Carlos. *"Title IV, The Means of Social Commentary on the Code of Canon Law, Vol. III*, no. 1, 296-297.

Ezekoka, Peter Onyekachi. "ICT as an Agent for E-Worship in Nigeria" in Emmanuel C. Anagwo & Kelechi Anyanwu (eds.), *Theory and Praxis of Sacred Liturgy in Nigeria: A Festschrift in Honour of Most Rev. Prof. Augustine Ndubueze Echema*, Umuahia: Sons Digital Press, 2021.

Fischer, Balthasar. "Active Participation in the Mass," in Alfons Kirchgaessner (ed.), *Unto the Altar: The Practice of Catholic Worship*. New York: Herder and Herder, 1963.

Francis, Pope. "Stop Taking Smartphone Snapshots During Mass, Pope Says" from https://www.ncronline.org/news/vatican/francis-chronicles/stop-taking-smartphone-snapshots-during-mass-pope-says. Accessed on 25th September 2022.

Francis, Pope. *Evangelii Gaudium, Apostolic Exhortation on the Proclamation of the Gospel in Today's World*. Vaticana: Libreria Editrice, 2013.

Francis, Pope. Plenary Assembly of the Pontifical Council for Social Communications, *Bringing Christ to the Digital Continent By Junno Arocho Esteves,* Vatican City, 23rd September, 2013 (Zenit.org).

Francis, Apostolic Letter, *Desiderio Desideravi* (On the Liturgical Formation of the People of God), Vatican City: Libreria Editrice Vaticana, 29th June 2022.

Gregory the Great, Pope. "Interpreting the Scriptures Continued" from https://prezi.com/efe37lioghms/interpreting-the-scriptures-continued/ accessed on 28th September 2022.

Jensen, Joseph. "Revelation, Concept of (in the Bible)," in *New Catholic Encyclopedia* 12 (Washington DC: Jack Heraty, 2003) 436-437.

John Paul II, Pope. *Proclaiming Christ*. Vatican City: Libreria Editrice Vatican, 2011.

John Paul II, Pope. *Redemptoris Missio*. Vatican City: Libreria Editrice Vatican, 1990.

John Paul II, Pope. Encyclical Letter, *Dominium et Vivificantem* (On the Holy Spirit) Vatican City: Libreria Editrice Vatican.

John Paul II, Pope. *Ad Limina Address*. Vatican City: Libreria Editrice Vaticana, 11th July 1998.

John Paul II, Pope. Apostolic Letter, *Rapid Development, To those Responsible for Communications*. Vatican City: Libreria Editrice Vaticana, 24th January 2002.

John Paul II, Pope. "Pope Tells WYD Youth that Salvation is an 'Invitation to be Part of a Love Story" from https://twitter.com/hashtag/Panama2019. Accessed on 28th September 2022.

Gruen, T. Osmonbekov, T. Czaplewski, A. "eWOM: The Impact of Customer-to-Customer Online Know-how Exchange on Customer Value and Loyalty," in *Journal of Business Research*, Vol. 59, 2006, 449-456.

Guardini, Romano. *The Spirit of the Liturgy*. New York: Crossroad Publishing Co., 1998.

History of ICT (Information and communications technology) from https://www.sutori.com/en/story/history-of-ict-information-and-communications-technology--N7J51bQqSU7vLWcVfdn5M9qa. Accessed on 15th August 2022.

Ihejirika, Walter C. *The e-priest: The Identity of the Catholic Priest in the Digital Age.* Owerri: Edu-Edy Publications, 2011.

Ilechukwu, Loenard & Uchem, Rose. "Application and Role of ICT in Religious Education" in *Research on Humanities and Social Sciences,* 4 (4) (2014).

Johannes Quasten, *Patrology. Christian Classics*, 1986, 30.

Kaaindio, M.P. & Wagithunu, M.N. "Integrating Information Communication Technology Skills in Preschool Education in Kenya" in *Mediterranean Journal of Social Sciences*, 5 (5), 89-102.

Kalaš, I. *Recognizing the Potentials of ICT in Early Childhood Education*, Russian: UNESCO Institute for Information Technologies in Education from http://iite.unesco.org/pics/publications/files/3214673.pdf. Accessed on 22nd November 2018.

Kanife, Ejike. "Why switching off phones during worship might not be the best policy for the Catholic Church in Nigeria" from https://technext.ng/2020/02/07/why-switching-off-phones-during-worship-might-not-be-the-best-policy-for-the-nigerian-Catholic-church/ Accessed 20th August 2022.

Kizza, Joseph Migga. *Ethical and Social Issues in the Information Age*. New York: Springer Media, 2003.

Köster, Wendelin. "Recovery Collective Memory in the Context of Postmodernism," in Pecklers, Keith (ed.), *Liturgy in a Postmodern World*. New York: Continuum, 2003, 32-35.

Kunle, Akinde Olusola & Opara Felix Kelechi, "Deployment of Digitized Packages Toward Engineering Education in West African Higher Institutions" in Joseph A. Ilori (ed.) *West African Journal of Higher Education: Christian Higher Education in African Context*. Ilorin: Modern Impressions, 2014.

Lang, Jovian P. "Bible and Liturgy" in *Dictionary of the Liturgy*. New York: Catholic Book Publishing, 1989.

Leeuw, Gerard van der. *Sacred and Profane Beauty: The Holy in Art*, trans. David E. Green. New York: Holt, Rinehart and Winston, 1963.

Leonard, Richard. "'Light! Camera! Worship! The Cinema and its Challenges to Roman Catholic Worship in Postmodernity" in Pecklers, Keith (ed.), *Liturgy in a Postmodern World*. New York: Continuum, 2003, 27-31.

Lightfoot, J. B. & Harmer, J. R. *The Apostolic Fathers*. New York: Apocryphile Press, 2004.

Lillie, Betty J. "Dreams" in Caroll Stuhlmueller, Dianne Bergant, Demetrius Dumm, *et al*. (eds.), *The Collegeville Pastoral Dictionary of Biblical Theology* (Bangalore: Theological Publications, 2011) 226-229.

Lincoln, Abraham. "The Best way to Predict your Future is to Create it" from https://www.wanderlustworker.com/the-best-way-to-predict-the-future-is-to-create-it/. Accessed on 26th September 2022.

John Lukwata, "Church and Mass Media: Harnessing Opportunities for Evangelization in Eastern Africa" in in *African Ecclesial Review* (AFER) Vol. 57, Nos. 3 & 4 Sept/Dec. 2015, 152.

Mayfield, Antony, *What is Social Media? iCrossing ebook* from https://www.coursehero.com/file/6882077/What-is-Social-Media-iCrossing-ebook/. Accessed on 25th August 2022.

Mazzalongo, Mike. "The Use of Media in Ministry: Communicating the Message" from https://bibletalk.tv/media-in-ministry. Accessed on 20th August 2022.

Mbiti, John. *African Religions and Philosophy*. London: Heinemann Education Books, 1969.

Mckenzie, John I. *Dictionary of the Bible*. London: Macmillan Publication, 1976.

McManus, Frederick. *Liturgical Participation: An Ongoing Assessment*. Washington DC: The Pastoral Press, 1988.

McNamara, Edward. "Follow-up: On Banners, Overhead Projectors and PowerPoint Displays" June 8, 2010 in http://www.zenit.org/article-29678?l=english. Accessed on 30th August 2021.

McNamara, Edward. "Using an Ipad at the Gospel" in http://www.zenit.org/article-34958?l=english. Accessed on 8th June 2022.

McNamara, Edward "Zenit: The World Seen From Rome" from http://www.zenit.org/article-35635?l=english). Accessed on 20th August 2022.

McNamara, Edward. "Follow-up: On Banners, Overhead Projectors and PowerPoint Displays" 8th June, 2010 in http://www.zenit.org/article-29678?l=english accessed on 20th August 2022.

McNamara, Edward. "Using an Ipad at the Gospel" 12th June 2012 in http://www.zenit.org/article-34958?l=english. Accessed on 30th August 2022.

Msafiri, Aidan. "Globalization of Concern: Opportunities and Risks of Using Cyberspace to Spearhead Evangelization in Tanzania," in Lukwata, John (ed.), *Search for New Paradigms of Evangelization in the 21st Century*. Nairobi: CUEA Press, 34-49.

Musa, Gerald. "Priests in Nigeria and the Use of Social Media" in Emmanuel C. Anagwo (ed.), *Journal of Inculturation Theology*, Vol. 16, No.1, 2019, 116-130.

Newman, Cardinal John Henry, "On the Development of Ideas" from https://www.newmanreader.org/works/development/chapter1.html. Accessed on 20th September 2022.

News Agency of Nigeria (NAN), "Using Bible apps on phone during church worship: Some say it is youth culture." In *The Vanguard* from https://www.vanguardngr.com/2018/09/using-bible-apps-on-phone-during-church-worship-some-say-its-youth-culture/. Accessed 20th August 2022.

Nichols, Arland K. "The Year of Faith: Recovering a Culture that is Genuinely Catholic" in *Homiletic & Pastoral Review*, from (http://www.hprweb.com/. Accessed 10th February 2013.

Niederwimmer, Kurt. *The Didache (Hermenia and Historical Commentary on the Bible)*. New York: Fortress Press, 1998.

Nwanze, "Art, Media and Literature as Catalysts of Socio-Political Change: The Nigerian Experience and the Role of the Church" in Bona Ikenna Ugwu, *Politics, Social Change and the Church in Nigeria Acts of the 12th SIST International Missiological Symposium, 2007* (Enugu: Kingsley's, 2011) 122.

Nwaigbo, Ferdinand. *The Holy Spirit and the Youth in Africa in the Era of COVID-19*. Mauritius: Blessed Hope Publishing, 2020.

Nwosuh, ChukwuEmekalum. "On Dispensing with the Kiss of Peace: Seeking Creative Liturgical Actions" Dominican Institute, Samonda, Ibadan, Nigeria, Unpublished Paper, 2nd May 2020.

Okeke, Hilary O. *Let us Celebrate the Mystery of Faith*. Onitsha: Goodmark Prints Production Inc. 2005.

Okeke, Hilary Paul O. *Living Our Culture in the Light of Faith Pastoral Letter*. Nnewi: CathCom Publishers, 2015.

Okonoboh, Rita. "Digital Christianity! Smartphones, smart pews, the changing phase of worship" in *The Nigerian Tribune* (22nd October 2017). from https://tribuneonlineng.com/digital-christianity-smart-phones-smart-pews-changing-phase-worship/. Accessed on 23rd October 2022.

Okure, Teresa. "A New Testament Perspective on Evangelization and Human Promotion" *in Journal of Inculturation Theology,* Vol. 1, No. 2, 1994, 126.

Okwuosa, Lawrence. "The Eucharist and Christian Formation" in Osarenkhoe, Agatha (ed.), *The Voyage: A Publication of the Conference of Major Superiors of Nigeria*, Vol. 3, Jan. 2006, 40-56.

Olusola, Emmanuel B. "The Christian Liturgy in the Age of Info-Technology: Prospects and Challenges" in Ijezie, Luke *et al.* (eds.), *Theology and Liturgy in the Life of the Church Proceedings of the 26th Annual Conference of the Catholic Theological Association of Nigeria* (CATHAN) 2012, 270-282.

Olusola, Emmanuel B. "Merits and Demerits of Information and Communication Technology (ICT) for Users of the New Media in Nigeria" in *Journal of Inculturation Theology*, Vol. 13, No. 2, 2012, 227-244.

Olusola, Emmanuel B. "Digital Church and E-Culture in the New Media Age: The Spectrum of Nigeria" in *African Ecclesial Review (AFER): ICT & Evangelization ~ Christianity in the Digital Culture*, Vol. 57, Nos. 3 & 4, Sept./Dec. 2015, 206-224.

Olusola, Emmanuel B. "The Church and Communication in an E-Age: The Matrix of *Inter Mirifica*" in *African Ecclesial Review* (AFER)*: ICT*

& Evangelization ~ Christianity in the Digital Culture, Vol. 57, Nos. 3 & 4 Sep./Dec. 2015, 169-185.

Oury, Guy. *The Mass*. New Jersey: Catholic Book Publishing Corp., 1988.

Ozonze, Joachin. "Learning to Live with Children of the Media Culture" in *The Chronicle Magazine 21* (December 2016 - December 2017) 17-19.

Paul VI, Pope. Apostolic Exhortation on *Evangelii Nuntiandi* (Evangelization in the Modern World) in http://w2.vatican.va/content/paul-vi/en/apost_exhortations/documents/hf_p-vi_exh_19751208_evangelii-nuntiandi.html accessed on 17th April 2022.

Paulus Episcopus Servus Servorum Dei Una Cum Sacrosancti Concilii Patribus ad Perpetuam Rei Memoriam, Decretum De Instrumentis Communicationis Socialis, Inter Mirifica from https://www.vatican.va/archive/hist_councils/ii_vatican_council/documents/vat-ii_decree_19631204_inter-mirifica_lt.html. Accessed on 10th September 2022.

Pecklers, Keith F. (ed.) *Liturgy in a Postmodern World*. London: Continuum, 2003.

Pickett, Thomas Aquinas. "Active Participation: Historical Continuity in the Church's Worship and Teaching" in https://www.academia.edu/11688578/Active_Participation_Historical_Continuity_in_the_Churchs_Worship_and_Teaching. Accessed on 22nd September 2022.

Pontifical Council for Social Communications, *The Church and Internet* in www.vatican.va/.../rc_pc_pccs_200202228_church-internet-en.html. Accessed on 12th August 2021.

Puthiadem, Ignatius. *Christian Liturgy: The Representation of the Greatest God – Human Story*. Mumbai: St. Pauls Publications, 2002.

Rolfes, Helmuth. *Communicatio Socialis Challenge of Ministry in the Church*. Kassel: Kassel University Press, 2007.

Sarfo, Charles Boampong, JNR. Eucharistic Celebration and Cyberspace in the Light of *Sacramentum Caritatis* 57: A Study in Kumasi

Ecclesiastical Province, Ghana. Unpublished PhD Dissertation. Port Harcourt: CIWA, June 2019.

Schaff, Philip. *Nicene and Post-Nicene Fathers Series 2, Vol 3*, CCEL, 2009, 558-572.

Second Vatican Council, *Sacrosanctum Concilium* (The Constitution on the Sacred Liturgy) in Flannery, Austin (ed.), *Vatican Council II*. Dublin: Dominican Publications, 1987.

Second Vatican Council, *Inter Mirifica (Decree on the Means of Social Communication*), in Flannery, Austin (ed.). *Vatican Council II*. Dublin: Dominican Publications, 1987.

Second Vatican Council, *Communio et Progressio* (Pastoral Instruction on the Means of Social Communication) in Flannery, Austin (ed.), *Vatican Council II*. Dublin: Dominican Publications, 1987.

Second Vatican Council, *Gaudium et Spes* (Pastoral Constitution on the Church in the Modern World) in Flannery, Austin (ed.), *Vatican Council II*. Dublin: Dominican Publications, 1987.

Sofield, Loughlan & Juliano, Carrol. *Collaborative Ministry: Skills and Guidelines*. Notre Dame: Ave Marie Press, 1987.

Spadaro, Antonio. *Cybertheology: Thinking Christianity in the Era of the Internet*, Trans. By Maria Way. New York: Fordham University Press, 2014.

The Catechism of the Catholic Church. Nairobi: Paulines Publications, 2001.

The Code of Canon Law. Bangalore: Theological Publications in India, 2001.

The General Instruction of the Roman Missal (GIRM). Nairobi: Paulines Publications Africa, 2003.

"The General Instruction on the Liturgy of the Hours" (GILH) in *The Divine Office: The Liturgy of the Hours According to the Roman Rite*. London: The Talbot Press, 1974.

The Roman Missal Renewed by Decree of the Most Holy Second Ecumenical Council of the Vatican, Promulgated by Authority of

Pope Paul VI and Revised at the Direction of Pope John Paul II, English Translation According to the Third Typical Edition. Nairobi: Paulines Publications Africa, 2011.

Tippett, Alan. *Missiology*. Pasadena: William Carey Library (1987).

Ukutegbe, Benedict E. "The Dignity and Place of Liturgical Books in Sacred Liturgy: An Evaluation in the Light of Digital Revolution" in in Ukutegbe, Benedict E., Anagwo, Emmanuel C. & Jamahh, Victor U. (eds.), *Abuse in the Liturgy and the Nigerian Context Today, Proceedings of the Annual Conference of the Catholic Liturgists' Association of Nigeria (CALAN) 2018*. Benin City: Floreat Systems Printing Press, 2018, 93-112.

US Bishops' Document on Church Art and Architecture, "Built of Living Stones" nr. 163 in http://www.usccb.org/liturgy/livingstonesind .shtml, accessed on 23rd August 2022.

Varghese, Ajay. "Jesus' Methods of Communication" from http://aja yvarghese.blogspot.com/2007/06/jesus-methods-of-communication.html. Accessed on 22nd August 2022.

Vorgrimler, Herbert (ed.), *Commentary on the Documents of Vatican II, Vol. 1.* New York: Herder and Herder,1966.

"What does ipad stand for/" from http://www.abbreviations. com/IPAD. Accessed on 1st April 2021.

Woods, Christopher. "Liturgical Formation: What is it and why is it important?" in http://www.westcott.cam.ac.uk/liturgical-formation. Accessed on 30th August 2022.

NAME/AUTHOR INDEX

Subject Index

ABOUT THE BOOK

In recent years there has been a groundswell of interest on how Information and Communication Technology (ICT) can best be harnessed to improve the efficiency and effectiveness of the Catholic liturgy. Accordingly, this book titled: *The Nexus between ICT and Liturgy in the African Context: Towards Consolidating Digital Worship in the African Context* grapples with the future of worship at a time of digital explosion in the Christian Churches, as expended through the lenses of the Second Vatican Council's interdisciplinary document titled: *Inter Mirifica* 13. Overwhelmed by digital revolution, media literacy and impact are only emerging. While the nexus of ICT may seem obvious, the deep connections and the many possibilities for the 21st century e-worship are yet to be significantly explored. The book examines the possible nexus and complementarity between ICT and Catholic liturgy. When not handled well, they will lead to cataclysmic destruction of liturgical heritage and patrimony. Nonetheless, exploring ICT for e-worship, the book advocates for adherence to guidelines in liturgical celebrations. Hence, the book discloses the meaning, theology, types, prospects, uses, and abuses in ICT for digital worship. This book will make a vital contribution not only to scholarship in liturgical studies in Africa but also as a catalyst towards a simplified consolidation, to the practice of Christian worship in the world today.

ABOUT THE AUTHOR

Emmanuel Chinedu Anagwo is a priest of the Catholic diocese of Nnewi, Nigeria. He did his Post-Graduate Programme at the Nnamdi Azikiwe University (UNIZIK), Awka, Nigeria and University of Port Harcourt (UNIPORT), Port Harcourt, Nigeria where he obtained Post-Graduate Diploma in Education (PGDE) and a Master of Education (MED) in Philosophy of Education respectively. He also holds a master's degree (MTh) in Theology and Licentiate in Sacred Liturgy (STL). He obtained two doctorate degrees, one in sacred liturgy, the other in philosophy of education, from the prestigious Catholic Institute of West Africa (CIWA), Port Harcourt, an affiliate of the University of Calabar (UNICAL), Nigeria; and from the University of Port Harcourt, Nigeria respectively. Dr. Anagwo has participated in several workshops and seminars in Nigeria, Ghana, Kenya, Liberia, and United States of America. He has also presented scholarly papers in international and interdisciplinary conferences, and some are published in referred journals. Among his publications include *Celebration of the Word of God: A Liturgical Enquiry* (Berlin: Peter Lang International Publisher, 2020) and *New Trends of Fundraising in Christian Worship: The Nigerian Pastoral Experience* (Berlin: Peter Lang International Publisher, 2022). He has also edited, co-edited and co-authored some professional books and served as Editor-in-Chief and Associate Editor of some professional journals. Currently, he is the Dean of Students' Affairs and Chairperson, CIWA Publications' Committee. His areas of research include the interface between liturgical renewal and biblical study, liturgical education and political liturgy, liturgical inculturation and ecological liturgy.

Africa in Theology – Theology in Africa
Afrika in der Theologie – Theologie in Afrika
L'Afrique en théologie – Théologie en Afrique
edited by Prof. Dr. Chibueze C. Udeani (Würzburg),
Prof. Dr. Claudia von Collani (Würzburg), Prof. Dr. Andreas Heuser (Basel)

Peter Ayoola Oderinde
Digital Spiritualities
Social Media and Nigerian Pentecostal Churches in Switzerland
"*Digital Spiritualities* answers many of the questions of the Christian faithful and scholars of religion about the sustainability of Christian fellowship in an era of COVID-19. Its deft analysis of the creativity of Christians on issues of online lived Pentecostalism, viz, online evangelization, online liturgy and online network formation make this book an invaluable text for scholars of African Pentecostalism. The book is a critical contribution to, and in the vanguard of, an emerging scholarship on online Christian fellowship among the African diaspora."
Olufunke Adeboye PhD, Professor of Social History & Dean of Arts, University of Lagos
vol. 3, 2022, ca. 280 pp., ca. 34,90 €, pb., ISBN-CH 978-3-643-91220-6

Lotanna Olisaemeka
Socio-Cultural and Religious Conflicts and the Future of Nigeria
A Mission for the Local Church
With the prevailing violent conflict situation of our world, perpetuated sometimes even in the name of religion, humanity today faces extinction. To reverse this ugly trend, humanity has no choice than to build a society where every tribe and tongue can coexist in peace. This work analyzed the violent conflicts from anthropological, behavioral, politico-philosophical, and theological perspectives, and makes a demand on humanity to save herself through proper education and dialogue with all men and religions.
vol. 2, 2022, 536 pp., 59,90 €, pb., ISBN-CH 978-3-643-90756-1

LIT Verlag Berlin – Münster – Wien – Zürich – London
Auslieferung Deutschland / Österreich / Schweiz: siehe Impressumsseite

Intercultural Theology and Study of Religions

edited by Prof. Dr. Chibueze C. Udeani (University of Würzburg), Prof. Dr. Klaus Zapotoczky (Linz), Prof. Dr. Friedrich Reiterer (University of Bonn), Prof. Dr. Dr. Claude Ozankom (University of Bonn)

Chibueze Udeani
Intercultural Hermeneutics – Understanding Culture and Religion
New hermeneutical challenges abound within the process of globalisation especially as they pertain to culture and religion. Consequently, a new form of hermeneutics approached from an intercultural perspective is needed. This requires, if not a new set of hermeneutical tools then, at least, a serious, profound and critical analysis and constructive adaptation of the already available set of hermeneutical tools. Intercultural hermeneutics in the understanding of religion and culture and among cultures and religions is being proposed here as this new form of art or science of understanding.
vol. 7, 2021, 322 pp., 39,90 €, pb., ISBN-CH 978-3-643-91454-5

Chibueze C. Udeani; Klaus Zapotoczky (Hrsg.)
Die Rede von Gott – Discourse on God
Interdisziplinäre und interkulturelle Zugänge – Interdisciplinary and intercultural Approaches
Gegenwärtig sind die Gottesfrage und ihre zuweilen zerstörerischen Folgen so konflikthaft geworden, dass bisweilen die Abschaffung Gottes zugunsten eines friedlicheren Zusammenlebens gefordert wird. So ist die „Rede von Gott" ein Themenfeld, das die *Internationale Gesellschaft für interkulturelle Theologie und Studium der Religionen (ISRIT)* diskutiert und dabei Expertinnen und Experten aus diversen Fachgebieten (Theologie, Psychologie, Physik etc.) mit historischen wie aktuellen Implikationen der Gottesproblematik aus interdisziplinären und interkulturellen Perspektiven zu Wort kommen lässt.
In our present time, talking about God with reference to its at times destructive consequences has become so much conflictive that sometimes even the abolition of God to the advantage of a more peaceful mutual co-existence is demanded. Hence the "Discourse on God" is another theme, upon which the *International Society for Intercultural Theology and Study of Religions (ISRIT)* deliberates involving experts from diverse fields of science – Theology, Psychology, Physics etc. – hereby focussing on the historical as well as the current implications of the God-problematic from interdisciplinary and intercultural perspectives.
Bd. 6, 2018, 318 S., 34,90 €, br., ISBN 978-3-643-90989-3

LIT Verlag Berlin – Münster – Wien – Zürich – London
Auslieferung Deutschland / Österreich / Schweiz: siehe Impressumsseite

Ästhetik – Theologie – Liturgik

hrsg. von Prof. Dr. Dr. h. c. Horst Schwebel (Marburg) und Prof. Dr. Albert Gerhards (Bonn)

Johannes van Acken
Christozentrische Kirchenkunst
Ein Entwurf zum liturgischen Gesamtkunstwerk. Herausgegeben, bearbeitet und ergänzt um eine Biographie von Ralph Eberhard Brachthäuser und eine kunsthistorische Einordnung von Manuela Klauser. Mit einem Geleitwort von Albert Gerhards
Bd. 74, 3., erw. Aufl. 2022, 304 S., 49,90 €, gb., ISBN 978-3-643-15197-1

Brigitte Enzner-Probst
Frauenliturgien neu entdeckt
Performative Potenziale in der liturgischen Praxis von Frauen. Mit einem Quellenanhang
Bd. 72, 2. Aufl. 2019, 472 S., 49,90 €, br., ISBN 978-3-643-14271-9

Teodor Puszcz
Das liturgische Gebet für Reisende und Pilger sowie Seefahrer
Ein Überblick bis zur Tridentinischen Liturgiereform
Bd. 71, 2019, 608 S., 59,90 €, br., ISBN 978-3-643-14225-2

Reinhard Leuze
Schönheit – Glaube – Vision
Eine theologische Ästhetik
Bd. 70, 2019, 256 S., 39,90 €, gb., ISBN 978-3-643-14137-8

Jörg Mohn
Osternacht
Spiegel und Impulsgeberin eines veränderten evangelischen Gottesdienst- und Liturgieverständnisses
Bd. 69, 2018, 408 S., 39,90 €, br., ISBN 978-3-643-14017-3

Wolfgang Vögele
Sono auribus viventium
Kultur und Theologie des Glockenläutens in Reformation und Moderne
Bd. 68, 2017, 258 S., 24,90 €, br., ISBN 978-3-643-13742-5

Christine Lungershausen
Anderssehen in räumlichen Wechselspielen
Wie lässt sich Sinneröffnung am Ort zeitgenössischer Kirchenfenster beschreiben?
Bd. 67, 2017, 320 S., 34,90 €, br., ISBN 978-3-643-13716-6

Erwin Löhr
Andere Bilder der Bibel
Bildliche Gedanken zum christlichen Glauben. Mit Beiträgen von Gerlind Knappmann, Heike Plaß und Thomas Sternberg
Bd. 66, 2017, 84 S., 24,90 €, gb., ISBN 978-3-643-13599-5

LIT Verlag Berlin – Münster – Wien – Zürich – London
Auslieferung Deutschland / Österreich / Schweiz: siehe Impressumsseite

International Practical Theology

edited by Prof. Dr. Chris Hermans (Nijmegen), Prof. Dr. Maureen Junker-Kenny (Dublin), Prof. Dr. Richard Osmer (Princeton), Prof. Dr. Friedrich Schweitzer (Tübingen), Prof. Dr. Hans-Georg Ziebertz (Würzburg) in cooperation with the International Academy of Practical Theology (IAPT)

Jan Albert van den Berg; Chris A. M. Hermans (Eds.)
Battle for the heart
How (not) to transform church and society
vol. 23, 2020, 202 pp., 39,90 €, pb., ISBN-CH 978-3-643-91306-7

Chris A.M. Hermans; Kobus Schoeman (Eds.)
Theology in an Age of Contingency
vol. 21, 2019, 208 pp., 34,90 €, pb., ISBN-CH 978-3-643-91108-7

Jaco Dreyer; Malan Nel (Eds.)
Practicing Ubuntu
Practical Theological Perspectives on Injustice, Personhood and Human Dignity
vol. 20, 2017, 272 pp., 34,90 €, pb., ISBN-CH 978-3-643-90848-3

Gorden E Dames
Towards a contextual transformational practical theology for leadership education in South Africa
vol. 19, 2016, 278 pp., 39,90 €, pb., ISBN-CH 978-3-643-90800-1

Pamela Couture
We Are Not All Victims
Local Peacebuilding in the Democratic Republic of Congo
vol. 18, 2016, 392 pp., 39,90 €, pb., ISBN-CH 978-2-643-90796-7

Pamela Couture; Robert Mager; Pamela McCarroll; Natalie Wigg-Stevenson (Eds.)
Complex Identities in a Shifting World
Practical Theological Perspectives
vol. 17, 2015, 284 pp., 29,90 €, pb., ISBN-CH 978-3-643-90509-3

R. Ruard Ganzevoort; Rein Brouwer; Bonnie Miller-McLemore (Eds.)
City of Desires – a Place for God?
Practical theological perspectives
vol. 16, 2013, 216 pp., 29,90 €, pb., ISBN-CH 978-3-643-90307-5

Edward Foley (Ed.)
Religion, Diversity and Conflict
vol. 15, 2011, 312 pp., 29,90 €, br., ISBN-CH 978-3-643-90086-9

Heid Leganger-Krogstad
The Religious Dimension of Intercultural Education
Contributions to a Contextual Understanding
vol. 14, 2011, 288 pp., 29,90 €, pb., ISBN-CH 978-3-643-90085-2

Annemie Dillen; Anne Vandenhoeck (Eds.)
Prophetic Witness in World Christianities
Rethinking Pastoral Care and Counseling
vol. 13, 2011, 248 pp., 24,90 €, pb., ISBN-CH 978-3-643-90041-8

LIT Verlag Berlin – Münster – Wien – Zürich – London
Auslieferung Deutschland / Österreich / Schweiz: siehe Impressumsseite